Second Edition

Local Economic
Development

TO OUR FAMILIES—past, present, and future

Second Edition

Local Economic Development

Analysis, Practices, and Globalization

John P. Blair
Wright State University

Michael C. Carroll
Bowling Green State University

Los Angeles • London • New Delhi • Singapore

For information:

 SAGE Publications, Inc.
2455 Teller Road
Thousand Oaks,
   California 91320
E-mail: order@sagepub.com

SAGE Publications Ltd.
1 Oliver's Yard
55 City Road
London EC1Y 1SP
United Kingdom

SAGE Publications India Pvt. Ltd.
B 1/I 1 Mohan Cooperative
   Industrial Area
Mathura Road, New Delhi 110 044
India

SAGE Publications
   Asia-Pacific Pte. Ltd.
33 Pekin Street #02-01
Far East Square
Singapore 048763

Printed in the United States of America

Library of Congress Cataloging-in-Publication Data

Blair, John P., 1947–
Local economic development: Analysis, practices, and globalization/John P. Blair, Michael C. Carroll. — 2nd ed.
       p. cm.
Includes bibliographical references and index.
ISBN 978-1-4129-6483-8 (clot: acid-free paper)
    1. Economic development. 2. Economic policy. 3. Local government. 4. Urban economics. I. Carroll, Michael C., 1958- II. Title.

HD82.B5543 2009
338.9—dc22   2008003508

This book is printed on acid-free paper.

08   09   10   11   12   11   10   9   8   7   6   5   4   3   2   1

Acquisitions Editor:	Al Bruckner
Editorial Assistant:	MaryAnn Vail
Production Editor:	Diane S. Foster
Copy Editor:	QuADS Prepress (P) Ltd.
Typesetter:	C&M Digitals (P) Ltd.
Proofreader:	Eleni-Maria Georgiou
Indexer:	Diggs Publication Services
Cover Designer:	Gail Buschman
Marketing Manager:	Stephanie Adams

Contents

Preface

The practice of local economic development (LED) has grown significantly as changing local, national, and international events have elicited local responses. The purpose of this book is to present the economics of economic development in a manner accessible to economists and noneconomists. It is written with an understanding that successful economic development programs require knowledge from a variety of fields including planning, political science, finance, sociology, and marketing. Nevertheless, economic processes are at the heart of local development efforts. Practitioners and academics should understand how market forces combine with noneconomic variables to shape economies and affect community welfare.

Information is presented in a straightforward manner. As a textbook, *Local Economic Development* will serve in either a development-oriented urban economics class or a regional development course. Concepts, theories, and tools are emphasized rather than specific programs. Programs change too frequently to provide a foundation. Theory without practice is sterile. Practice without theory is adrift.

This revision has an international orientation. Ideas are presented to show that local institutional and cultural contexts can greatly influence the course of local development. Consequently, no homogeneous cultural setting is assumed. Instructors are tasked with fitting the concepts to specific local circumstances.

Traditional topics such as location of activities, growth and development, economic structure, land use, neighborhood development, and governance are presented in ways that connect theory to "on-the-ground" realities. Theoretical discussions are not so abstract that the welfare of individuals and communities gets lost in the analysis.

Economic problems including transportation, poverty, immigration, education, urban management, and housing are covered within the context of regional development.

Numerous quantitative tools, including location quotients, shift-share analysis, local multipliers, input-output analysis, statistical modeling, cost-benefit studies, discounted cash flow analysis, and so forth are described in an easy to understand manner. The description of how to apply tools is sensitive to their limitations. Cutting-edge issues are integrated with traditional topics rather than treated as mere appendages.

LED attracted us because it is "people centered" and analyses a world that we see everyday. The impacts of policies on how people live can be visualized. We hope that the subject will continue to be taught and studied in that sprit.

Thanks are due to colleagues at our institutions. Particular thanks are due Fern Freeman and Pat Sherman, who provided important secretarial assistance. Also, the folks at Sage made major contributions. Al Buckner, MaryAnn Vail, and Diane Foster helped ramrod the manuscript through the marketing and production processes. Thanks also to Shamila Swamy and her team from QuADS Prepress (P) Ltd for their copyediting. Finally, appreciation is extended to our students, whose comments and insights contributed to the pedagogy.

1

Local Economic Development in a Global Market

The vast majority of decisions affecting local economic development (LED) are made by private individuals or institutions. Often the decisions are made by persons living half a world away from the affected locality. These choices are generally made on the basis of self-interest after consideration of the costs and benefits. Many economic development practitioners seek to understand how market processes operate so that they can help their organizations make good decisions. Others seek to influence private economic decisions by affecting the real or perceived costs and benefits of decisions so as to stimulate economic development. In both cases, it is essential to understand how the market economy operates. This chapter describes how economists view economic activities and serves as a point of departure for understanding the development process.

How Economists View the World

Students who have not studied economics sometimes fail to understand the role of models and assumptions in economic analysis, the economist's view of individual behavior, and how disagreements about policy can arise. A sketch of these important aspects of the economic paradigm will set the stage for further analysis.

MODELS AND ASSUMPTIONS

Economists often build deductive models to help understand economic processes. Models are deliberate simplifications of reality because the economy includes so many variables that interact with each other in so many ways that

1

we can understand process only by focusing on a few variables at a time. The variables not under consideration are usually assumed to stay the same, the well-known "ceteris paribus" or "other things equal" assumption. For instance, when thinking about how quality of life may affect job growth, it is necessary to assume that the state of the national economy and other critical variables do not change when comparing areas. Otherwise, a city with very poor quality of life located in a fast-growing area might show higher job growth than a city with high quality of life in a slow-growing area.

An important application of the "other things equal" assumption is found in the law of demand. It states that if the price of a good falls, the quantity individuals are willing and able to consume will increase, holding other things equal. Figure 1.1 is a demand curve consistent with the law of demand; it slopes downward. Changes in tastes and preferences, incomes, the price of other goods, expectations, and market size could result in a situation where the relation between price and quantity demanded could appear to violate the law of demand. For instance, price and quantity demanded could increase at the same time if the size of the market also increased. Therefore, to focus only on the relationship between price and quantity sold, it is necessary to make explicit the assumption that everything stays the same except price and quantity.

Students often object to the many assumptions that are incorporated in economic models because they are unrealistic. In reality, other things do not

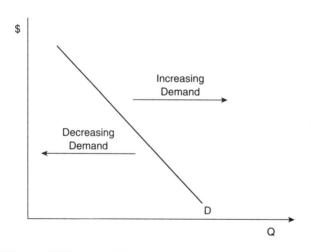

Figure 1.1   The Demand Curve

NOTE: The demand curve shows how many units of a product consumers will purchase at various prices. Under some conditions, the demand curve represents social benefits. Thus, someone would value the 10th unit at $5. Changes in income, market size, price of other goods, preferences, and expectations could cause the demand to increase or decrease.

remain equal, so why do economists assume that they do? The value of the assumptions is that they provide a systematic framework for analysis, and they may be relaxed so that the impact of changing certain assumptions may also be analyzed. For instance, the assumption that the size of the market or incomes do not change may be replaced by the assumption that market size or incomes increase. Then it can be shown that increases in market size or incomes will shift the entire demand curve to the right (called an increase in demand).

Spatial economic models are often predicated on unrealistic assumptions, such as perfect knowledge, profit-maximizing behavior, uniform transportation costs, consumers with identical tastes, and homogeneous space. The insights gained from these models can be increased if consideration is given to how the models will be affected if the assumptions were changed. Changing the assumptions of a model provides insights about the variables that were being held constant.

INDIVIDUAL BEHAVIOR AND UTILITY MAXIMIZATION

For most economists, individuals are the building blocks from which group actions emerge, so it is important to understand what motivates them. The powerful assumption that economists make is that individuals are motivated to maximize their own utility. Money provides utility, but so do other things, such as love. In the sphere of economic development, money is usually the most powerful motivator, but individuals also receive satisfaction from things such as helping their community.

Adam Smith highlighted the importance of self-interest:

> It is not from the benevolence of the butcher, the brewer, or the baker, that we expect our dinner, but from their own self-interest [in trying to get these things]. . . . We address ourselves, not to their humanity but to their self love, and never talk to them of our own necessities but of their advantages.

According to Adam Smith, a market system creates rewards and incentives that encourage utility-maximizing individuals to do what is in the public interest as if they were guided by an "invisible hand."

Disagreements about the extent to which individuals seeking their own self-interest actually serve the public interest are at the heart of the debate between those who believe in "letting the market operate" and those who believe that government involvement is important for successful economic performance.

Economists also assume that individuals are rational in their efforts to maximize utility. The rationality assumption is essential if economic models are to predict behavior. If individuals did not act rationally, then all behavior could be explained as the result of irrational actions.

Students sometimes object to the concept of *utility-maximizing man*. One objection is based on the mistaken idea that utility-maximizing behavior is selfish. In fact, economists recognize that altruistic behavior can provide satisfaction to some individuals. The second objection is that the utility maximizing assumption does not examine how tastes and preferences are formed or why individuals differ in how they attain satisfaction. Economists tend to assume that individuals have a set of preferences, but little attention is given to how preferences are formed. It is likely that if economic life and social life were different, individuals would have a different set of preferences. Urban and regional economists often rely on the work of psychologists, sociologists, and planners, who are more informed about questions of preference formation.

IDEOLOGICAL PERSPECTIVES ON MARKET OPERATIONS

Economists explore two distinct types of questions. On the one hand, positive questions address the world as it is. On the other hand, normative questions inquire about how things should be or ought to be and involve value judgments. Economists disagree about appropriate policies either because of different analyses of how the economy operates (positive) or because they have different values (normative).

Sometimes policymakers are more concerned with economic growth than static efficiency, particularly individuals involved in economic development. A community that operates inefficiently but grows rapidly may be better off in the long run than a community that maintains a high level of static efficiency but does not grow rapidly.

Economic development policies are cast in a way that forces policymakers to choose between static efficiency and economic growth. Some critics of economic planning suggest that too much planning stunts growth because unemployed resources are necessary for innovation and the development of new products.

Equity refers to fairness. When a policy change hurts some individuals but benefits others, questions of fairness arise. If income is tilted too much toward one group, it may be difficult to maintain social stability. Imbalances in the distribution of income may reduce economic prosperity. Economists are not very good at deciding which actions are more equitable, because such decisions cannot be made on scientific grounds. Nevertheless, the appropriateness of most changes must be decided, at least partly, on the basis of fairness.

There are two alternative perspectives on the extent to which government involvement in the economy may improve economic welfare—conservative and liberal.

The conservative perspective places a high value on economic freedom and economic efficiency. Many conservatives agree with Friedman (1962) that capitalism is necessary for political freedom. The analyses of conservative economists tend to show that the laissez-faire market works well. When competitive market conditions exist, individuals seeking their own self-interest act in society's interest. Consequently, conservatives tend to oppose government involvement in regional and urban problems. Even when their analysis leads them to believe that market outcomes are imperfect, conservatives tend to believe that imperfect market outcomes are preferable to government-imposed solutions (which may also be imperfect).

Liberal economists tend to place a high value on economic equity when viewing market operations as sometimes both inefficient and inequitable but still useful. Blinder (1987) referred to the liberal philosophy as combining respect for the efficiencies of the free market with concern for those the market leaves behind. Consequently, liberals tend to believe that government action is important for solving urban problems and securing a more equitable distribution of income. Fundamentally, liberals want to maintain the basic framework of market decision making; but they believe that there is substantial potential for government actions to improve market outcomes. In particular, government regulations and taxes may help when markets are not operating as they should.

Conservatives and liberals constitute the mainstream of economic thinking. Both perspectives rely on the market to provide information and establish the basic incentives that encourage socially desirable behavior. Most of the policy issues discussed in this text are within the liberal-conservative framework.

Radical economic analysis is outside mainstream thinking and often provides interesting challenges to traditional economic thinking. Radical economists are distrustful of the market. Many radical economists believe that the market is not an impartial mechanism that helps organized economic activities. Rather, the market is a means of social control. They are less concerned with whether market mechanisms are efficient than they are with whose interests the market serves. Government programs that affect economic outcomes often help the wealthy because the same interests that control the market also control government. Radicals tend to see urban problems as a reflection of class conflicts. Radicals see greater government involvement in the economy, including direct ownership of productive resources, as a more preferable solution to problems than either a policy of laissez-faire or government modification of market outcomes.

How Markets Work

Markets are a process (not a place) through which buyers and sellers conduct transactions. Markets coordinate numerous economic decisions and provide incentives that influence behavior. To emphasize these important functions, Milton Friedman has claimed that no one in the world knows how to make a pencil. He meant that no one knows how to complete all the steps in the process—cutting the trees, mining the graphite, and so forth. Yet the market helps coordinate these decisions, and many more. Prices tell producers which components of the pencils are needed, what kinds of pencils folks want and provide an incentive for production and an incentive to use less.

When the market is working well, the incentives generated by the market encourage individuals to behave in a way that benefits society. For instance, when a community's economy starts to decline, local resources become idle. Prices of land, labor, intermediate goods, and other resources may fall. The declining prices send two signals. (1) If you own productive resources, do not bring them to this region because the resources can earn more elsewhere. Thus, new workers may not relocate to the area, and current residents may consider leaving. (2) At the same time, falling resource prices might encourage producers, wishing to employ resources, to consider relocating or starting in the region.

The example of community decline illustrates a situation where the market is working well. However, the market does not always generate outcomes that are socially beneficial. When markets create suboptimal or perverse outcomes, government officials attempt to intervene. Sometimes the interventions involve small changes in incentives, or "tweaking" the market, and at other times the market may be completely overridden.

Bartik (1990) contended that appropriate interventions in market outcomes is the hallmark of successful LED policy. Accordingly, an understanding of how markets operate is a prerequisite to understanding the forces that shape local economies and development policies.

SUPPLY AND DEMAND

Figure 1.2 illustrates how supply and demand operate. The demand curve shows how consumer purchases will be affected as prices change, other things being equal. Similarly, the supply curve shows the quantity of output producers would be willing and able to sell at various prices. The higher prices will induce businesses to produce greater output, other things equal.

Let D_0 be the operative demand curve. Price will be determined at the point where the quantity supplied and quantity demanded are equal, Point a in Figure 1.2. The price will be $5. At that price, consumers will produce 100 units, and consumers will purchase 100 units. At any other price, there will be either a shortage or surplus of the product. The $5 price is considered an equilibrium price because once it is attained it will not change unless the supply or demand curves shift. It may take the market a long time to find the equilibrium price; so at any given time, the actual price may not be in equilibrium.

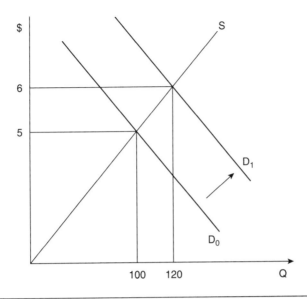

Figure 1.2   Supply and Demand

NOTE: The initial price and quantity of a product are determined by the initial demand and supply curves D_0 and S, respectively. Equilibrium price and output will be $5 and 100 units, respectively. If demand increased to D_1, price and output of the product would increase to $6 and 120 units, respectively.

Suppose that economic development caused the population and incomes of residents to increase. As a result, the demand curve will increase from D_0 to D_1. Price and output will increase. Immediately, we can visualize one of the impacts of economic development on the demand for local products. Similarly, factors that increase the demand for the output of local establishments can contribute to LED. For example, if demand for American-made cars increased, communities with automobile production facilities would probably experience increases in employment as the output of automobiles increased.

SUPPLY, DEMAND, AND EFFICIENCY

When there are many well-informed buyers and sellers, prices and output levels are determined by the interaction of supply and demand. Competitive markets can be very efficient. Economists believe that the sum of individuals' marginal private benefits (MPB) from consuming additional units of a product determines the demand curve in Figure 1.2. The demand curve slopes downward because benefits from <u>additional</u> units of a product fall as more units are consumed. Furthermore, if only the purchaser captures the benefits from the good or service, then the demand will reflect the benefits to society, the marginal social benefit (MSB). (The purchaser is part of society, so the benefits are considered social benefits.) Thus, individuals will purchase goods up to the point where price equals marginal benefits, $P = MSB = MPB$. The relationship between demand and MSB in a world where third parties are unaffected by the use of the good is shown in Figure 1.3.

When producers bear all production costs, the supply curve, which shows how many units they will sell at various prices, will equal the marginal social cost (MSC) curve. The costs paid by producers to make each unit reflect the cost of bidding for the needed resources from alternative uses. Those alternative uses are opportunity costs. Therefore, if the producers bear all the relevant costs of production, then $S = MSC = MPC$ when quantity is q_1.

In a competitive, free-market economy, the price of each good reflects the value society places on the resources used to produce it. In Figure 1.3, the market-determined level of output will be q_1 because the quantity supplied will equal the quantity demanded. If q_1 is the actual output, in what sense is it optimal? If we assume that all relevant costs and benefits are borne by either the producer or the consumer, then the actual output, q_1, will also be at the point where $MSB = MSC$. Producing beyond $MSB = MSC$ will result in producing output where the social costs of producing extra units are greater than the benefits, so

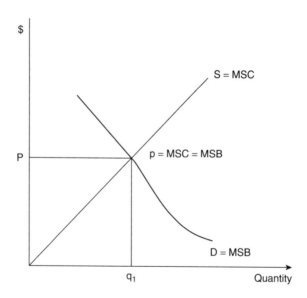

Figure 1.3   Model in an Efficient Market

NOTE: In a competitive market, when all relevant costs are borne by the principles to a transaction (no externalities), output will tend to be optimal.

producing beyond q_1 would be undesirable. If the output level were below q_1, increases in output would be desirable because MSB would exceed MSC.

MARKETS ARE NOT ALWAYS EFFICIENT

If markets worked as effectively as suggested by the analysis underlying Figure 1.3, the role of governments in LED would be very small. There would still be an income redistribution role, but most interference with market outcomes would be inefficient. However, there are several realities that prevent markets from operating efficiently. This section discusses some widely recognized market failures and provides examples of how they may motivate LED activity.

Public Goods

Sometimes markets will not provide goods that citizens want because there are inadequate payment mechanisms. This is a particular problem for the goods we share. For instance, how could roads be provided if not for the government? Few individuals would voluntarily pay for roads if they thought they could use them for free. Maybe some toll roads could be built privately, but their scope would be much more limited than today's highway and feeder road system. Furthermore, the cost of collecting tolls would be too high in the case of local streets, with their numerous entrance and exit points, so private businesses would not finance construction of local roads and similar infrastructure. If they are to be built at all, government must finance them. Goods that must be provided by local government include fire protection, health services, police protection, and amenities such as parks. Usually, provision of public goods in an area is necessary before private investment and businesses can be attracted. At the same time, economic development often increases pressure on governments to build more public infrastructure.

Externalities or Spillovers

When all the costs and benefits fail to accrue to the principles of a transaction (buyers and sellers), third parties will be affected. Often governments need to intervene to protect these third parties. Polluting firms are an excellent example of a spillover effect. Private providers will often overproduce goods that have pollution as a by-product, because the producers will not be concerned with the costs of the pollution, which is borne by others. Negative externalities are a particular problem in high-density urban areas, because one negative spillover harms so many persons.

Local governments may also provide, or subsidize, many services that provide positive spillovers to encourage more production than would be provided by the market. Education is an excellent example, because an educated citizenry provides benefits not only to the person receiving the education but to others in the community. Local officials may seek to reduce negative externalities and increase positive externalities. Furthermore, economic development carries with it a set of externalities. When the local economy improves (declines), many individuals benefit (lose), even if they had nothing to do with the change. Officials are often concerned with which groups may benefit or lose from LED.

Externalities are particularly an urban problem. Urban areas are characterized by high density and the negative (and positive) effects of externalities are amplified in high-density places for two reasons. First, the greater the population is, the more the externality events that will occur. Second, the greater the population, the more the persons harmed by each externality event. For instance, an automotive breakdown may occur once in 50,000 miles. Also, the number of persons hurt by a breakdown will depend on the number of cars on the road. Say, 1/10 of the passengers will be affected by each breakdown. Thus, in a small rural area there will be fewer breakdowns than in high-traffic urban areas, and fewer persons will be inconvenienced by each breakdown. Based on this observation, it may be concluded that harm from externalities will increase faster than the rate of population increase. Conversely, benefits from positive externalities will also increase faster than the population does.

Monopolies

The market will not work efficiently if there are only one or a few producers (or purchasers). Consequently, governments often intervene to control monopolies. The regulation of public utilities is an instance where government has intervened in the market process to ensure that firms do not take advantage of their market power. Monopolies can be a problem at the local level even in industries that are competitive at the national level. For instance, the hotel-motel industry is very competitive nationally, but in a small town in a sparsely populated region, there may be only one motel, a monopoly. Under some circumstances, local monopolies might be an impediment to economic development. Sometimes an LED official seeks to bring new businesses to a community that may increase the competition for existing businesses. Building on the hotel-motel illustration, it is possible that a community that had too few hotels could lose convention business.

Imperfect Information

If some consumers or producers are uninformed, the market will not operate to maximize welfare. Therefore, governments sometime intervene to improve consumer and producer knowledge. Public relations and advertising associated with economic development are attempts to better inform (or misinform) business about the benefits of locating in a particular area. An important task of many economic development practitioners is to gather information that is difficult to find about the local economy and provide it to businesses seeking to make local investments. At the same time, some local officials may exaggerate or distort information in an attempt to make their region appear better than it is in reality. Such information is often included in pamphlets that promote the area.

THE ROLE OF PROFITS

In the market economy, profits drive production and employment decisions. Producers normally will not hire workers or establish businesses unless they anticipate earning a profit. In competitive markets, profits are assumed to be zero because total cost includes a normal return to the business owner or entrepreneur. To understand business decision–making, it is important to understand the concept of profit. The formula for profit is

$$P = TR - TC, \tag{1.1}$$

where P = profits; TR = total revenues; and TC = total costs, both explicit and implicit.

Total revenue equals the price(s) of the output(s) times the number of units sold. One way to sell more output is to lower the price. However, if the price decline offsets the sales increase, then total revenue will fall. If the increase in sales offsets the price decline, total revenue will increase.

Total cost represents all the private costs of production, including the opportunity cost of the owner's efforts and an adequate return on the owner's investment. Thus, the cost of inputs or the wages paid to workers are explicit costs, while the owner's time and the return that could be earned on the capital if it were invested elsewhere are implicit costs. Hence, there is a distinction between profits as used by economists and profits as used by accountants. Accounting profits do not deduct payment for the owner's time, efforts, skills, risks, and so forth.

To understand the nature of the profit equations, consider a person who owns a business with the following costs and revenues:

Total revenue = $100,000

Cost of material = $25,000

Cost of hiring workers = $25,000

Other out-of-pocket costs = $10,000

Other opportunity costs = $50,000 (The other opportunity costs include foregone opportunities the owner could receive if the capital invested earned a normal return interest and if the owner worked for another employer instead of running the business.)

To an accountant, this firm would be earning a profit because the accounting costs would be $60,000 (total explicit costs that do not include other opportunity costs) and the total revenue would be $100,000, so accounting profits would be $40,000. However, the accounting analysis is misleading, because the total costs include the opportunity costs of the owner's capital and labor. If the firm were to operate, the investor-owner would give up opportunities to earn $50,000. Thus, the opportunity cost of $50,000 should be included to provide a comprehensive total cost estimate. After accounting for all costs, this business actually generates an economic loss of $10,000.

Equation 1.1 is very useful in understanding business decisions. Suppose a firm is considering a decision to add to its output. Profits would increase only if the additions to total revenue (called marginal revenue) are greater than the additions to total cost (called marginal costs). Conversely, if marginal revenues are less than marginal costs, firms will not undertake the action under consideration. Accordingly, in thinking about how to increase profits, extra costs as well as extra revenues must be considered. Improving product quality or increasing advertising might increase sales and hence total revenue; but if these steps increase costs more than they increase revenues, profits will decline. If a business sells most of its products outside the area, policymakers have very few tools to help boost revenues. On the other hand, if a firm sells its product locally, most types of local economic growth will contribute to sales. On the cost side, both direct measures, such as business subsidies or tax breaks, as well as indirect methods may reduce costs.

Economic development practitioners are frequently concerned with attracting business by lowering costs, increasing revenues, or altering the perceptions of costs and revenues. Equation 1.1 has two important limitations. First, there are exceptions to the profit-maximizing assumption. Economists usually assume that business managers will behave to maximize profits because maximizing profits is one way to maximize utility. Sometimes, however, businesses may make decisions that may not increase profits but will enhance the utility of the business manager. For instance, a corporate executive may influence the company to donate a million dollars to a local charity. Such an action could reduce income for the stockholders (owners), but the prestige and community recognition that the manager receives may provide direct utility. Particularly, when managers run companies for stockholders, managers may put their own utility ahead of corporate profits or the owners' utility.

Second, future costs and benefits are often not well-known, and some things are impossible to predict. A business may give to charity because it is good public relations, which may increase profits in the long run. Such reasoning may be correct, but it is impossible to quantify. Often business decisions, such as the location of a new venture are undertaken on the basis of a hunch rather than careful calculation of the marginal costs and benefits.

Economic development officials may influence business decisions by describing how an action could increase revenues or lower costs in the long run without having to quantify the impact.

Economic Development Defined

Economists distinguish between economic growth and economic development. Growth is an increase in the overall size of a local economy. Development requires that qualitative improvements occur (Partridge & Rickman, 2003). To illustrate the difference, consider, for instance, the location of a plant that paid very low wages. The plant location might result in growth because the size of the economy would likely increase. However, a diminished level of satisfaction for most residents at the time the plant was opened might also result. Thus, development might not always be associated with growth.

Economic development implies that the welfare of residents is improving. Improvement might be indicated by increases in per capita income (adjusted for inflation). However, economists recognize that income alone is an incomplete indicator of how well residents of a region are doing. Many other quantitative and qualitative factors are associated with welfare.

Some observers attempt to measure quality of life. However, measurement of quality of life is very amorphous. Hajiran (2006) showed that an adequate measure of quality of life requires measuring everything that we value in various "domains," including some very subjective and difficult to measure facets of life such as recreation, spirituality, environment, safety, knowledge, and liberty. These domains are very subjective but important. The evidence that economic growth is associated with increases in subjective well-being, particularly in developed countries, is tenuous (Kenny, 2005).

Equity is another indicator of economic development. Even if average incomes did not grow, a change from a very unequal distribution of income to one that most people considered fairer could be a form of development. Similarly, improvements in the quality of life, such as better transportation systems, education, and cultural facilities, are also indicators of economic development. Sometimes indicators of economic development are difficult to quantify, but they are nonetheless important.

Sustainability is another component in the definition of development. Sustainable development suggests that if growth is excessively destructive to the environment, it cannot maintain itself and hence is not true development. Unfortunately, sustainability is difficult to quantify (Howarth & Farber, 2002)

Beauregard (1993) pointed out that when we focus on the *economics* of economic development, there is a tendency to ignore the broader political and social issues that also affect the quality of life in a community. Since many aspects of economic development are difficult to measure, they are often ignored or devalued. In this book, the theory and tools of economic development will focus on production, consumption, and other resource allocation issues. However, we will not lose sight of the fact that LED is part of a larger process of community development.

Economic development and growth are tied together in significant ways. Growth is usually an important element in the economic development process because growth provides the resources needed for development. Growth helps economies afford improvements in the quality of life and poverty reduction programs. Without economic growth, there would be insufficient jobs to support even a slowly growing population, and forced out-migration may result.

Careers in LED

Numerous career fields require knowledge of LED. Some jobs are concerned with directly establishing or implementing LED policies. Many more jobs combine local economic knowledge with knowledge in other areas because understanding local economic conditions is an important tool for achieving other ends. Thus, the field is built on an interdisciplinary base. In the practice of LED, economics is combined with insights from other areas of study.

Most areas, from large states to small cities, hire economic development officials charged directly with improving the local economy. Their jobs are primarily concerned with stimulating economic growth in a variety of ways, including direct business attractions, provision of a variety of subsidies, improving infrastructure, education and training, and so forth. Private organizations such as chambers of commerce also employ individuals charged with attracting new businesses and improving the conditions of existing businesses. National governments also employ LED experts to grapple with how to improve local economic conditions, often as part of national economic development efforts. In many cases, the efficiency of the national economy may depend on economic development activities at the local level. Federal departments dealing with commerce, housing, international affairs, labor markets, and public service delivery employ individuals who specialize in local economics at both the entry level and the most senior levels.

Many jobs require knowledge of economic development as part of a "kit of tools" needed to achieve other goals. For example, community development workers and many others employed in the private, not-for-profit sector seek to strengthen the local economy in order to improve the housing stock or local job programs. Local government officials must assess the local economy to make better decisions. For instance, the advisability of a spending or tax decision may depend heavily on local economic performance. Business and government forecasters need to understand LED in order to tailor their forecasts to local economic conditions. Local officials recognize that the success of decisions may hinge on the local economy and that the decision will have an impact on the future local economy.

Private businesses are interested primarily in the success of specific enterprises. Knowledge of local economies is often an important tool in achieving that success. Property development companies, utilities, and transportation groups employ persons familiar with LED because the nature of the local economy influences the prospects of their business.

Consulting firms employ individuals to assist companies in location decisions and to advise local governments regarding how to increase economic activity. Banks and other financial institutions employ persons with knowledge about the local economy to assess the risks associated with large ventures and to place loans. Individual investors interested in property development regularly assess the strength of local areas before making an investment. Consider a farmer who sells a product in a market where prices are set by international supply and demand forces. It may seem as though the farmer may not be affected by the local economy. Yet in most cases, the farmer's assets are primarily embedded in his land. Decisions about whether to sell the land or buy more are related to the question of how the local economy will fare. Even the decision about which job to take may depend on the expected future of the local economy.

The great majority of LED jobs require individuals to relate economic insights to concerns in other fields. Accordingly, skilled practitioners should be equipped to relate economic knowledge and an understanding of the local economy to a variety of issues, some of which may not be the principal concern of academic economists. The practice of LED requires the ability and willingness to take an interdisciplinary perspective.

During the course of a career, there will be numerous instances where local economic issues intersect with social and political concerns. For instance, crime can be a deterrent to economic progress when working and middle-class people leave a certain neighborhood because of fear. Thus, sociological and economic knowledge as well as knowledge from other fields must be combined to address the problem. For most real-world concerns, economics may be part of the answer, but economics alone seldom provides the complete answer.

The Nature of Regions

Region is a chameleon word, taking meaning from the context of its use. For instance, the phrase "the region around my house" normally connotes a neighborhood region. However, if someone were to say he or she lived in a cold region, the phrase would connote a multistate area. As trade between nations increases, international regions are becoming more important, and economists are more concerned with multinational regions. In keeping with common usage, both large and small regions will be examined in this text.

Urban is also a term that has different meanings. An urban area, no matter how it is defined, is a region, although not all regions are urban. Urban places are normally associated with large, high-population-density cities. Yet some places with populations as small as 2,500 are considered urban by the Census Bureau. Thus, a small village with only a few stores could be considered urban by the Census Bureau, although such a place might not be considered an urban area as used in everyday conversation.

Many social scientists define *urban* in terms of lifestyle rather than density. Urban society is often contrasted with traditional society. In this sense, urbanization reflects a social change in which diversity, rationality, tolerance, impersonality, functional relationships, and bureaucratic organizations become important characteristics. According to the sociological perspective, the farmer who uses a variety of advanced technologies in production, has major capital investments, buys and sells grain futures in a world market, and watches T.V. broadcasts from around the world via satellite is considered urban.

TYPES OF REGIONS

The three types of regions are functional, homogeneous, and administrative.

Functional Regions

Functional regions are distinguished by the degree to which they are integrated internally. If interaction of components within a region is significant compared with interaction with other places, the basis for a functional economic region exists. An area in which local businesses traded with each other more than they traded with the rest of the world would constitute a functional area. Often a functional region is characterized by a major center and the contagious areas that are economically linked to the center, or node. Most metropolitan areas have a central core. Transportation systems are usually anchored at the core, and key financial and governmental activities are also located there.

Metropolitan areas exhibit hierarchical patterns that characterize functional regions. Specifically, employment activity and retail activity tend to be concentrated in the central business district and in other subcenters throughout the metropolis. The nodes of concentrated economic activity complement and contrast with residential areas. However, the business concentrations and residential areas are dependent on each other. Many LED policies are best implemented at the metropolitan level because of the interdependence within the region.

Standard Metropolitan Statistical Areas

The concept of a functional economic area has been operationalized in the statistical construct of metropolitan statistical areas (MSAs). These areas are defined on the basis of a core area containing a large population nucleus and adjacent communities having a high degree of economic and social integration with the core. Because of the importance of MSAs to analysis and policy, it may be useful to describe their structure in detail.

Central cities are the heart and node of the MSA. Each MSA must include one city with 50,000 or more residents or a Census Bureau–defined urbanized area of at least 50,000 inhabitants and a total MSA population of at least 100,000 (75,000 in New England).

Counties are the building blocks of MSAs. The central county(ies) (containing the central city) plus all contiguous counties that have close economic ties to the central county and are metropolitan in character are included in the MSA. The extent of economic linkage among counties is measured by transportation and communications patterns. The metropolitan character is measured by population density and percent urban. MSAs in New England are based on groups of cities and towns because there are no counties in New England.

MSAs contain suburbs, or urban communities that are closely linked to the central city. Suburbs include satellite communities and bedroom suburbs. Satellite communities (sometimes referred to as "edge cities") normally have an active local economy, often including a substantial manufacturing base. Frequently, businesses in satellite cities developed independently of the central city. In contrast, bedroom suburbs lack an independent economic base. While a few retail and service stores may be located in bedroom communities, their primary function is to provide a residence for individuals who work elsewhere. Because bedroom communities often provide an environment sheltered from many urban problems, an anonymous wit referred to bedroom communities as a "womb with a view." In addition, there is usually some agricultural activity within the outlying counties of most MSAs. Figure 1.4 presents a stylized picture of an MSA.

An advantage of collecting MSA data by county only rather than by cities or by the urbanized portion of an MSA is that the geographic boundaries of a county seldom change. Although counties may be added or dropped from particular MSAs, it is relatively easy to establish a consistent time series by aggregating data collected for individual counties. In contrast, when city boundaries change or an urbanized area increases, it is usually very difficult or impossible to reconstruct a consistent time series. However, the use of counties as the units from which MSAs are built results in more diversity within the MSA than would be the case if only the most urbanized areas were included.

As urbanization has increased, metropolitan areas have grown together. As urban areas have overlapped, commuting and other economic relationships have extended beyond the original metropolitan area.

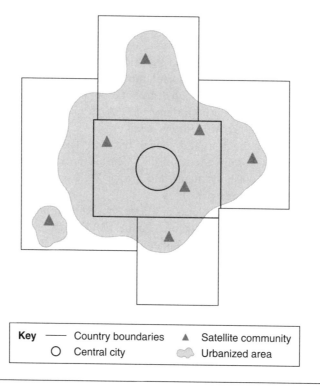

Key —— Country boundaries   ▲ Satellite community
      ○ Central city   Urbanized area

Figure 1.4   Anatomy of an MSA. Metropolitan areas include inner cities, central business districts, various types of suburban areas, and even farms.

A consolidated metropolitan statistical area (CMSA) is a combination of contiguous metropolitan areas. It is defined as a metropolitan area that has a population of at least 1 million. The metropolitan components of CMSAs are designated as primary metropolitan statistical areas (PMSAs). For instance, the Cleveland-Akron-Lorain CMSA is composed of the Akron, Cleveland, and Lorain-Elyria PMSAs. PMSAs are similar to MSAs except for their inclusion in a larger metropolitan complex.

Homogeneous Regions

Economic development officials sometimes deal with homogeneous regions that are designated on the basis of internal similarity. The many informal belt regions—corn, bible, rust, sun, snow, and so forth—are homogeneous regions based on common activities or climate. Likewise, the Appalachian region is distinguished by common economic development problems.

Many neighborhoods are distinguished by ethnic or economic similarities and, hence, are basically homogeneous regions. The census provides data on census tracts, which are small areas consisting of several blocks. While census tracts are not necessarily established on the basis of homogeneity, data on homogeneous neighborhoods are often derived from census tract information.

Administrative Regions

Administrative regions are formed for managerial or organizational purposes. Both private organizations and governments find administrative regions useful. Whereas observers might disagree regarding the exact boundaries of functional or homogeneous regions, administrative regions are normally more clearly delineated because they are used to delegate spheres of activity for businesses or governmental organizations. Administrative regions are also important because they frequently become the basis for policy. Cities, states, and counties are important administrative regions.

Administrative regions often overlap or evolve into functional or homogeneous regions. For instance, a company may establish a set of sales districts based on similar (homogeneous) tastes for product lines within each district. If regional offices provide support services for local sales offices, the administrative region will assume the characteristics of a functional area as well. Furthermore, once an administrative region is formed, the various components may develop commonalities that make the region more homogeneous, and chains of communication, trade, and control that are characteristic of functional regions may emerge.

The number of governmental regions is numerous. There are approximately 85,000 units of local government in the United States. Within the Chicago metropolitan area, for example, there are 1,214 units of local government, ranging from well-known governments such as cities, counties, and school districts to many special-purposes districts that are nearly unknown to average citizens, such as water control districts, lighting districts, recreation districts, and so forth. With so many districts, it is rare that workers in an urban business have the same district profile. In the Chicago area, there are 1.7 units of local government per 100,000 people. Many observers believe that political fragmentation is a major impediment to good government, while others believe that diversity of governmental units contributes to wise decision making.

Local, National, and Global Economic Development

Previously, economists have studied LED as a subject distinct from national economic development. Textbooks addressing the problems of poor countries had a national perspective, seldom emphasizing the localities within those countries. Today, observers view local economies as the critical building blocks of national development. There is a need for national governments to not only

address the needs of specific areas but also ascertain which localities can support economic development and which areas will generate the greatest bang
from assistance. Efficient use of economic development resources should be
the goal when planning and implementing national development policies.

A theme of this book is that appreciating the process of LED is integral to
understanding national and global development. Scott (2001) examined the
relationship between increased globalization and the increasing importance of
urban regions. He contended that as international trading agreements have
reduced trade barriers, unimpeded capital flows and population mobility have
reduced the economic importance of national borders. Thus, the significance
of national entities to economic development has diminished. Simultaneously,
localities are economically linked by a variety of networks that are central to
cost-efficient production and innovation. In other words, the economic ties
that bind nations have weakened, while similar linkages within regions are
becoming more important.

Summary

The vast majority of economic development decisions are based on private
costs and benefits. Sometimes market forces align individual costs and benefits
with outcomes that enhance welfare, but sometimes they create perverse
inducements. This book is predicated on the proposition that understanding
of market forces is critical to understanding LED. Largely through market
forces, local economies are linked to national and international events. At the
same time, LED is integral to understanding and improving national and
global development.

Economists build models based on assumptions. "Other things being equal"
is one of the most useful assumptions. This assumption allows economists to
focus on a few variables by assuming other factors to be constant. As the cost
to customers increases, the quantity of a product consumers will be willing and
able to purchase declines, *other things being equal.* The other things being equal
assumption may be relaxed to provide a more complex analysis of how other
variables affect quantity. Economists also assume that individuals are motivated by self-interest; they seek to maximize utility or satisfaction. Satisfaction
is sometimes interpreted broadly to include things such as emotional satisfaction or narrowly to include only income or profits.

Market processes coordinate numerous economic decisions between buyers
and sellers. Market processes set prices and determine outputs. Price changes
transmit signals to market participants and thereby influence behavior. Supply
and demand curves are used to illustrate how prices and outputs are determined
in competitive markets.

The operation of supply and demand free of governmental restriction may generate efficient outcomes. However, public goods, externalities or spillovers, monopolies, and imperfect information can result in inefficient markets. Correcting these market failures may improve local economies.

Profits influence business decisions. Profits equal total revenues minus total costs. In a simple case, total revenues are prices of output times quantities. In a simple case, total revenues equal the prices of output times quantities sold. When considering costs, analysts must recognize opportunity cost—alternatives foregone in order to produce.

Economic development includes economic growth, but it can also include issues of quality of life and income distribution. Qualitative measures of economic development may be difficult to measure, but they are important.

There are various types of regions. A functional region is defined on the basis of the degree of economic integration. Standard metropolitan areas are based on high levels of interaction between the central city(ies), suburbs, and nonurban areas in the region. Counties are the building blocks for regions. Homogeneous regions are based on internal similarity. Neighborhoods are often defined on the basis of common characteristics of the residents and may, therefore, be considered homogeneous regions.

Knowledge of LED is important not only in careers directly developing and implementing policies but also in many careers where knowledge of local economies must be combined with expertise in other fields.

2

Business Location, Expansion, and Retention

Economic development officials historically paid overwhelming attention to attracting new firms or existing firms that were considering relocation. More recently, many local development officials concluded that communities can generate more jobs by encouraging local businesses to expand or at least maintain their current location. Most of the location factors that contribute to a firm's decision to locate in an area also influence its ability to grow at that location.

The purpose of this chapter is to develop a perspective on a firm's decision to locate or expand in an area and to provide a knowledge base for influencing such decisions. Although the chapter emphasizes profit-oriented firms, the discussion has implications for the location choices of nonprofit organizations.

Location Factors

Every organization will be influenced by many of the location factors discussed below, but with varying degrees of influence. When selecting a location, organizations are generally required to make trade-offs among desired locational features. The trade-offs will differ depending on the establishment's characteristics. For instance, profit-making organizations will be influenced by profit considerations, political institutions by public opinion, and charitable organizations by particular aspects of their mission.

INERTIA

Inertia is perhaps the strongest location factor, yet it is often unrecognized. Once a firm is established at a site, many forces operate to keep it where it is, even when a new facility is required. First, the reasons for the initial location may not have changed. The same factors that supported the original choice could cause a firm to select that location again. This is particularly true if success has made a new facility necessary to increase capacity.

Second, the economic and social structures of an area may evolve to reinforce the initial choice. In a symbiotic or "coevolutionary" relationship, the local community develops in ways that support the firm, and the firm adapts to take advantage of the local area (Norgaard, 1984). In concrete terms, a firm will develop ties to other producers, buyers, and employees in the area. For instance, a firm may have a local supplier that can accommodate unusual fabrication needs. The business ties may even be cemented by personal friendships. Building on what is already in place is a staple of local economic strategies.

Third, a firm that relocates will lose some of its workers. Such a loss may not be extremely important to some firms. However, for other businesses, certain skilled workers may be essential. For instance, a research facility may be hesitant to relocate to another region for fear of breaking up a research team. Schmenner (1982, p. 91) reported that more than 60% of plant expansions were motivated, in part, by the desire to keep the management team together rather than risk separations if a larger facility were built elsewhere.

TRANSPORTATION–COST-MINIMIZING MODELS

Transportation costs are the most thoroughly analyzed location factor because manufacturing activities are sensitive to transportation costs, and they are relatively easy to quantify. Transportation cost models can be analyzed with the tools economists have. Products that have high shipping costs (for either inputs or outputs) relative to the value of the final product tend to be sensitive to transportation costs or "transportation oriented."

Market and Material Orientation

Market or material orientation implies a locational tendency that could be altered by other considerations. Market-oriented producers tend to locate near their market, in part because the final products tend to be more expensive to ship from the production site to the market. Therefore, it saves transportation costs if the products are produced near their intended market. Similarly, activities that add an input resource that is more or less equally available everywhere (ubiquitous) tend to locate near markets. For instance, soft drinks are considered weight gaining because the materials, such as glass, syrup, and so forth, are shipped to the bottler, where water, the ubiquitous input, is added at the production locations. Thus, by locating near the market rather than near the sugarcane, or some other supplier, the producer avoids shipping the water all the way to the market. Products that are hazardous to transport, bulky, perishable, or fragile also tend to be market oriented because of the relatively expensive costs of shipping these products to the market.

Material-oriented activities tend to locate near material inputs. Many material-oriented activities tend to be weight losing—the final product weighs significantly less than the principal input. It makes sense for a sawmill to locate near the forest because in the process of milling, the inputs lose weight and bulk. Likewise, chemical producers who use coal in their production process locate in coal-producing regions because most of the coal burns during production. It is less expensive to ship the chemicals than to transport the tons of coal necessary to produce the chemicals. Meat packing is material oriented because it is cheaper to ship the butchered meat than to transport live cattle. In addition to weight-losing products, producers tend to locate near the inputs when the inputs are bulky, heavy, fragile, perishable, hazardous, or otherwise expensive to transport relative to the final product.

End Point and Transshipment Locations

The discussion of material- and market-oriented activities implies that a location at either the market or the material source would be equally likely if the transportation costs of shipping the raw material to the market equaled the costs of shipping the final product to the market. In this case, the transportation costs would be equal at the market and material sites and all points in between. Such an equality of transportation costs would occur only by coincidence.

The pull of the market and material sites is bolstered by two additional factors: (1) extra handling costs and (2) nonlinear rate structures (long-haul economies). First, a location between the two sites would normally require extra terminal (loading and unloading) costs. If the production site were located between the materials site and the market, (1) the inputs would have to be loaded at the material site; (2) transported to the production site; (3) unloaded, processed, and reloaded at the production site; and (4) the final product transported to the market and (5) unloaded at the market. Thus, a midpoint location requires an extra handling process.

A second factor that favors the market or material site rather than midpoint locations is that transportation systems frequently charge customers less per mile for long hauls than for short hauls. It costs less than twice as much to travel 200 miles as it does to travel 100 miles. Thus, it is less expensive to transport a product or input the entire distance between the material site and the market than to make two short trips.

Transshipment points represent an important exception to the general location advantage of market and material sites. They are junctures in the transportation network where loading and unloading cannot be avoided. Since some shipments would have to be interrupted in any event, production locations at transshipment points may not increase transportation costs. For instance, before the technology developed to construct bridges that could span major rivers, goods transported by land routes had to be unloaded and placed on barges to cross the rivers. The transshipment function contributed to the development of St. Louis. Port cities on the East Coast and West Coast also have transshipment functions. Airports are increasingly important transshipment points in the globalized commercial network.

The Principle of Median Location

The tendency for establishments that produce outputs with high transportation costs to locate at the market has been explained. But what if the market itself is dispersed? In that case, such establishments tend to locate in the center of their market. This tendency is known as the principle of median location. An example will illustrate the principle. Assume that the production costs, quantity demanded, and price are not affected by location. Transportation costs of the output are assumed to be proportional to distance. This might be approximated by the case of a pizza parlor that delivers at a uniform price anywhere in an area. Assume that the customers, denoted by dots, are distributed as shown in Figure 2.1. Each numbered hash mark indicates a block. Assume further that each delivery requires one trip; doubling up to serve both Blocks 2 and 4 in one trip is not allowed.

Where should the market-oriented activity locate if Figure 2.1A represented the market? Intuitively, many people believe that a location on Block 11 would be the best choice because it is close to the middle of the market. But that solution is incorrect. Block 4 would be the transportation-cost-minimizing location.

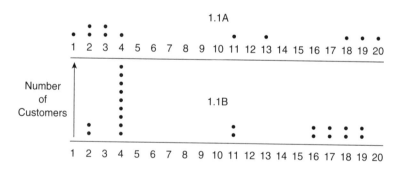

Figure 2.1   The Principle of Median Location

NOTE: The principle of median location illustrates the tendency of market-oriented activities to locate at the point where half the customers are on either side. A large population cluster tends to attract market-oriented activities even if other customers are not located at the point of the population cluster.

To see why Block 4 is optimal, suppose the firm relocated from Block 4 to Block 11. On the one hand, the shift would save 5 blocks' travel when serving customers on Blocks 11, 18, and 19 and 20, a total saving of 15 blocks traveled. On the other hand, an extra 5 blocks of movement would be added for customers on Blocks 2, 4, 5, and 6, or a total of 20 travel blocks. Thus, the total travel costs would increase with the move. Likewise, any move from Block 6 to lower-numbered blocks would increase the total travel costs. If Block 4 were a large residential center, say with 9 customers as show in 2.1B, the median point would be very stable. In general, market-oriented block activities will tend to locate at the median (where half the customers are on one side and half are on the other side) rather than in the geographic center of a market.

Road Systems and Multiple Inputs

Let's complicate the situation by introducing road systems, multiple input sources, and markets. The concept of locational weights can be useful in analyzing these situations.

The "locational weight of the product" is the cost of shipping one unit of the product 1 mile. The "locational weight of an input" is the cost of shipping enough of the input to produce one unit of the product one mile.

Figure 2.2 illustrates several possible road systems and shows how the concept of ideal weight—the cost of transporting the inputs or output needed for one unit of the product—can be used to analyze various situations. Case A is an instance where the firm would locate in the middle of the pulls. Moving north of the minimum transport cost point would increase transportation costs per unit by $8 ($5 + $3) per mile while saving only $7 per unit per mile. In contrast, Case B illustrates an instance where the ideal weight at the end point offsets the counterpulls. Moving away from the end point would save only $8 ($5 + $3) while costing an extra $10 per unit per mile. Case C shows how a midpoint location with a small ideal weight may minimize transportation costs if the other weights pull in opposite directions. Case D illustrates the effects of a dominant weight, even though there are several small inputs or markets.

Case E is interesting because it represents a classic locational triangle with roads connecting only the cities. In this case, the largest weight, 7, would be sufficient to attract production to that site. In contrast, as the triangle flattens to approach the line, as in Case F, the situation becomes more like Case A, and the midpoint location tends to minimize transportation costs.

Of course, reality presents even more complicated problems than those addressed in Figure 2.2. In practice, a location planner may have to choose between good and bad roads, alternative routes, and so forth. Nevertheless, the kind of analysis shown in Figure 2.2 provides a foundation for understanding more complicated situations.

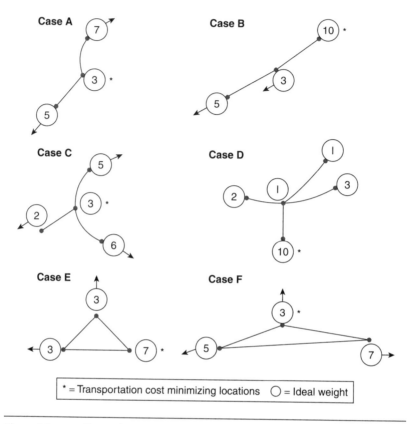

Figure 2.2   Alternative Transportation Systems

NOTE: A fixed transportation system limits possible locations, but ideal weights are still important in determining the transportation-cost-minimizing points.

PRODUCTION COSTS

Transportation costs have traditionally received more attention than other location factors because of their importance in many critical manufacturing processes, such as iron and steel production. The early studies of location placed primary emphasis on the need to minimize transportation costs. However, transportation costs are becoming relatively less important, for three reasons. First, manufacturing, which depends heavily on transportation, has decreased in importance. Second, technology has lowered the cost of transportation compared with other inputs. (Currently, transportation costs are starting to increase as fuel costs rise, so the long-term trend may be reversing.) As the value of the product increases compared with the cost of transportation, less importance will be attached to shipping costs relative to other costs. Finally, the range of spatial variance in other costs of production has become more widely recognized.

Production cost differentials have traditionally been analyzed by examining whether the lower production cost differentials offset the higher transportation costs. In Figure 2.3, the transportation-cost-minimizing point is indicated as "TCMP." Around this point are lines that show the increased transportation cost associated with moving away from the minimum transportation cost point. These lines are known as isodopanes (*iso* means equal and *dopane* means cost), or isocost lines. Let Point L be a low-cost production point. Perhaps energy and/or labor costs are cheaper at L. If the per-unit cost savings are greater than $3, the establishment should locate at L rather than at TCMP. If the savings are less than $3, then TCMP is the most profitable location.

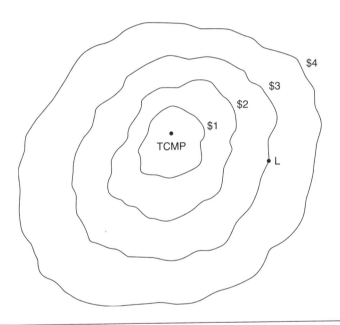

Figure 2.3   Location at a Low-Production-Cost Area

Labor Costs

Firms that have significant labor costs relative to the value of the final product tend to be labor oriented. Leather, insurance services, and many services are examples of labor-oriented industries. A tendency for some companies to seek low labor costs in less developed countries throughout the world has accompanied globalization. Labor costs also vary locally. Many office activities are relocating from the central city to the suburbs to gain access to the "pink collar" workforce that has developed due to the increase of the two-wage-earner families.

A region's prevailing wage rates are an important indicator of labor costs. They represent the wage of a typical worker in a given job category. An area has many prevailing wage rates because there are many different categories of labor. A firm employing unskilled workers would be interested in a different prevailing wage than a firm employing typists.

Wage rates alone are not sufficient to accurately reflect labor costs, for several reasons. First, wage rates are only part of the compensation package. Benefits such as health insurance and retirement are also important. Second, productivity differences can cause labor costs to differ between regions, even when hourly compensation is equal. If workers in Area A produce twice the hourly output as workers in Area B while using equal amounts of other inputs, the compensation rate in Area A could be higher than in Area B and yet labor cost per unit of output could be lower in Area A.

Although it is important, labor productivity is difficult to measure, particularly in the service sector. Data that allow researchers to calculate the total dollar value of output divided by the size of the labor force (a measure of productivity) are available in most developed countries. While this information can be used to approximate labor productivity, it does not account for the different amounts of capital or other inputs used in production. Furthermore, if a region's high productivity is due to better management rather than a capable workforce, the productivity difference will not justify higher compensation for workers.

A third difficulty in using prevailing wage rates as a measure of labor costs is that employers may be able to hire workers at amounts substantially below an area's prevailing wage rate. A study by White (1987) found that workers in Milwaukee who had experienced substantial spells of unemployment were willing to work for wages well below their previous wage and below the prevailing wage in the area. The longer the length of unemployment, the lower the reservation wage. A firm that measures labor costs by the prevailing wage in the industry would overlook the fact that unemployed workers will accept substantially less pay. Of course, some employers may fear that workers will not remain satisfied with wages below the local prevailing rate. Therefore, firms may choose to assume that wages will increase to the prevailing level. Considerations of future wage levels cannot be rigorously quantified, but neither can they be ignored.

Unionization is often mentioned as a location factor related to labor cost. The common perception is that unions increase compensation, promote work rules that reduce productivity, and contribute to work interruptions. While some empirical studies have found negative relationships between unionization and local economic performance (Schmenner, 1981, p. 7), the decline in union power in recent years has likely mitigated the adverse affects of unions.

Quality of Life

Increasingly, economic development officials believe that if the local quality of life could be improved, economic development would be enhanced. The emerging importance of quality of life is indicated by a Sarasota County, Florida, survey, where more than 70% of location decisions considered the quality-of-life factor. Many businesses were found to be willing to accept "somewhat" higher operating costs in order to obtain a better quality of life (Moulder & Hall, 1995). Richard Florida (2002) argued that businesses prosper and tend to locate in areas with a creative labor force. Creative people want to live in areas with diverse and high-quality amenities. Hence, good amenities will contribute to economic development.

Florida (2002) extended the concept of a "good place to live" to include community tolerance. Thus, communities open to blacks and gays and non-traditional lifestyles will have an edge in attracting some firms, according to Florida. Amenities refer to features that enhance quality of life. Regional amenities include good weather, access to museums, sunshine, good roads, schools, other public services, and a variety of other factors that may only indirectly influence production costs. Amenities have become more important because many industries, particularly in high-tech sectors, have become liberated from traditional, cost-oriented locational pulls. A locational decision maker may choose a site with more amenities or a better quality of life if other direct-cost factors are about equal, and many firms will select amenity-rich environments even when other things are not equal.

Amenities may allow firms to recruit more productive workers or recruit workers at lower costs. Technically skilled researchers and creative employees value communities with a good quality of life. Since individuals at the top of their professions can often obtain jobs almost wherever they choose to live, they would work in an area with a poor quality of life only if the wage compensation was substantially higher than elsewhere or if the job satisfaction was particularly high. A good quality of life may help attract and retain less skilled workers at lower wage rates as well.

Amenity-rich areas may experience increases in the demand for property, causing real estate values and rents to rise. In this case, production costs in amenity-rich areas may be high because the company's land rents and taxes (to pay for public amenities) are high. Roback (1982) used weather-related variables, such as the number of cloudy days and the number of heating degree days (days that are cold and require heating), to measure quality of life. She concluded that increased amenities both lower wages and increase rents. In spite of higher rents, business behavior indicates that amenities exert a strong pull. The recognition that quality of life is an important contributor to economic development has led many local economic development (LED) officials to "market" their communities to improve the media's representation. For instance, *Money Magazine* regularly publishes a "best places to live" index, and officials consider strategies to boost their ranking. The rankings are usually very subjective and based on the preferences of an unrepresentative sample of people. Nevertheless, media stories take a life of their own, and local officials often spend public money trying to improve their rankings (McCann, 2004).

Taxes

Traditionally, many economists have not considered taxes a major location decision factor because they represent a small percentage of business costs. However, several recent studies have challenged this position. Currently, most observers believe that state and local taxes appear to have at least a moderate influence on industrial location and economic growth (Bartik, 1992).

There are a variety of taxes that influence the location of a business, and they all have varying impacts on the location decision. Personal income taxes may indirectly affect labor costs as workers require higher compensation to offset higher taxes. Personal income taxes may also influence high-paid executives who directly affect the firm's location choice. These executive decision makers may be more concerned with their personal tax situation than that of the business. Wasylenko (1984) and Romans and Subrahmanyam (1979) have both shown that high personal tax rates have detrimental effects on regional growth. Corporate income taxes directly affect after-tax profits and may have a more direct effect on the location decision. Bartik (1984) found that capital-intensive industries were particularly sensitive to state taxes on corporate profits. Real estate and property taxes are especially important intraregional location factors because there are substantial variations in property tax rates within a region (Charney, 1983).

Government Incentives and Infrastructure

Governments provide a variety of special incentives or subsidies for businesses to encourage location in a certain area. Examples of special governmental incentives include state interest subsidies, loan guarantees, regulatory exemptions, sale of land below market prices, tax credits, special infrastructure constructed at public expense, and provision of construction-ready sites. Most major locational decisions involve some type of governmental assistance. Special incentives are offered by so many places that they are almost a ubiquity (Sweeney, 2004). Major downtown hotels or office projects almost always receive special governmental incentives, often from more than one level of government. Like taxes, government incentives are both an intra- and an interregional location factor. There is no strong empirical evidence regarding the effectiveness of direct business subsidies, although most economic development practitioners consider them essential. However, some neighborhood advocates argue that business subsidies drain money from neighborhood programs and human services.

Infrastructure development (roads, water and sewer facilities, telecommunication, public buildings, and so forth) also plays an important role in creating an environment that retains and attracts business. A good stock of public infrastructure will make local firms more productive.

Local Business Climate and Regulations

Recently, business climate has been identified as an important location factor. Businesses often refer to excessive "red tape" as an obstacle to expansion. Excessive or poorly administered regulations can be particular impediments to new business formation. Like quality of life, business climate is a somewhat vague concept because it is intended to include not only tax and expenditure programs but also the less tangible aspects of a community's attitude toward business. An area's willingness to accommodate potential and existing businesses also exemplifies a good business climate. Hanson and Berkman (1991, p. 213) referred to the state business climate as a "poor and crudely measured" concept.

The scope of regulations imposed on businesses often measures business climate. Important areas of regulation include finance, communication, the environment, transportation, labor markets, and property development.

Energy Costs

Energy prices directly affect transportation costs and consequently affect the location of transportation-oriented activities. Energy is also a direct input in the production process. Carlton (1983) examined the birth of new branch plant locations and concluded that electricity prices were a major location factor.

Energy costs are highly regulated, and many development officials hope to attract business by keeping costs as low as possible. However, there are important quality dimensions to energy that should also be addressed. For instance, businesses may be concerned with the availability of some energy sources. Concerns include access to natural gas and the possibility of blackouts or brownouts. As businesses rely increasingly on computers, the quality of electrical energy, including the minimization of electrical surges, is an important locational consideration.

Site Costs

The cost of a particular site may be expressed in terms of rent or purchase price of land and building. Site costs include land and buildings. Site costs are not an important interregional location factor because almost all regions offer a variety of sites at a wide range of prices, but site costs are a major factor in the competition among jurisdictions within a region. Warehouses and office facilities are particularly sensitive to site costs. Site costs can be greatly affected by terrain and other physical features that influence construction costs.

NATIONAL POLITICAL CLIMATE AND STABILITY

National political stability is a regional location factor that is generally the same in regions throughout a nation. As the world economy becomes increasingly interdependent, establishments are considering locations throughout the world. One of the most important considerations a foreign investor has is deciding whether the government is stable and whether the political climate is compatible with a satisfactory return on investment. Fear of new governmental regimes has impeded foreign investment (Nel, 2003; Obwona, 2001). Corruption is also a substantial drag on development (Pellegrini, 2004). Currency stability is also important. The political stability of the United States partly explains the continuing inflow of foreign investment despite international trade deficits. Economic freedom indicators vary significantly across nations. Various observers have constructed indicators that measure economic freedom. Key indicators of political and economic freedom, such as freedom of speech and contract, correlate strongly with indicators of prosperity, such as per capita income, GDP growth, unemployment, and so forth (Gwartney & Lawson, 2006). Like quality-of-life indicators, economic freedom measures consist of a long list of variables. The decision regarding what to include as measures of economic freedom is subjective. While economic freedom indicators are more likely to distinguish between nations rather than regions within a nation, location decisions often involve selection among cities in different countries.

Political factors may also help one area within a country compete with other regions, particularly for establishments that do business with the federal government. In such cases, the strength of the region's representatives to the national government may be a very important site selection factor for businesses that deal with the government. These concerns may have occasion to request assistance in obtaining government business.

OPPORTUNITY CREATION

Firms may seek locations in areas that provide unspecified future opportunities. The overwhelming preponderance of location literature has focused on cost factors. Even the need to be near a market is normally described in terms of the effect on transportation costs for customers and/or the firm. Increasingly, site selection experts are considering the advantages of seeking locations that either provide future opportunities or at least do not restrict future possibilities. A retail firm that moves to an area in anticipation of population increases or other cost-reducing/market-expanding events is an example that can easily be incorporated into the traditional location considerations.

However, firms may also seek locations that promise more opaque opportunities. In particular, simply being "where the action is" may place a firm in a position where it can take advantage of innovations better. Specifically, Christensen and Drejer (2005) suggest that a firm's location affects innovation and knowledge acquisition. In an era of rapid change, lack of access to knowledge streams will be a locational disadvantage.

The Decision-Making Process

The locational choice can be complex, because the decision may involve a variety of motives and affect a substantial portion of the workforce. This section examines the motives of locational decision makers and the corporate decision-making process.

MOTIVATIONS

In economics, the most widely used motivational assumption is that businesses seek to maximize profits. Since profit maximization is a cornerstone for understanding behavior, it is appropriate, at least as a first approximation, to assume that it is the main criterion in choosing a location. However, there are three instances where profit-maximizing explanations will fail or provide only part of the explanation.

First, the profit-maximizing assumption fails to account for the choices of nonprofit institutions. Fire stations and other public facilities are located on the basis of quick service and the political pulls of citizens in various parts of the city. Politics can also be a very important locational determinant for many facilities, such as military bases.

Second, some managers may choose to locate a facility in an area that has a good climate, low personal tax rates, or other advantages that have a personal appeal, even if the location is not strictly profit maximizing. In other words, managers may place their personal interests above stockholder interests (which is not surprising if you believe managers maximize utility and have some insulation from being fired if profits are not maximized). Because there are many uncertainties in location decisions, evaluating a location decision based solely on profit forecasts may be difficult.

Third, business owners and managers may prefer a safe location (a high probability of generating satisfactory profits) rather than high-risk/high-return locations; if the high-risk location fails, the managers may be fired or the business may fail.

PRACTICAL LIMITATIONS ON THE CHOICE PROCESS

The amount of time and study devoted to locational decisions varies drastically. At one extreme, an individual may open a business after comparing rents between a few buildings and making sure that there are no competitors in the area. It may be rational not to devote much time, effort, or money to a locational decision if the profitability of the enterprise is not sensitive to location. Even profit maximizers want to maximize profits net-of-location search costs. However, other locational decisions involve extensive analysis and negotiations. New businesses are less likely to engage in a careful, profit-maximizing analysis of locational choice than branch plants. New businesses often locate where the founder lives, which suggests that personal factors may be as important as location factors that might increase profits. However, a successful and enduring business site may have attributes of a profit-maximizing location, even if it was initially selected based on personal factors. Yet locations based purely on personal choices, in areas that cannot support satisfactory profits, will perish. As Hoover (1948, p. 211) put it, "A good analogy is the scattering of certain types of seeds by the wind. These seeds may be carried for miles before finally coming to rest, and nothing makes them select spots particularly favorable for germinations." Because of the survival of those that happen to be well located, the resulting distribution of such plants from generation to generation follows closely the distribution of favorable growing conditions.

Hoover's analogy is appealing but probably overstates the case. Nonoptimal locations may or may not be quickly eliminated. In fact, bad locational choices could remain in place for decades. The local economic environment could change in ways that support the initially suboptimal location, perhaps through the process of coevolutionary development.

STEPS IN THE CORPORATE SITE SELECTION PROCESS

Although there are a variety of motives involved in selecting a location, large businesses tend to follow similar steps in the site selection process. Schmenner (1982) identified six basic steps: (1) need recognition, (2) establishing a site selection team, (3) developing criteria, (4) narrowing the choices, (5) local discussions, and (6) the final decision.

Need Recognition

Locational decisions are seldom "only location decisions." They are usually part of a broader corporate planning process and occur at critical junctures in a firm's life cycle. A change in corporate strategy, such as the introduction of a new product or process, or changing market conditions often motivate a location decision. Sometimes the development of a new facility will be the motivating factor.

Establishing the Selection Team

The organization of the company affects the nature of the site selection process. Corporations with a centralized staff will generally form a team at the corporate level. Team members will include representatives from key corporate departments, such as transportation, distribution, personnel, engineering, real estate, or planning. Decentralized companies may carry out the locational study at the divisional level. For small companies, the CEO is more directly involved in the decision because the small company cannot afford a team of "in-house" specialists. Small companies also normally search within short distances of their existing plants so that information costs may not be as significant.

Consulting firms specializing in locational decisions are used in about one third of the locational decisions for Fortune 500 companies. The proportion may be even higher for small- and medium-sized firms that do not have the internal staff needed to conduct a locational study. In addition to being more cost-effective than an in-house staff, the advantages of employing consulting firms rather than doing the work in-house include the insulation of the site selection team from internal pressures and greater anonymity for the company.

Developing Criteria

The site selection team will develop a list of important locational "must have/want" characteristics for the new facility. The role of the proposed facilities in the overall corporate strategy will be considered in developing and revising the list of criteria. The "must have/want" list will include both quantitative and qualitative location factors. The location factors may be weighted to indicate which locational features are the most important.

Trade-offs occur between the information that may be theoretically ideal and information that is realistically available.

Narrowing the Choices

Once the criteria have been established, data must be collected. Often a preliminary screen is used to narrow the choices. The preliminary screen will rely on data that are readily available.

The search is normally made sequentially. The first stage involves the choice of a multistate, state, or urban region. Once a region or state has been selected, a more microgeographic focus will be taken, narrowing the areas under consideration to a short list of one or a few communities. At this stage, the search for an exact site will begin. Individual suburban and central city jurisdictions within a metropolitan area often compete with one another as well as with sites in other regions.

In selecting a broad region, the site selection team will focus on variables that have significant variations, such as state taxes, climate, proximity to customers and suppliers, and other features.

Location factors that vary at the microgeographic level of detail, such as land costs, access to major roads, and good local schools, are less important in the macroregional screen but are important in determining where the final parcel of land will be.

Once the number of sites has been narrowed to a manageable few, a specific site must be found. At this stage, published data are less useful than the telephone and legwork. Information costs limit the number of sites that can be examined in detail.

Normally, a firm making a major locational decision will gather detailed information on several specific sites. A company may make its requirements or needs known to state or local agencies and let them respond. Regional and city planning agencies, local utilities, banks, railroads, and chambers of commerce are all sources of information. The features of each site will be compared against the "must have/want" list. Sites will be eliminated as more detailed and difficult-to-obtain information is gathered on the remaining sites after each elimination round. Site visits and collections of nonstandard or unpublished data will help narrow the number of sites.

Discussions With Local Public Officials

Most communities are anxious to attract new economic activity. The firm may require assurances from local officials that zoning or other land use regulations will not become impediments if it decides to locate in the area. Firms may negotiate special incentives to locate in a particular area. Incentives include tax abatements, land below market price, and a variety of indirect subsidies.

Several consulting firms use large-scale computer models to aid in the winnowing process. In constructing such a model, weights are first assigned to the "must have/want" list of characteristics. The more important the attribute, the higher the weight. A particular site will be assigned a score on each location factor. The better the regional attribute, the higher the score. By multiplying the weight for each factor by the region's location score and summing the results, an overall desirability index can be obtained. The use of computer software does not guarantee optimal site location, and the large-scale computer-generated site selection method has been criticized for lack of rigor and accuracy (Erickson, 1987; Skora, 1985).

Reaching a Final Decision

The final decision is normally formalized in the firm's capital budget. Preliminary estimates of land acquisition and construction costs will be developed for inclusion in the corporation's capital budget. In a large corporation with several divisions, each unit may have to compete with other divisions for a share of the capital budget. A feasibility analysis will normally show that the proposed facility will earn a sufficient rate of return to justify the construction costs.

Changing Relative Importance of Location Factors

In an effort to determine the most important location factors, researchers have asked decision makers what location factors are most important to them. It is difficult to generalize from these studies, because each study used a different research design. The differences in the studies include the types of selection factors examined, the time period examined, the types of businesses analyzed, and the techniques used to draw a conclusion.

SURVEYS OF LOCATION FACTORS

There are several factors to consider when evaluating survey responses. First, questions must be designed carefully to avoid ambiguous responses. For instance, quality of life has been found to be important in many surveys, but researchers are still not clear as to the definition of a good quality of life. Second, respondents may provide answers that they believe will influence policy in their favor or that they believe the surveyor wants to hear. Taxes, for instance, are often ranked high on surveys even though they are not a major cost element for most activities. Possibly this is because respondents believe that if taxes are considered "important," governments will reduce them. Third, only existing firms can be surveyed. Firms that made bad choices and went out of business cannot be contacted. Finally, the choices given by the survey researcher can affect the response. Suppose all the labor-related location factors—labor cost, productivity, cost of skilled labor, fringe benefits, changes in the wage rate, presence of clerical workers, unionization, and right-to-work laws—were listed in great detail. Possibly no single factor would be considered as important by more than a few respondents. However, every firm might respond that "labor" was an important factor if labor were a choice by itself. This problem makes comparison of findings very difficult.

SURVEY FINDINGS PAST TO PRESENT

Early location theory treated transportation costs as the dominant location factor. Morgan (1964) examined the results of 17 locational studies conducted prior to 1963. He found four significant factors: (1) markets, (2) labor, (3) raw materials, and (4) transportation. Other factors such as taxes, quality of life, and financial incentives were not found to be significant. The direct, cost-oriented location factors exerted the dominant influence on industrial location. Morgan's study is dated, but it provides an excellent reference point for examining how location factors have changed since the mid-1960s.

More recent surveys (Alexander Grant, 1985; Fortune, 1977; Gabe and Bell, 2004; Heckman, 1982; Kieschnick, 1981; Premus, 1982; Schmenner, 1982) indicate that many additional factors affect location choices. Six important generalizations can be made by contrasting the recent findings with surveys conducted prior to 1970.

First, the traditional location factors—(1) markets, (2) labor, (3) new materials, and (4) transportation—remain the most important location factors.

Second, the relative importance of the traditional location factors has diminished compared with that of other location factors. For example, unlike studies in the 1940s and 1950s, most of the recent location studies found factors such as education, unionization, personal reasons, business climate, energy, and familiarity with local conditions on the "must have/want" list. In contrast, Morgan's (1964) review of 17 location studies conducted prior to 1963 found the traditional location factors to be practically the only factors that mattered.

Third, the primary impact of technological change has been to reduce the significance of proximity to raw materials and transportation costs as location factors. Technology has increased the number of steps in the production process, reduced the importance of raw materials, and lowered transportation costs. One consequence has been a shift in the growth of U.S. manufacturing activities from the resource-rich Midwest to areas of the country where markets are expanding, such as the Southwest and Far West.

Fourth, studies have found that state and local taxes have had an important effect on business location, particularly within metropolitan areas, where business property taxes can vary substantially among jurisdictions. Thus, contrary to what the earlier literature has suggested, it would be imprudent to ignore taxes as one of the important factors that influence the industrial development of regions (Alexander Grant, 1985; Heckman, 1982). However, low taxes offset by low public services may actually reduce the locational appeal, particularly at the local level (Gabe & Bell, 2004).

Fifth, the range of places that businesses evaluate has expanded to the global scale. Two places with vastly different characteristics might both be competitive in the site selection process. As the difference between places under consideration has increased, trade-offs may become more ambiguous. Differences in labor costs or political stability are much smaller within a nation than globally, so it is easier to make decisions at the margin. It is easier to imagine "other things equal except for, say, wages," when considering similar locations. It is more difficult to say how much of a cost reduction will compensate for, let's say, a stable middle class.

Finally, "soft" factors are becoming more important. Observers mention quality of life, education, and diversity of the population as important location factors for particular types of enterprises.

Conducting Business Retention and Expansion Programs

Business retention and expansion (BR&E) strategies have emerged as one of the most effective tools for generating strong local economies. Among other things, the programs promote job retention and growth by identifying barriers to business survival and growth among firms already located in the community. The growth of BR&E programs recognizes that the majority of new jobs come from internal expansions rather than by attracting new firms.

The BR&E programs are basically a process whereby community representatives meet with local firms in an effort to understand how they can be better assisted by local governments. The outcome of these visits include building an ongoing relationship with local businesses, identifying "red flag" issues that require quick resolution (Morse, 1996), generating information on business needs that can be used in LED planning, and providing assistance in the resolution of specific concerns. When a business expresses interest in expansion or suggests that it may be considering relocation, LED officials make a special effort to encourage the firm to expand locally. There are a few simple steps in the typical BR&E study:

Step 1: Develop a questionnaire and an interview team.

The interview team should initially be assigned to visit local businesses. Team members may be either community volunteers or professional staff. Normally, a site visitation team will include two or more team members so that one can take notes and the other can maintain eye contact and move the interview along the lines suggested in the interview protocol work.

A survey instrument should be developed to guide the interview team and to collect information in a formal way. Often the interview begins with open-ended, "ice-breaking" topics. In the course of the discussions, the interviewer may skip some questions if the answer is obvious in the course of the conversation. Furthermore, if a follow-up is appropriate, interviewers may be encouraged to explore the issue even if there is no specific question on the interview form.

Step 2: Conduct interviews.

Site visitation teams will visit firms. Sometimes, business are delighted to cooperate. Often they express the idea that "this is the first time the government has shown an interest in my business." Some BR&E teams reported difficulty in getting businesses to cooperate because businesses saw "the government" as an enemy. Pearland, Texas, for example, overcame initial business resistance by carefully explaining the purpose and limitations of the program, devoting adequate time to make the business connections, and providing immediate follow-up when the business had a problem. Even if the follow-up does not solve the business' immediate problem, it builds trust and helps the business recognize that the community officials are serious about the desire to assist. (Dickson, 2005). As businesses endorsed the program, other businesses cooperated more readily. It may be important to coordinate the business interviews, particularly if several local governments within a metropolitan areas are conducting their own BE&R studies. In one Ohio county, business owners complained that organizations were repeatedly asking the same questions and their time was being wasted. Coordination among local governments will also be important to avoid interjurisdictional competition. When local governments compete, there is a danger that subsidies might be provided for a business to move from one part of the region to another with no new job creation for the region.

Step 3: Analyze the results of questionnaires and develop a long-term strategy.

However, the BR&E programs are also intended to guide longer-term LED efforts. Once sufficient data are collected, economic development officials should design and implement plans to address the important concerns that were identified. For instance, if local merchants complained about unruly youths "scaring" customers, the school or the police department might be made aware of the problem. Often the policies will involve helping local businesses deal with other governmental agencies to ease some regulatory requirement. Popular activities that have resulted from BR&E studies include conducting seminars for business on timely topics and providing businesses with "networking" opportunities.

Step 4: Continual follow-up.

While an intensive interview effort may be appropriate when a program is first introduced, one of the most important aspects of BE&R programs is that they need to be ongoing so that businesses don't feel that they have had their say and now it's over. New issues will continue to evolve and should be identified so that they can be incorporated into future economic development planning. The most important long-term benefit from the BE&R strategies program is that it builds the capacity to maintain an ongoing relationship with local businesses.

Summary

Location factors affect a community's ability to attract and retain economic activity. Increasingly, local location policies are oriented toward improving existing business rather than taking a business located in another area. Businesses are influenced by a variety of location factors, but to differing degrees, depending on the characteristics of the organization.

Inertia is a major, often unrecognized, location factor. The reasons the firm located in an area in the first place may continue to be important and economic. Coevolutionary development explains how businesses develop in ways that reinforce existing locations. When a firm moves out of an area, it risks loss of business contacts and valuable workers. Building cooperative working relationships among businesses can be a business retention strategy.

Transportation-cost-minimizing models are based on the idea that firms will locate at a transportation-cost-minimizing point. Market-oriented firms produce finished products that are expensive to transport, so they locate near markets. Material-oriented activities locate near materials because the materials needed in production are expensive to transport. The principle of median location explains the location tendencies of market-oriented firms serving several markets.

Low production costs may encourage a firm to locate away from the transportation-cost-minimizing point. Principal production cost factors include (1) labor costs (including prevailing wage, productivity, and unionization), (2) quality of life, (3) taxes, (4) government incentives and infrastructure, (5) political climate (including stability), (6) local business climate, (7) site costs, and (8) energy costs.

Economists normally assume that profits drive locational decisions. This is generally true. Nevertheless, profits may fail to account for the choices of nonprofit institutions. Profit-maximizing models also fail to account for possible conflicts of interest between corporate managers and stockholders. Finally, decision makers may prefer safe locations (a minimum, nearly guaranteed profit) to high-risk, high-expected-profit locations.

The corporate decision process can be divided into five steps. First, a need for a new location must be recognized. Location decisions are seldom *only* location choices but are often associated with other business changes. Second, a site selection team can be formed to include key corporate officers and, possibly, site selection consulting firms. Next, a "must have/want" list can be developed. Location factors may be weighted according to relative importance. Fourth, a winnowing and focusing stage, in which computer models may be used, will narrow the locational choices. Negotiations with local policymakers over details such as costs and subsidies may also be necessary to reduce the shortlist to a particular site. The final decision is often recognized in the company's capital budget.

The most important selection factors continue to be transportation costs, access to materials, access to markets, and labor costs. However, the list of important location factors has increased significantly in recent years. Consequently, the relative importance of the "big four" has declined. The nature of location factors will continue to change as technology and other factors change the production process.

Maintaining ties with existing local businesses can be enhanced through BR&E studies.

3

Markets, Urban Systems, and Local Development

This chapter is focused on the economic relationship between places. Patterns of trade and information exchange form complex networks. These networks tend to overlap in cities. An area's place within a network influences its economic function and prospects.

First, the concept of a market area for a single product is developed. The second section describes how the production sites for a variety of products can result in a system of cities in which cities form a hierarchy with specialized functions and hinterlands. The third and fourth sections evaluate the theoretical model and consider its application in the global economy. The final section describes some techniques that can be used to measure the extent of market areas and discusses hinterland expansion strategies.

Demand and Market Areas

A market area is the geographic region in which a product is sold. To focus on the economic forces that shape a product's market area, it is useful to assume the following:

1. An economy exists on a homogeneous plane. In other words, natural resources, climate, population density, and other location features are the same.

2. The plane is initially populated by self-sufficient families. That is, they produce all their own food and clothing and do not rely on outside producers.

3. Transportation costs are equal in all directions and proportional to distance.

After considering the implications of this restrictive model, certain assumptions may be relaxed. As the assumptions are relaxed, a framework will exist to help understand the important economic forces that shape development.

Under the above conditions, some of the original self-sufficient families would specialize and make products at lower costs than their neighbors by taking advantage of economies of scale. The area in which they sell their output would constitute their market area, and producers would be the only sellers within their area. The market area would be limited, because the larger the area serviced, the greater the transportation costs at the market fringe. Thus, unless economies of scale are substantial, transportation costs would prevent one family from servicing the entire nation. To see how the above implications are derived from the initial economic assumptions, it is useful to first understand how demand is affected by distance.

Demand in a Spatial Setting

The nature of market areas can be better understood by considering demand in a spatial setting. "Textbook" demand analysis ignores space. Making space explicit in demand analysis is essential to understanding local economic forces. Figure 3.1 shows a typical demand curve for an individual. The typical consumer will purchase q_1 units per period at price P_1. How does space influence the analysis?

Suppose a producer operating on the "homogeneous plane" initially priced a product at P_1, as in Figure 3.1. The price represents the selling price at the establishment's point of sale. A consumer buying the product must pay the point-of-sale price plus the transportation costs. Transportation costs include monetary and nonmonetary costs. In this model, time and aggravation are "transportation costs," just as gasoline and automobile depreciation are transportation costs. There are two important implications from the existence of transportation costs. First, transportation costs drive a wedge between the cost to consumers (the price plus transportation costs) and the revenue received by producers. Second, the cost to consumers will differ depending on how close to the seller they live, even though the point-of-sale price may be equal for everyone. Consumers pay a greater cost the farther they are from the point of sale.

Assume that consumers located next to the store or plants have no transportation costs. Therefore, an individual next to the plant could be expected to purchase q_1 units. However, consider a customer located distance d from the plant, and let d_r equal the transportation costs for this customer. Thus, the person living at distance d will bear a total cost of P_1 (the point-of-sale price) plus d_r. Clearly, individuals living farther from the point of sale will purchase fewer units, q_d in this case. The inclusion of distance in traditional demand analysis helps us understand that two things happen when a firm lowers its price. First, customers within the existing market will consume more. Second, the size of the market area will increase as new customers are willing to travel longer distances to make purchases.

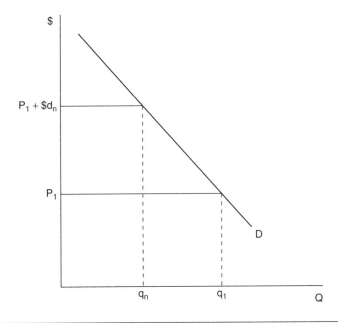

Figure 3.1   Demand With and Without Transportation Costs for a Consumer Living Distance d From the Plant, Where q_d = Quantity Demanded at distance d, P = FOB (Free on Board or at the Door)) Price, and r = Transport Cost Per Mile

NOTE: The inclusion of transportation costs as part of the price can be represented as a movement up the demand curve.

COMPETITION FOR MARKETS

The spatial perspective implies that as distance from a store increases beyond some point, transportation costs will add enough to the price so that individuals will not buy from that location. The geographic space in which a product is sold is the firm's market area. Suppose a producer is successful in an enterprise and earns excess profit. Excess profits are profits in excess of what could be earned if the resources were employed in a comparable investment. The producer may also have established a market area and will have some monopoly power within that market area because customers will have some preference for a nearby seller. Figure 3.2a shows the average cost curve (AC) and demand of the producer. Since the price at the profit-maximizing level of output is above the average cost of producing the output, the firm is earning excess profits. (In keeping with the economic tradition, "normal profits" are included as a cost in the average cost curve.) The marginal cost and marginal revenue curves are not shown in the figure. Figure 3.2b shows the corresponding market area for the producer. Notice that initially there are no nearby competitors encroaching on the firm's market area.

A Spatial Monopolist

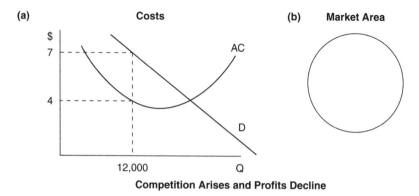

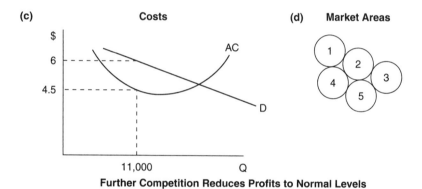

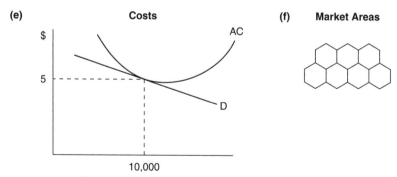

Figure 3.2   Costs, Competition, and Market Areas

Will the excess profits remain in the long run? Assuming that other potential producers have both knowledge of market opportunities and the ability to open similar facilities, new producers will enter the industry in search of excess profits. Producers will initially locate away from each other to avoid competition. Thus, new producers will carve out their own market areas and earn profits similar to those of the representative firm. However, as still more producers enter the industry, they will squeeze the initial producer, reducing the excess profits and market area. New firms will reduce the demand for the original producer's product. Figures 3.2c and d show this situation. In this case, profits will be reduced, but they may still attract other producers. As more producers start businesses, the landscape will become increasingly crowded. Eventually, profits will fall to a level at which no more firms will enter the industry. One possible equilibrium is shown in Figures 3.2e and f.

Hexagons, as shown in Figure 3.2f, are an efficient shape for filling an area. However, they are not the only possible outcome of spatial competition. Suppose every firm was earning very slight excess profits when the market areas were tightly packed, an additional producer would not be able to operate profitably. This situation may also represent an equilibrium. Therefore, there is a degree of indeterminacy about market size. The important point is that as firms enter the industry in search of excess profits, the profits of existing firms fall, and the size of market areas shrinks.

The equilibrium shown in Figure 3.2e is similar to the outcome suggested for firms in monopolistically competitive industries. Even if all producers sold identical products, the spatial perspective indicates that demand for the product would be downsloping—not horizontal as suggested in the traditional discussions of the purely competitive industry. The spatial analysis indicates that monopolistic competition may better depict markets that would otherwise be classified as competitive. Essentially, producers are differentiated by location. Consumers have preferences for producers' locations just as they have preferences for particular brands of very similar products.

THRESHOLD DEMAND AND RANGE

"Threshold" and "range" are useful concepts for understanding market areas. The threshold demand is the minimum quantity a producer must sell to earn at least normal profits. It is the spatial equivalent to the break-even point. Figure 3.3 shows the geographic threshold associated with quantity demanded of 10,000 (the break-even output in Figure 3.2 when the firm was earning just sufficient profits to stay in operation). The threshold quantity can be associated with a threshold population. For instance, if the average individual in the market area consumes 10 units per year at a price of $5, the threshold population associated with Figure 3.2 would be 10000/10, or 1,000. The threshold population is also associated with a threshold geographic market, often called the inner range. For a firm that is producing an amount just sufficient for the threshold market, the price, average total cost, and average revenue are equal.

Variations in threshold size explain why some economic activities are more common than others. Activities with very low demand thresholds, such as filling stations, food stores, churches, and restaurants, are more common than activities with high thresholds, such as undertakers, public accountants, and specialized physicians.

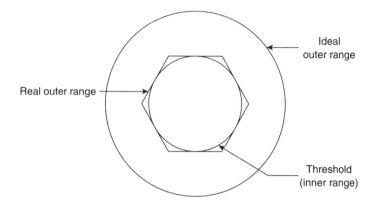

Figure 3.3   Threshold and Range

NOTE: The threshold is the market size that will allow a firm to break even. The ideal outer range is the distance at which the transportation cost makes the product prohibitively expensive. The real outer range represents the actual market area.

The "ideal outer range" of a good is the maximum distance individuals are willing to travel to purchase a good at the lowest possible average cost. At the perimeter of the ideal outer range, consumer costs (including transportation costs) are so high that demand for the product is zero. Competition from other producers normally reduces the distance a consumer will travel below the ideal outer range. The "real outer range" is the maximum distance a customer will travel in an environment with competing establishments. It is the actual market area of a firm.

The real outer range describes the firm's actual market area. In Figure 3.3, the firm has an opportunity to make excess profits because the real outer range is larger than the threshold level. Of course, if the producer is inefficient and produces at above the minimum necessary average costs, the opportunity to earn excess profits will be lost. When threshold and real outer range are equal, only normal profits (normal return to the owner) are possible, even if the producer operates efficiently.

In practice, retail firms can earn excess profits even in equilibrium. For instance, when a population in a market area is sufficient to support one establishment but inadequate to support a second establishment, the second establishment will probably not enter the market and erode the existing establishment's excess profits.

DETERMINANTS OF MARKET SIZE

Three factors determine the size of the market area for a particular product. (1) If *economies of scale* are significant, producers will be able to offset some or all of the additional transportation costs of serving distant markets. Thus, establishments in industries with significant economies of scale will have large market areas. Economies of scale are often associated with high fixed costs. (2) *Demand density* is the quantity demanded per unit of land area or the quantity demanded per person times the population density. The larger the demand density, the greater is the number of producers that can operate in a given area. Hence, high-demand-density activities, such as convenience groceries, will have smaller market areas than automobile dealerships. (3) The effect of *transportation costs* on market size is ambiguous. On the one hand, if scale economies exist and transportation costs decline, the product could be provided cheaper everywhere, including beyond the market fringe. Thus, the decreased transportation costs would allow firms and consumers to take advantage of both scale economies and lower transportation costs by expanding the market. On the other hand, if the representative firm faces increasing cost conditions, a decrease in transportation costs will increase profits *initially* and may eventually attract more firms into the industry. In this case, the increasing production costs may offset the lower transportation costs, so that it becomes more expensive, per unit, to serve an expanded market. Accordingly, smaller market areas may result.

Forces are continually operating to change the size of market areas. For instance, there has been a long-term tendency for incomes and population to increase. As a result, market areas for some products, particularly retail goods, have become smaller. At the same time, economies of scale have increased in some manufacturing industries, increasing the market areas for some products. If gasoline prices continue to increase, smaller market areas can be anticipated for many products.

The Urban Hierarchy and Urban System

The previous section described the formation of market areas for a single product. This section shows how economies from having joint market centers lead to the development of cities and trading patterns among cities. Once production becomes concentrated at the center of a particular market area, the economic landscape will no longer consist of families distributed evenly over a homogeneous plane. Cities will form. Some cities will be small because they are the production points of only a few products with a few economies of scale. Furthermore, economic forces will influence the size and spatial distribution of cities and the relationships among them. This section shows how a hierarchy of central places will develop and a system of cities will emerge.

CENTRAL PLACES

To understand the development of cities of various sizes, it is necessary to recognize the economic advantages that accrue when two or more establishments locate together. These advantages are termed "agglomeration economies" (see Chapter 4). Producers will trade off some of the advantages of locating at the exact center of a market to gain advantages from locating near other producers. Examples of agglomeration economies include shared parking among retail stores, shared roads, and other shared public infrastructures. The desire of customers to reduce their costs by bundling trips also encourages producers to locate together. Fixed transportation systems and geopolitical barriers will reinforce the tendency of establishments to share market areas. Thus, different activities may have similar, but not identical, market areas; yet they may find it advantageous to locate together and serve the same market areas even if they have different ideal ranges. Accordingly, there will be fewer market areas than products.

Assume that there is a fixed number of different market sizes reflecting the trade-off between achieving agglomeration economies from locating near other businesses and being at the center of a unique market area. Market sizes will range from small areas for convenience goods to markets that include entire regions or multiregion areas providing high-order services such as advanced medical care. Commodities or services with similar geographic markets will locate together, and market areas will be shared. Furthermore, some producers with small threshold markets will locate in the same place as producers serving large market areas to attract customers who would normally be beyond their threshold. Additional spatial concentration will allow for sharing of infrastructure and make other agglomeration economies possible.

A hierarchy of central places will result from the sharing of common locations. Many cities will be the site of only a few producers serving small market areas. These first-order central places—hamlets—will provide services such as grocery stores, drug stores, churches, and so forth. The rural population is the hinterland (market area) for the first-order central places. Second-order central places will provide all the services provided by first-order places because residents and the rural population near the second-order cities represent an effective demand. In addition, second-order central places will provide services that have larger threshold markets. Clothing and furniture stores are examples of additional functions that might be offered by second-order central places. The market area of the second-order goods and services producers will include several first-order places. For example, if a resident of a first-order central place needed a new suit, it might be purchased in the nearest second-order city. First-order places are part of the second-order central place's hinterland.

Second-order cities will be part of the hinterland of third-order cities, and so on, up the hierarchy. The largest cities will be the production centers for establishments with the largest market areas, but regional centers will also provide lower goods and services. Greater economic activity supports a larger population. Hence, the central-place model also explains population size. A functional regularity exists in the system of cities. Higher-order cities will provide some services to lower-order places in their hinterland. There will be a spatial regularity to city systems as well as a functional regularity. If establishments in first-order central places have market areas of radius r, then first-order towns will be $2r$ apart. Higher-order places will be farther apart than the first-order place because some of the establishments in these cities serve larger market areas. Furthermore, each second-order city includes some first-order cities in its hinterland. Likewise, since first-order cities have smaller market areas, more first-order places will exist than second-order places.

Figure 3.4 is a stylized map of a system of cities in our theoretical urban hierarchy. It shows villages, towns, metropolitan areas, and one capital. In other words, there are only four different market sizes, and producers locate according to the size of the area they serve. The market areas of higher-order places are also identified. Each town has six villages in its hinterland; each metropolis has six towns and thirty-six villages in its hinterland. The largest city is the "capital" of the region. Its hinterland includes six metropolitan areas, 36 (6×6) towns, and 216 (36×6) villages (not all the villages are pictured).

GOODS AND SERVICES ACCORDING TO URBAN RANK

Figure 3.5 illustrates a hypothetical distribution of activities according to the rank of the central place. It shows that higher-order central places have a greater range of activities. In reality, the distribution of activities will not be so regular. A profile such as Figure 3.5 may be a useful economic development tool. An analyst might wish to collect data on activities that are similar among a group of central places. If a function is unexpectedly absent and a more detailed study fails to uncover a reasonable explanation for the absence, that activity might be a successful new business possibility. The number of establishments will also increase as the size of the urban place increases, but not necessarily in a proportional manner. Will doubling the population allow for

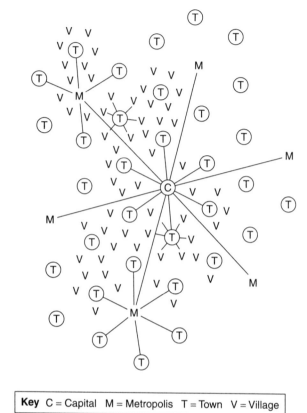

Key C = Capital   M = Metropolis   T = Town   V = Village

Figure 3.4   Stylized Map of Urban Places

NOTE: Central-place theory describes an ordered region with snowflake-like symmetry.

double that number of stores? For instance, if a population of 500 supports one grocery store, will a population of 1,000 support two groceries? Not necessarily, because as the population of a central place increases, say, beyond 500, the existing grocery store may achieve an economy of scale. When the population grows to 1,000, a new store may not be able to undersell the existing business (Wensley & Stabler, 1998).

Since the model is designed around retail and service activities on a homogeneous plain, a real-world distribution of activities will not be so regular. Also, there are many different types of "clothing stores" or "eating places." A small place may support a diner but not a five-star restaurant. Furthermore, as urban places come closer together, proximity will influence functions. Usually, large retail centers offer amenities and other shopping attractions not found in stand-alone businesses. Individuals may prefer to travel to a nearby large mall

	Order of Central Places					
Economic Function	**6**	**5**	**4**	**3**	**2**	**1**
Minimum convenience						
Filling station	X	X	X	X	X	X
Grocery store	X	X	X	X	X	X
Full convenience						
Eating places	X	X	X	X	X	
Hardware store	X	X	X	X	X	
Drug store	X	X	X	X	X	
Low-order specialty						
Laundry		X	X	X	X	
Clothing store	X	X	X	X		
Appliances	X	X	X	X		
Hotel, motel	X	X	X			
Shoe store	X	X	X			
Sporting goods	X	X	X			
High-order specialty						
Radio		X	X			
Paint store	X	X				
Music store	X	X				
Antique store	X	X				
Wholesale						
Lumber supplies	X					
Professional service						
equipment	X					
Groceries	X					
Bulk oil	X					
Number of cities in class (nesting factors = 3)	1	3	9	27	81	243

Figure 3.5   Economic Functions and the Urban Hierarchy

NOTE: Bigger cities have more functions and serve lower-order places.

to purchase goods. Accordingly, a larger population threshold will be needed for local retail activity in a town near a large metropolitan area than in a similar-sized town that is more isolated. These and other limitations imply that an analysis of the expected economic activities of a town requires more than a mechanical approach.

CHANGING URBAN PATTERNS

The model can be used to understand how economic change may cause the urban system to change. Since the system of cities is based on market areas, the same factors that cause market areas to change will cause the hinterlands of cities to change. Thus, changes in transportation costs, changes in the scale economies of production, and increases in demand density influence the urban hierarchy.

In general, when the optimum size of a market area declines because of an increase in demand density (income and population increases), decreases in optimum plant size, or increased transportation costs, activities will shift toward lower-order central places. Economic activities will shift down the hierarchy, and goods previously provided exclusively by higher-order places will now be provided by lower-order places. In effect, the dominance of higher-order urban places will be weakened. For instance, when MP players were introduced, they could be purchased only in specialty shops located in large metropolitan areas. As consumer acceptance increased (increasing demand density), they became available in lower-order central places. When market areas increase, possibly due to improved transportation or increases in economies of scale, the location of services will shift upward and lower-order central places will be weakened compared with larger cities.

When one or a few functions become available at a different level of the hierarchy, the economic functions of cities will change. If the location of a large number of economic activities shifts upward or downward, an entire category of central place could disappear. Stabler and Williams (1973) documented the disappearance of some intermediate places in Saskatchewan that lost their role in serving smaller areas. The rural ghost towns—or near–ghost towns—apparent in many parts of the Midwest may be attributable to the tendency of farmers to bypass grocery stores and other service establishments in small hamlets, preferring the greater variety and other advantages of shopping in towns only slightly farther away. Improved transportation and the mechanization of agriculture (lowering demand density) probably contributed to this phenomenon. In metropolitan areas, improved transportation due to beltways have contributed to the rise of regional shopping centers and the decline of neighborhood stores.

The changes discussed above should not obscure the overall stability of the urban hierarchy. If we examine a region over a period of 1 or 2 years, we would find little change in the relationship among central places. It is unlikely that a central place would completely disappear or that a new place would emerge. Although cities will grow at different rates, it is very rare that the primary or highest-ranking city will change. The system of cities changes slowly, partly because of inertia and the long economic life of capital investment, particularly infrastructure, and partly because new activity will have incentives to fit into the existing urban grid.

The stability of places in the urban hierarchy may be explained by channels of interdependence. Once urban or regional linkages are created, they transmit growth from one place to another. Cities lower in the hierarchy may grow; but as they do, opportunities for growth among linked cities within the hierarchy will be created. Roads and wire connections (telegraph and telephone) are important physical linkages that support economic linkages. The hierarchy of cities was less stable in the Southeast than in other regions both before and after the Civil War because of an underdeveloped hierarchy of cities. The stability of urban ranks has been attributed to the fact that growth in one place often generates growth in larger cities in the hierarchy (Pred, 1977). Increases in economic activity in small places will cause people in these small towns to purchase more from larger places that sell specialized goods to small places. The urban hierarchy in regions that lack an integrated system of cities will be less stable.

An Evaluation of the Central-Place Approach

Central-place theory described a well-ordered region with snowflake-like symmetry that does not exist in reality. The conclusions, however, follow from the model's initial assumptions, which emphasized economic factors operating on a homogeneous plane:

1. There are the same number of size classes of cities as market sizes.

2. Cities of the same rank have equal hinterlands, offer similar services, and have similar population sizes.

3. Higher-order cities provide the goods and services that lower-order cities provide, plus the functions of producers serving the next-larger-size market.

4. Smaller cities with smaller hinterlands are more numerous and closer together than larger cities.

5. Central places of the same order will be at equal distance from one another.

6. Residents of lower-order cities may purchase goods and services from producers located in higher-order cities, but commodities will not flow from lower-order places up the urban hierarchy.

CONSIDERATIONS EXTRANEOUS TO CENTRAL-PLACE THEORY

The combined results of the assumptions imply market-oriented locational decisions by firms. Accordingly, cities are also market oriented. While this model highlights very important tendencies and provides insights into the forces that influence urban development, factors extraneous to the model warrant consideration.

Spatial Differences in Production Costs

The abstract central-place model implicitly assumes that the costs of production are the same at all locations. Therefore, a firm's location decision is driven primarily by the need to be near its markets. In fact, some places are more suitable as production sites than others. Production processes requiring raw materials may tend to locate near the materials, firms may locate near suppliers or purchasers, and land has different levels of productivity.

Some producers serving large market areas may operate most profitably in small towns because of lower labor costs, access to raw materials, and so forth. In this case, goods made in smaller places will be sold to larger cities. Manufacturing activities are particularly sensitive to spatial cost variations. The location of manufacturing activities has been described as a "wildcard" within the hierarchy because large manufacturers may locate in small towns as well as major cities. Central-place theory is more applicable to activities that are market oriented in location than activities that are cost oriented. Thus, central-place models describe the location of service centers (where activities such as retailing, wholesaling, and business dominate) much better than the site selection of manufacturing.

The location factors excluded from central-place theory can create a situation where two towns have similar hinterlands and similar functions except that one of the towns may be the site of a manufacturing plant with a very large market area. Thus, the manufacturing town will be larger than the other place, even though, with the one exception, they are similarly situated in the urban hierarchy.

Transportation Costs

The central-place model included the assumption that transportation costs are uniform in all directions. In reality, transfer costs are cheaper along established routes, and market areas are extended along transportation routes. Discontinuities in transportation costs will arise due to disruptions in the transportation system caused by rivers, mountains, and other geographic features. For instance, a mountain may increase transportation costs and cut off part of what would otherwise have been part of a city's hinterland. Accordingly, actual urban systems will not always reflect the ideal central-place pattern.

Transport companies often charge block rates rather than continuously increasing rates. Consequently, a producer located 50 miles from a village may experience the same transportation costs as a firm located 150 miles away. This can lead to market overlap and indeterminate market boundaries, because producers may deliver a product from different distances at the same price. Long-haul economies may also contribute to market overlap.

Market Overlap, Rate Absorption, and Price Discrimination

The central-place model assumes a unique market area for each product. In reality, firms located in different places sell in the same markets, and people travel outside their local markets to make purchases. Instances of market overlap can be caused by rate absorption, price discrimination, and product differentiation.

Sellers may absorb some of the transfer costs themselves to extend their markets, or they may price discriminate by charging distant customers lower prices. An example of rate absorption would be a producer who sold a product at a uniform delivery price to all customers in the region instead of charging a higher delivery cost to distant consumers. There may be promotional or menu cost savings due to charging a single price. Price discrimination may also be a deliberate market strategy. Economic analysis suggests that firms price discriminate (i.e., charge higher prices) against customers with inelastic demands for two reasons. First, distant customers tend to be closer to competitors and are therefore in a better position to purchase from alternative suppliers. Second, as price increases, demand becomes more elastic.[1]

Product Differentiation

The abstract model included the assumption that products were undifferentiated, so it was reasonable to assume that consumers would buy the least-cost item. If all firms charged the same FOB price, the nearest producer would be the least-cost supplier. However, if consumers have a preference for one brand over another, some customers would be willing to pay a premium to purchase the preferred brand. Thus, market overlap is likely to occur. The more intense the brand loyalty, the greater the extent of market overlap. Pure market overlap can occur if the products are indistinguishable.

Agglomeration Economies

The cost reductions from having a group of retail stores clustered together is large, particularly when customers like to comparison shop or purchase complementary goods, such as a dress and shoes. For most retail goods, proximity to a metropolitan location increases the population size necessary to support retail establishment in a nearby small town (Wensley & Stabler, 1998). It takes a smaller population to support a basic retail cluster in a remote rural area than in a suburb connected by good highways to a major mall.

When firms practice freight absorption, market overlap may occur. Furthermore, distant consumers are more likely to be near competing sellers than customers located near the facility. Thus, producers will have an incentive to charge lower prices to distant customers.

Institutional Factors

Numerous political factors can affect urban networks. Liquor stores may be underrepresented in a state with stringent laws or high liquor taxes, whereas a cluster of similar stores may be found on the other side of the state border. Interstate commerce within the United States is relatively free of barriers to trade, but not entirely so. "Buy at Home" campaigns, tax policies, licensing, and inspection regulations are a few institutional impediments that affect market area.

Institutional factors are more important in international commerce. Languages, tariffs, quotas, customers, and differences in legal systems are just a few impediments that prevent a firm located in one country from extending its market area abroad. Some regions, such as the European Economic Community, are trying to reduce institutional impediments. However, progress is slow. There is a tendency for products with larger market areas and export impediments to locate near the center of a country's population to avoid border problems.

Nonemployment Residential Locations and Commuting

Central-place theory suggests that large production centers will be large cities because of the implicit assumption that people live where they work. However, cities can grow for reasons unrelated to employment. Retirement and amenity-oriented communities in the South and Southwest are examples of growth outside the central-place framework. Likewise, "bedroom" communities can grow without local employment because of increase in the number of commuters who work in other central places.

EMPIRICAL EVIDENCE

How well does empirical evidence support central-place theory? There are many more small cities than large, as suggested by central-place theory. Larger cities are farther apart and provide a greater variety of services than smaller places. These generalizations support central-place theory. However, whether the theory explains economic geography sufficiently depends on individual judgment rather than a definitive statistical test.

One of the first empirical tests was undertaken by A. Losch (1954), who used the 1930 census data to analyze urban places in Iowa. He divided cities into various orders and found that the central-place model predicted the number of places in each order, the size of centers, and their distance apart. Since Losch, numerous other empirical studies of central-place theory have been reported. Central-place theory even explains settlement patterns in communist (Skinner, 1964) and traditional (Steponaitis, 1981) economies. These studies agree on the following points:

1. Central-place theory explains the size and spatial distribution of cities in homogeneous agricultural regions such as the United States or Western Canada. It does a poor job in explaining urban patterns in complex regions such as the megalopolises of New York/Washington, D.C. In metropolitan areas, places of work are often separated from places of residence.

2. The distribution of service activities can be explained by central-place theory reasonably well. Manufacturing, extractive, and governmental activities are not explained by central-place theory. These goods and services are likely to move up as well as down the urban hierarchy.

3. The central-place model has also been tested using data from shopping centers in metropolitan areas (Morrill, 1987; West, Von Hohenbalken, & Kroner, 1985). The authors obtained the expected hierarchies of shopping centers, although they observed stores of the same type replicated in the same centers, possibly due to the economics of comparison shopping. Accordingly, the forces at work in the central-place hierarchy explain both intra-urban and interurban tendencies.

Globalization and Urban (City) Systems

Scholars have described an emerging global system of cities that have similarities to central-place systems (Castells, 1996). The flow of information and the control of multination organizations have hierarchical tendencies. Yet the global hierarchy is not structured as orderly as suggested by central-place theory. For instance, many small places may be linked directly to global markets, bypassing regional or national urban systems (e.g., a manufacturing plant of a multinational corporation).

Empirical research on global urban networks has been growing rapidly. Sassen (1991) found that London, New York, and Tokyo were at the apex of the global hierarchy, based on the size and variety of connections with the world economy evident in those cities. Scholars with the Globalization and World Cities (GaWC) study group and others have developed theoretical models and an extensive database in an ongoing effort to describe the global network of cities. Important conclusions include the following:

1. Economic variables are only one dimension of the linkages that connect cities throughout the world. Other types of linkages include cultural, social, and political variables. The rank of a city in the global hierarchy depends on the dimension being considered. For instance, Geneva and Nairobi have a strong connection when considering indicators of social globalization, but connections are weaker for economic connectivity (Taylor, 2005).

2. The set of connections among companies is not as predictable as might be implied by the central-place model. For instance, an international bank in Tokyo may have branches in London and New York but not in nearby Okinawa.

3. Taylor (2004) concluded that globalization has not and will not generate a homogeneous global space as implied by many supporters of the global hierarchy model. "McWorld has to give way to local and national hybrid ties," where local features will also be important (p. 361). National and local economic linkages, cultures, and institutions strongly influence the structure of the hierarchy.

4. Cities that are centers of urban networks tend to be located near coasts and tend to be in Europe, the United States, or the Pacific Rim.

Globalization creates a new set of challenges for local economic development officials. An inventory of an area's linkages to other places in the world can be important to understanding the forces that will shape its economic prospects. Such a description might include local companies that are branches of a multinational organization. Knowledge of which local establishments export (directly or indirectly) abroad would also be vital to the inventory.

Local development officials also need to construct and strengthen linkages with international economic nodes. Globalization has made local air connections much more important for transport of both passengers and time-sensitive goods. Development of cultural events, educational programs (especially language) for children of foreign workers, "sister-city" relationships, and other innovative programs can make an area more inviting and affect how a community is viewed by the world.

How to Measure Areas of Influence

The concepts of market area and hinterland are similar. Market area refers to the region in which a particular product is sold. The size of a market area, of course, depends on the product. The concept of a hinterland is broader than the concept of a market area. It recognizes that larger places provide a variety of goods and services to the hinterland. They also exert a general influence on their hinterland that includes transmission of culture, political influence, and knowledge.

SURVEY TECHNIQUES

There have been numerous attempts to measure the range of a city's hinterland. Early efforts examined the circulation of major daily newspapers between major cities, reasoning that newspapers accurately reflect retail trade patterns and social orientation among cities.

Indications of whether a small city is in another city's hinterland might be found by examining newspaper circulation or television markets. In addition to newspapers, Green (1959) examined a variety of indicators of influence, such as railroad ticket purchases, freight movement, telephone calls, place of origin of vacationers, addresses of directors of major firms, newspaper readership, and associations of hinterland banks. He found that the various indicators did not give a constant definition of a city's hinterland. For instance, newspaper circulation might suggest a place is in the hinterland of one area, while freight shipments might not. A generalized sphere of influence is a meaningful construct, but it should be considered a composite of a variety of indicators.

Shopping patterns are an important indicator of the hinterland. Surveys have also been used to determine shopping patterns within a metropolitan region or for specific product groups. The market area for a single business or a shopping center can also be found directly by examining sales patterns. Direct measurement is particularly easy when producers have records of their customers' addresses.

Several generalizations can be drawn from the empirical studies:

1. The proportion of consumers shopping at a central place varies with distance from the shopping area. The closer individuals are to a shopping area, the greater the proportion of individuals shopping there. Refinement of this idea includes the use of travel cost rather than distance alone.

2. The distance consumers are willing to travel increases as the size of the shopping area increases. Indicators of size include the number of stores and the number of square feet of shopping space.

3. The distances that consumers travel vary for different types of products. The greater the cost of the product, the greater the distance the consumers are willing to travel.

4. The "pull" of any shopping area is influenced by the nature of competing shopping areas (Huff, 1964).

The first two generalizations are similar to the law of gravitational attraction. The pull of gravity decreases with distance and increases with the size of the object. This similarity has given rise to gravity models of spatial interaction, as described below.

REILLY'S LAW OF RETAIL GRAVITATION

W. J. Reilly (1931) applied a gravity model to determine the scope of a city's hinterland. Similar techniques have been used to estimate traffic flows between various points. Although Reilly's law is dated, the initial formulation serves as the basis for modern techniques for measuring spheres of influence. Simply stated, the model postulates that an individual's tendency to shop at Center A will increase as the size of the center increases and will decrease as the square of the distance between the customers and Center A increases. The law of retail gravitation states that the breaking point where trade is equally divided between two cities runs through a point where the ratio of the distances squared equals the population ratio:

$$P_a/P_b = D_a^2/D_b^2, \tag{3.1}$$

where P_a is the population of the major city and D_a is the distance from the major city to the intermediate place.

Reilly's law may be restated to express the distance between a major city, say Center A, and the outer limit of its trading area with another central place, B:

$$S_h^a\, D_{ab}/(1 + \sqrt{P_b/P_a}), \tag{3.2}$$

where S_h^a is the scope of A's hinterland (distance from A to the breaking point); D_{ab} is the distance from A to B, where B is the nearest competing city; and P_a and P_b are the population in Cities A and B, respectively.

In terms of the hypothetical cities shown in Figure 3.6, the breaking point for A's sphere of influence would be

$$56 \text{ miles} = 100 \text{ miles}/(1 + \sqrt{(30000/50000)}). \tag{3.3}$$

The breaking point is closer to B than to A because A is the larger city. Thus, individuals halfway between A and B would make most of their trips to A. After all, consumers could probably purchase anything in A that they could purchase in B and purchase some things in A that could not be purchased in B.

The term *law of retail gravitation* incorrectly implies that Reilly's formula is almost universal in applicability and generates highly accurate results. This is not the case. It does not come close to the precision of a physical law. Furthermore, development officials should be aware of three shortcomings that weaken the model's practical use. First, the model implies a sharp break point. In reality, a central place's influence tapers off, and hinterlands overlap.

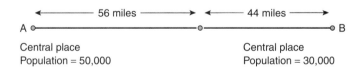

Figure 3.6   Generalized Sphere of Influence

NOTE: The attraction of an area increases with size and decreases with distance. Using Reilly's law of retail gravitation, the point at which half the trips are to A and half are to B can be estimated.

Second, the distance parameters (the squares of distance) may not be the same for all types of trips. Previous research has shown that the coefficient on the distance term, D, can vary depending on local conditions. Essentially, distance reflects the costs of travel. Thus, the "distance discount" may be greater if travel is expensive or inconvenient. Also, people will travel farther for expensive goods, implying a smaller distance discount. Most market researchers will estimate the distance discount independently depending on the circumstances. Third, travel time or cost may be more appropriate than miles as a measure of trade barriers. Some of these criticisms have been addressed by the development of more sophisticated statements of Reilly's law.

PROBABILISTIC MODELS

Without modification, Reilly's law is limited by the inherent uncertainty of consumer behavior. Huff (1964) developed a probabilistic model to determine the influence of shopping areas within metropolitan regions. He estimated the likelihood that an individual in place i would shop at a particular central place j. The probability depended on (1) the distance (usually expressed in time) between the consumer and the destination, j; (2) the number of competing central places; and (3) the size of the central place, j. The measure of size is usually either population or square feet of shopping space. Huff's formulation is expressed as follows:

$$P_{is} = S_s/(T_{is})^b \bigg/ \sum (S_j/T_{ij})^b, \tag{3.4}$$

where P_{is} is the probability of an individual living at i shopping at s, the subject center; S_j is the size of the shopping place, j (includes the subject shopping center and others); T_{ij} is the distance between other shopping centers, j, and places i expressed in time; b is an exponent (similar to the squared term in Reilly's law); and $\sum$ is the sum over all places j.

Ideally, a survey of customers should be conducted to determine the value of b, because it may differ depending on the particular situation. The need for a survey is a major impediment because of the extra time and cost involved. However, studies have found that b equals about 2 for most general merchandise goods. Goods and services for which individuals are willing to travel longer distances will have lower coefficients (lower distance discounts). Often, distance is measured in terms of time rather than miles because time is more relevant in urban travel decisions. In empirical studies, time is usually measured by dividing the distance into 5-min time zones. Within 5 min, $T = 1$; between 5 and 10 min, $T = 2$; and so forth. Huff's (1964) probabilistic model results in retail trade areas defined in terms of probability contours, as shown in Figure 3.7. The point of 50% probability is Reilly's midway point.

RETAIL SPENDING

The model is often extended to estimate the total retail spending that would occur at a shopping center. Thus, it is an important tool for commercial developers and planners. To understand how a real estate planner might use the model, assume that the number of potential customers at each location, POP_i, is known (locations are often defined as census track areas within a metropolitan statistical area, so the data are available). Assume also that the annual available expenditures per person, per year for the types of goods sold by the center equal E. These variables can be determined from surveys or published sources. Estimates on the annual household budget by product category for various levels of income are available from data published by the U.S. Bureau of Labor Statistics. The "Survey of Buying Power," published by *Sales & Marketing Management*, has similar data. Total spending, by individuals located at i, at shopping area j, would equal the probability of shopping at i, P_{ij}, times total spending:

$$TS_{ij} = P_{ij} \times POP_i \times E. \tag{3.5}$$

By summing the total spending for all areas, i, an estimated total spending at a particular location may be derived. Thus, gravity models are useful for economic development officials who wish to consider potential market opportunities in their area.

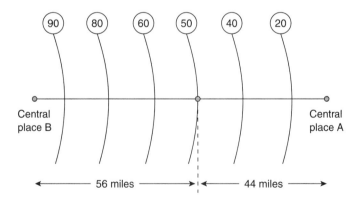

Figure 3.7   Retail Trade Areas Determined by Probability Contours

NOTE: Probability contours show the probability that a shopping trip for a resident located anywhere on the "map" will be to A. The closer to A the shopper is, the higher the probability of shopping at A.

AN EXAMPLE

To see how the model can be applied, assume that a developer is planning to construct a small neighborhood shopping strip of 10,000 sq. ft in census tract j, as shown in Figure 3.8. There are two existing centers, A and B. What is the likelihood that an individual located in census tract i will shop at the proposed center? Assume that the distance measure, T_{ij}, increases by 1 for each 5-min distance increase and the exponent has been determined to be 2. Applying the probabilistic gravity model yields

$$P_1 = (10000/2^2)/((10000/2^2) + (15000/3^2) + (20000/4^2)) = .46.$$

We may interpret the results as indicating that the average shoppers in location i will make 46% of their trips to the proposed center in j. (We are assuming that the point in the center of the customer area represents the location of all consumers in i. The finding would be less accurate if the bulk of the population in i lived closer to or farther from the shopping center.)

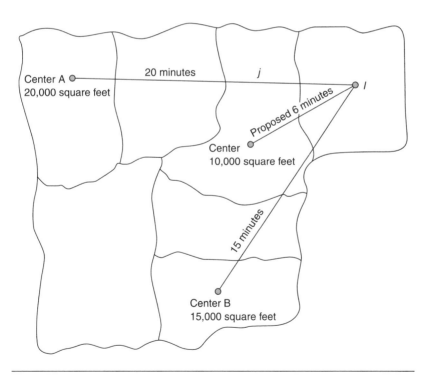

Figure 3.8   Location of Customers and Competitors

NOTE: The size and location of other establishments should be considered when estimating the likelihood that a resident located at i will shop at the proposed center.

The estimate of the likelihood of shopping at the proposed center must be supplemented with additional data before the volume of retail trade can be calculated. Specifically, we would need to know (1) the population size of area i (POPi) and (2) the annual expenditures per capita (E).

To estimate the volume of retail trade at the proposed center, assume that the population of census track i is 8,000 and the average family in i spends $700/year on the type of retail goods anticipated for the proposed center. Then, the amount of trade estimated for the proposed center from area i would equal

$$.46 \times 700 \times 8000 = \$2,576,000.$$

The above example indicates only the sales likely to come from individuals in area i. To develop an estimate of potential total sales, the same procedure would have to be followed for every area in the region.

Mechanistic application of shopping models can be problematic. Local cultures, demographics, measures of distance, and competitive environments should be carefully evaluated in the calibration process. Turner and Cole (1980) warn that, unfortunately, few, if any, checks are made on the forecasts of planning consultants and others using shopping models or otherwise. Their "track record" is not known (p. 146). This observation might be applied not only to retail studies but also to a variety of forecasts and projects that economic development officials must confront.

Hinterland Expansion Strategies

Areas of urban influence are elastic. Urban development officials may increase relative sales in their area by expanding the distance over which individuals will travel to make purchases. Hinterland expansion may be particularly beneficial to merchants in small or medium-sized cities in agricultural regions where many families have choices (albeit limited choices) about which city will be their primary market center. Similarly, managers of shopping centers in metropolitan areas may engage in hinterland expansion strategies to increase the scope of the local business sector. Neighborhood and suburban merchants may also benefit by increasing the distance individuals will be willing to travel to shop in an area.

The theoretical models suggest that the principal lever for increasing an area's hinterland are (1) improving transportation and (2) increasing the variety of goods offered for sale. Accordingly, policymakers should be particularly attuned to ways of improving transportation along routes traveled by customers who may be nearly indifferent between one shopping area and another. They may also seek to encourage new merchandizing lines that are absent in the hinterland area in which they hope to expand. Efforts to expand a district's hinterland may include changing perceptions as well as changing reality.

One approach to hinterland expansion is to change perceptions of distance or travel time. If individuals are familiar with an area, including how to get there, where to park, and which stores can best serve their needs, they may perceive the area as being closer than a place that is at equal distance but unfamiliar. Generally, the more frequently individuals travel to an area, the more familiar they feel about it. Sometimes a cumulative process can occur whereby trips to an area diminish the perception of distance, which then contributes to additional trips. Following this line of reasoning, cities may sponsor festivals or other special, regional events designed to attract shoppers who might otherwise be unfamiliar with an area. Simply creating a welcoming attitude will also help. Small rural towns offering services that competing towns do not have may use this advantage to expand their hinterland. Since individuals must travel to the town on some occasions if they wish to purchase the particular items, their level of familiarity will increase. Hence, communities may extend their market area by building on uncontested products or services.

Consumer perceptions of size and the variety of goods available are also susceptible to influence. Suburban shopping centers have frequently attempted to attract customers beyond their initial market area by promotions that emphasize the variety of goods available or the number of stores at their location. Small towns and urban neighborhood shopping areas have similarly tried to promote themselves as areas that offer a large variety of merchandise. For instance, many communities have developed specializations in crafts, dining, antiques, automobile sales, and so forth. Hence, such communities have successfully extended market areas by building on specialties.

Summary

This chapter described a global set of relationships among urban places. When demand is considered in a spatial context, both price and distance from customers determine a firm's sales. If a producer is earning excess profits, other firms will enter the industry, decreasing the existing profits. At the same time, the spatial market area of the original firm will decline.

The minimum geographic area a firm must serve to break even is the inner range. The real outer range is the firm's actual market area. If a firm's actual market area is larger than the inner range, the firm may earn excess profits. Three factors operate to determine market size—economies of scale, demand density (population density and per capita spending), and transportation costs.

Market areas for producers of different products overlap. The overlap allows firms to locate in the same area to achieve agglomeration economies as producers locate near each other. Central places are centers of one or more market areas, with producers locating at the centers. Large cities will be the home of many producers, including some producers with very large market areas. Smaller cities are the production site of fewer firms with a smaller market area. Market areas form the basis of an urban hierarchy of cities.

Factors that change market areas will alter the system of cities and the hinterland for individual cities.

Evaluations of the central-place model have concluded that the predictions of the model have some validity. However, there are many exceptions to the pristine, symmetrical conclusions. Spatial differences in production costs, transportation cost variations, price discrimination, institutional factors, product differentiation, and nonemployment residential choices are some of the factors not accounted for by the theoretical model.

The empirical evidence suggests that urban patterns in homogeneous agricultural regions fit the theoretical predictions better than activity patterns in dense coastal regions. The model explains the distribution of service and retail activities better than the distribution of manufacturing activities. The theoretical model also explains some shopping center patterns within metropolitan areas.

There are several methods for measuring areas of influence. Such techniques are important because developers, planners, and others may wish to estimate the attraction of new enterprises. Models based on three principles have been useful. Areas of attraction (1) increase with size, (2) diminish with distance, and (3) diminish with intervening competitors.

An urban hinterland expansion strategy may be a useful economic development tool. Such a strategy could be based on changing the reality or perceptions regarding travel costs to the area and the goods and services available in the area.

Note

1. The price elasticity of demand is $\%\Delta Q / \%\Delta P$, where $\%\Delta Q$ is the percent change in the quantity and $\%\Delta P$ is the percent change in price. Distant customers are likely to be paying a higher price and consuming a smaller quantity simply due to higher transportation costs. Hence, a given absolute change in price will be a small percentage of change for distant customers, and a given absolute change in quantity will be a small percentage of change.

4

Economic Interdependence and Local Structure

Repulsion among competing firms was a principal economic force described in the discussion of market areas. However, cohesive forces also operate in regional and metropolitan economies. The complexity and functionality of these local interdependencies contribute to the image of a city as a productive growth machine. Production and marketing interdependencies tend to attract firms toward each other. Economic development officials need to understand existing linkages between firms, how to strengthen existing linkages, and how to establish new, beneficial relationships among firms.

Agglomeration Economies

Agglomeration economies are cost reductions that occur because economic activity is carried on at one place. Alfred Marshall used the concept of agglomeration economies to explain the concentration of specialized industries in particular localities in the 19th century. While critical to local development, agglomerative forces are not well understood. This section will focus on the importance of agglomeration economies but will also discuss some conceptual ambiguities. There are several types of agglomeration economies, ranging from savings that accrue to only one establishment to agglomeration economies that spread throughout an entire region.

INTERNAL AGGLOMERATION ECONOMIES

Internal agglomeration economies are cost reductions that accrue to a firm that expands activity at a particular place. For instance, the expansion of a plant could result in internal agglomeration economies. Since the firm that expands also receives the benefits of the expansion, the agglomeration economies are "internal"; that is, the benefits are captured by the firm engaging in the expansion.

The spreading of fixed costs over a larger output, greater division of labor, the potential for using alternative technologies, and saving through bulk purchases are sources of internal agglomeration economies. Better use of a manager's time or better use of specialized machinery can result in lower average costs due to increased output. The concentration of headquarters activity undoubtedly allows a substantial internal agglomeration economy.

Economists sometimes refer to economies of scale as efficiencies that result from the expansion of a *firm*. For economies of scale to represent agglomeration economies also, the expansion must be spatially concentrated.

DIRECT SALE/PURCHASE LINKAGES

The tendency for firms that trade with each other to locate in the same region is one of the most important causes of agglomeration. Interindustry agglomeration occurs through forward and backward linkages. Buyers may attract suppliers to a region, or suppliers of inputs may attract a firm more forward in the production chain.

The question of whether sellers are attracted to areas where buyers are located or vice versa is important to development planners. If forward linkages are more important, then a regional policymaker might choose to concentrate on the development of primary production activities such as oil extraction, raw material production, and agriculture, thus eventually attracting firms that use these inputs in the production process. If backward linkages are more effective, then an economic strategy might focus first on the development of final products such as apparel or food canning. Once established, these activities would induce further growth through backward linkages.

Hirschman (1972) argued that underdeveloped countries (and by implication, underdeveloped regions) are characterized by weak interdependencies. Agriculture and extractive activities are major productive activities in less developed countries, and they have weak forward linkages within these economies. The few forward linkages—principally, refining of raw materials—that might be generated by these activities do not encourage significant development that spreads elsewhere in the economy. Oil, mineral, and agricultural products have been exported without encouraging significant additional local economic activity in many African and Arab countries. In some countries where wealth is highly concentrated in the hands of a few, final products such as luxury automobiles, high-end electronics, or branded clothing are imported. Such imports merely create activities that put finishing touches on imported products and create few effective backward linkages that generate further growth.

Are forward or backward linkages more effective in attracting linked industries? Local economic developers (EDs) now believe that generalizations about whether forward or backward linkages are more effective are inadequate. Whether forward linkages are more powerful than backward linkages depends on the industry pairs and specific sets of local circumstances. The issue of how to use linkages in the development process calls for additional empirical research.

LOCALIZATION ECONOMIES

Interindustry linkages among direct trading partners are a special type of localization economy, but localization economies can encompass much broader-based agglomerations. Localization economies occur when increases in the output of an entire group of firms at a particular place result in lower costs for firms in that industry at that location. Economic development officials often design strategies to create a group of closely related industries in order to attract further growth from firms seeking localization economies.

Localization economies are often easier to describe in theory than to operationalize. An imaginative theorist can describe connections between most industries, but local developers need to know whether the theoretical linkages are significant in practice. Observing patterns of expansion and contraction among industries is one way to determine which industries are closely integrated (Cutler, England, & Weiler, 2003).

An enhanced labor pool, specialized machinery, imitation, and the chance to comparison shop are important sources of localization economies.

Labor Pool

When firms in the same industry locate together, they may contribute to the development of a skilled labor pool that benefits all firms in the industry. Employment fluctuations may increase the location advantage of an area with a concentration of skilled labor. If many firms in an industry were located in the same region, then variations in demand for one firm's output might be offset by countervailing increases in another firm's production. Hiring peaks might even out. Furthermore, if a local industry had sufficiently large skill requirements, it might even be feasible to develop a school to train workers. Such schools or training programs would not only improve the quality and availability of labor but also enhance the retraining. Thus, community colleges often have excellent training programs designed to meet local labor-market requirements. Labor agglomerations are particularly important to advanced technology clusters because advances in knowledge increasingly require cooperation among persons in a variety of subjects.

Specialized Machinery

The ability to share specialized machinery and other factors of production is another source of localization economies. For example, an area may start developing as a distribution and warehousing center. When the area attains a large enough volume of activity, the market may be sufficient to support a distribution equipment firm that sells, repairs, or modifies loading and handling equipment. (Notice the backward linkage effect.) As a consequence of the improved availability of specialized distribution equipment, all distribution and warehousing firms in the area may operate more efficiently. Currently, specialized air cargo shipment facilities offer a similar type of specialization.

Imitation, Modification, and Innovation

Firms in the same industry may be able to imitate and copy one another more readily if they are located together. Therefore, they may be able to respond to changes in their industry quicker than if they were isolated from their competitors. Of course, the firm that is copied may be harmed, so in this instance, it would be better off in an isolated location, where copying would be more difficult. However, managers may not know which firm will develop leading innovations. On average, the "sharing" of information may benefit the group. In industries with numerous and scattered innovations, such as fashion or computer games, all firms may be better off if they have locations that allow them to imitate quickly. Furthermore, a firm that copies two changes is in a better position to innovate additional changes by combining or modifying changes that were taken from other firms. Thus, particularly in fast-changing industries, economies from industrial imitation, modification, and innovation tend to be important sources of localization economies.

Comparison Shopping

Another localization economy can be traced to the desire of individuals to compare products. Individuals may prefer to shop for shoes in a regional shopping mall because they can compare the merchandise in four or five different stores in fewer trips. Firms selling similar products may repel one another under some circumstances, but when consumers have a demand for display variety, similar competing establishments may locate together. An additional shoe store in a regional shopping mall may actually benefit all the shoe stores by making the mall a more desirable place to shop for shoes. The additional store may lower the percentage of mall shoe shoppers who purchase at each existing store, but total sales may increase due to the greater number of shoppers. Retail establishments selling complementary products may also tend to cluster. For instance, theaters and restaurants often locate together, reflecting the fact that people like to eat out before or after seeing a show.

Households are the direct beneficiaries of display variety because their shopping costs are reduced. But some of these advantages may be captured by retailers due to greater sales. Shopping center developers may also benefit if they can charge retailers higher rents because of the popularity of the shopping center. Automobile alleys and urban restaurant areas are examples of agglomerations based on display variety. Display varieties of agglomeration that are national or international in scope include the Khan Film Festival, the Paris Air Show, and numerous sales-oriented conventions.

URBANIZATION ECONOMIES

Urbanization economies are the most diffuse type of agglomeration economy. They are cost savings that accrue to a wide variety of firms and households when the volume of activity in an entire urban area increases. The firms that share in urbanization economies may be unrelated. Urbanization economies may be attributed to several sources.

Infrastructure

Urbanization economies may result from potential economies of scale in public infrastructure, such as roads, sewers, and public services. A region's infrastructure becomes inputs into a wide variety of private production and consumption activities. When significant economies of scale exist in infrastructure provision, increase in the size of an urban area will allow lower per-unit infrastructure costs. These cost savings may be passed to producers and consumers, perhaps in the form of lower taxes.

Division of Labor

Urbanization economies may also result from a more extensive division of labor. In a small town, many stages of production and distribution must be carried out within a plant because the local market cannot support specialty firms. Activities that cannot be carried out within the plant must be purchased from elsewhere or not performed at all. The extra costs of importing will tend to place the firm at a competitive disadvantage relative to other producers.

Internal Economies

Establishments that sell to a variety of firms and households may also achieve cost reductions as the urban area expands because larger markets will allow firms to achieve internal economies of scale. Internal economies may be passed forward to customers in the form of lower prices or backward to the factors of production in the form of higher compensation.

Averaging of Random Variations

Larger urban markets allow for an averaging of variations in economic activity, a larger group of industries than suggested by localization economies. A drop in sales to one customer or group of customers may be offset by new orders from other customers. Mills and Hamilton (1984) summarized this aspect of agglomeration economies:

> [The] most important of such agglomeration economies is statistical in nature and is an application of the law of large numbers. Sales of outputs and purchases of inputs fluctuate . . . for random, seasonal, cyclical and secular reasons. (p. 18)

Thus, to the extent that business ups and downs are uncorrelated, a firm in an urban area will have fewer scheduling production problems than if it were located in a smaller place. Similarly, labor changes can be accommodated more easily in a large urban area. If a chief financial officer or a tax accountant quits, finding a replacement will be a more significant problem in a small town than in a metropolitan area.

Urban Diseconomies

As the size of an economic concentration increases, diseconomies appear, so urbanization economies may be offset by urban diseconomies. Examples of urban diseconomies may be inconvenience, anxiety, delay, and aggravation, which many people associate with metropolitan regions. The higher wages paid in large cities may reflect the compensation necessary to offset the negative psychological costs of work in congested areas.

Some enterprises are more disadvantaged by suburban diseconomies than others. However, there does not appear to be a size so large that overall urban diseconomies outweigh the economies associated with size. For instance, productivity generally increases as metropolitan size increases. Therefore, urbanization economies tend to outweigh urban diseconomies over the range of city size observed in the world today.

RECAP

The impacts of agglomeration economies range from specific to diffuse. The most specific agglomeration economies accrue to a plant. Agglomeration economies affecting pairs of firms are also rather specific. Economies that result when an industry or an industrial cluster expands are slightly more diffuse. Urbanization economies are the most diffuse type of agglomeration economy. They depend on the size of the entire urban area, and the benefits of the agglomeration are shared by a wide variety of businesses.

External economy industries such as fashion, publishing, and financial activities tend to concentrate in large urban areas because they require diverse inputs and information. These are generally rapid-change industries where inputs (including information) must be rapidly obtained.

Cluster Analysis

The concepts of agglomeration have been incorporated into the broader concept of cluster economies. Economic clusters are a new paradigm for analyzing an interdependent group of activities that make up an area's economic core. Michael Porter (1998b) is credited with one of the major components of the cluster concept, the "competitive diamond," shown in Figure 4.1. The diamond was originally developed to explain a nation's advantage in trade. Currently, it is recognized that the intensity of the interactions among elements of the triangle are enhanced by geographic proximity. Hence, clusters are considered to be the drivers of many local economies.

Consider the four major components of a cluster:

1. *Firm strategy, structure, and rivalry:* Vigorous competition among firms can strengthen all firms in the group. Furthermore, the success of the local cluster depends on strategies of individual firms as they position themselves in a national and international market. Thus, cluster analysis includes focus on firms as well as industries.

2. *Demand conditions:* Local consumers who anticipate national preferences or who demand products that "catch on" elsewhere provide advantages to local producers. For instance, a Mexican restaurant chain is more likely to get a successful start in the Southwest because the local demand may favor Mexican foods. Areas with high incomes often anticipate demands as incomes in other regions increase.

3. *Related and supporting institutions:* A group of suppliers of intermediate inputs that is engaged in competitive efforts to produce higher-quality or less costly inputs are integral to a successful cluster. These institutions not only include direct supplies of intermediate inputs but also include tangential enterprises that employ similar technologies or production processes.

4. *Factor input conditions:* This element includes not only the cost of factor inputs such as labor, land, capital, and entrepreneurship but also the quality and terms of the inputs available. Available resources for new ventures, such as equity capital, appropriate labor, and supporting public institutions, are considered particularly important.

How is cluster analysis related to agglomeration economies? Cluster analysis clearly evolved from agglomeration economies, and agglomeration economies

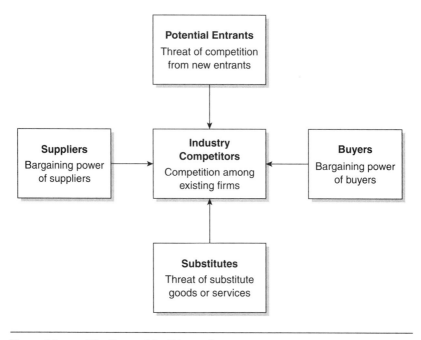

Figure 4.1   The Competitive Diamond

are critical to most clusters. Some observers have wondered whether clusters are merely a new terminology for an established idea (Martin & Sunley, 2003). One distinctive feature of cluster analysis is the emphasis on the dynamics of competitive advantage. Comparative advantage suggests that a region should produce products at a low cost relative to other areas. Competitive advantages include static cost efficiency and also the ability of a cluster to differentiate and innovate new products and product lines in order to remain competitive as markets change. Competitive advantage connotes a dynamic process. Another feature of cluster analysis is the recognition that beneficial relationships between firms can be very subtle. For instance, a community might establish a reputation as a cultural center. This reputation might affect firms in a variety of industries, including manufacturing.

In practice, cluster analysis at the local level involves determining which groups of firms are important to the region and identifying the nature of the linkages among them. Sometimes the linkages are difficult to uncover in the absence of direct market transactions. Once the diamond has been identified, actions to strengthen and build on the existing institutions and linkages can be considered. However, the implementation of cluster analysis remains largely subjective, so policy analysts must use their best judgment in implementation.

Measures of Economic Structure

While agglomeration economies are an important theoretical concept for understanding economic structure, we also need means to measure and analyze economic activities. This section describes some of the important empirical tools used by urban and regional economists. We start by describing a widely used way of categorizing industries. Next, location quotients (LQs) are explained, and then, techniques for using LQs for estimating exports are illustrated. Coefficients of specialization are the final topics discussed in this section.

NORTH AMERICAN INDUSTRIAL
CLASSIFICATION SYSTEM (NAICS)

"Tell me your industries and I'll tell you your future," said Wilbur Thompson. Understanding how firms are grouped into industries is important because economic development officials often analyze communities according to what industries they have. The North American Industrial Classification System (NAICS) is a commonly used means of categorizing economic activities. It was developed in consultation between United States, Canada, and Mexico to provide comparability between the three countries. Business *establishments* (think plants, not firms) are assigned to an industry based on the type of output they produce. Each industry has an NAICS code. Establishments are assigned to industries based on what they produce. The codes "nest," so that the first two digits identify the broadest sector and additional digits narrow the activity. For instance, NAICS 33121, "Iron, steel pipe, and tube from purchase steel," is a subsector of NAICS 3312, "Steel product manufacturing from purchased steel." All primary metal manufacturing is included under NAICS 331, "Primary metal manufacturing." Data for international trade are available based on industries classified according to the UN's SITC (Standard International Trade Classification) code system, which is very similar to NAICS.

Most production facilities have unique qualities. Conceptually, no matter how detailed the level of desegregation, many plants in the NAICS category will produce different products. Aggregation of things that are not alike is an important limitation on the use of NAICS or any other effort to categorize businesses according to what they produce. Furthermore, establishments often produce outputs in more than one NAICS category. A farm may produce both poultry and corn, just as a manufacturing facility may produce paper and cardboard boxes. Because a plant may produce more than one output, NAICS categorizes all employment and sales of a facility according to the major product line. A local analyst who considered only the official employment reports would not fully understand the local employment structure. NAICS can lead to an underestimation of the variety of goods and services produced in an area.

Another problem is created by disclosure rules. Governmental data collection systems normally avoid providing information that could disclose data about a singe plant. Thus, if a county has only one facility that produces bread, no information will be revealed about that NAICS code. However, information about the bakery will normally be included in the aggregated data on food manufacturing. When researchers seek to describe the economic structure of an area based on secondary data, they face a trade-off between a detailed level of industrial desegregation and a detailed level of geographic desegregation. The disclosure rule presents a particular problem for small areas, where detailed information is scarce.

LOCATION QUOTIENTS

The LQ is a tool for assessing a region's specialization in an industry. The industrial composition of a local economy may be better understood by comparing the local industrial structure with that of other cities or with the country as a whole than by examining a local economy in isolation. For instance, suppose it was determined that fabricated metals accounted for 12% of total employment in a community. While this information may be useful for some purposes, it does not indicate whether the economy is concentrated in metal fabrication compared with other places.

The employment LQ is the ratio of (a) the percentage of regional employment in a particular industry to (b) the comparable percentage in a benchmark area. The country is usually the benchmark area, although states or a group of similar regions may also be used as reference points. Accordingly, the LQ for industry i is generally expressed as

$$LQ_i = \frac{e_i/e_t}{US_i/US_t},\qquad(4.1)$$

where LQ_i is the location quotient for industry i, e_i is the local employment in industry i, e_t is the total local employment, US_i is the national employment for industry i, and US_t is the total national employment.

LQs can be useful tools for identifying industries in which a region has a disproportionate level of employment. An LQ equal to 1 for a particular industry means that the region has the same percentage of employment in that industry as the nation. An LQ less than 1 implies that the area has a less than proportionate share of employment in a particular industry, while an LQ greater than 1 implies a greater than proportionate concentration of employment.

The reasons a community has a concentration of employment in particular industries can often be traced to a current or historical location advantage. If an industry is underrepresented locally, a development planner might investigate why employment is low and what can be done to increase it. This is not to say that communities should strive to develop economies with structures that are similar to the U.S. average. Therefore, good judgment is important in determining how to interpret LQs.

Table 4.1 shows the LQs for three major metropolitan regions. They are roughly consistent with our casual knowledge of these regions. For instance, New York has high LQs in apparel, printing, and FIRE (finance, insurance, and real estate). The Los Angeles LQ in transportation equipment reflects the area's heavy concentration in aerospace production. The dominance of petroleum and chemicals in Houston is consistent with our perception of the Texas economy.

The picture of industrial structure given by the LQ will change depending on the level of industrial detail used in the calculations. For instance, the data in Table 4.1 reflect the two-digit level of industrial detail. Houston is obviously highly concentrated in the chemical industry when the classification is limited to two digits. However, Houston does not have high concentrations in all aspects of chemical production. If the two-digit chemical industry were divided into more narrowly defined sectors, Houston would be seen to have LQs significantly less than 1 for some chemical activities and a very high LQ for petrochemicals.

LQs are a versatile tool. The variable being analyzed and the area used for comparison can be tailored to fit the research question. While employment is the most frequently considered variable, measures of activity have included value added, sales, and occupation, and others. Furthermore, while the nation is normally used as a benchmark, a comparison of a region's percentage of activity in industries with that of similar cities or a state has been useful. For instance, ED officials may wish to compare their areas' economic structure with the average employment structure of other cities of similar size. Finally, EDs have used an LQ for linked activities, LQ_L. For instance, grain storage facilities could be used as an indication of specialization with reference to grain production:

$$LQ_L = \frac{(g_s/g_p)}{(G_S/G_P)}, \qquad (4.2)$$

where LQ_L is the location quotient for linked activities, g_s is the local grain storage in cubic feet, g_p is the local grain production, G_S is the U.S. grain storage in cubic feet, and G_P is the U.S. grain production.

Table 4.1   Location Quotients in Three Major Urban Counties: 2005

Industry	Cook County, Illinois	New York County, New York	Los Angeles County, California
Base Industry: Total, all industries	1	1	1
NAICS 11, Agriculture, forestry, fishing, and hunting	0.02	0	0.2
NAICS 21, Mining	0.08	0	0.2
NAICS 22, Utilities	0.38	ND	0.73
NAICS 23, Construction	0.64	0.25	0.64
NAICS 31–33, Manufacturing	0.9	0.18	1.04
NAICS 42, Wholesale trade	1	0.86	1.2
NAICS 44–45, Retail trade	0.79	0.53	0.86
NAICS 48–49, Transportation and warehousing	1.45	ND	1.1
NAICS 51, Information	1	2.61	2.13
NAICS 52, Finance and insurance	1.45	2.92	0.88
NAICS 53, Real estate and rental and leasing	1.12	2.19	1.15
NAICS 54, Professional and technical services	1.38	2.29	1.13
NAICS 55, Management of companies and enterprises	1.32	1.8	1.26
NAICS 56, Administrative and waste services	1.11	1	0.99
NAICS 61, Educational services	1.62	2.13	1.29
NAICS 62, Health care and social assistance	1.01	0.85	0.81
NAICS 71, Arts, entertainment, and recreation	0.9	1.58	1.14
NAICS 72, Accommodation and food services	0.87	0.82	0.9
NAICS 81, Other services, except public administration	1.11	1.19	1.7
NAICS 99, Unclassified	0.75	1.94	0.08

NOTE: ND, not disclosable.

In this case, a very low LQ for grain storage facilities might lead a development planner to attempt to encourage someone to start a grain storage enterprise since there may be a local need for storage facilities.

ESTIMATING EXPORT EMPLOYMENT WITH LOCATION QUOTIENTS

One of the most important aspects of regional structure is the distinction between activities that sell goods and services to nonresidents (export activities) and activities that provide goods and services to local residents (nonbasic activities). This section describes how a region's export industries can be identified. The next chapter elaborates the importance of export activities in the local growth process.

To establish the link between LQs and estimates of export employment, consider an LQ greater than 1. An LQ greater than 1 means that the region has more individuals employed in the particular industry than would be expected based on benchmark patterns. A likely explanation for a higher-than-average proportion of regional employment in a particular sector is that some of the sector's workers are producing exports—products that are sold outside the region. If this explanation is valid, an LQ greater than 1 means that some percentage of the employees in that industry are producing for export. Conversely, an LQ less than 1 means that the product is underproduced locally and, hence, must be imported. Exact self-sufficiency is signified by an LQ equal to 1.

Let s_i equal the self-sufficient employment level, and set the LQ equal to 1.

$$LQ = 1 = \frac{(s_i/e_t)}{(US_i/US_t)} \tag{4.3}$$

or

$$s_i = (US_i/US_t)e_t, \tag{4.4}$$

where US_i represents U.S. employment in industry i, US_t is the total employment in the country, and e_t equals total local employment. Equation 4.4 may be modified to show export employment as the employment in excess of the self-sufficient level in industry i.

$$x_i = e_i - s_i \tag{4.5}$$

or

$$x_i = e_i - e_t (US_i/US_t), \tag{4.6}$$

where x_i is the employment in industry i. Total export employment in the region is the sum of the export employment in the individual sectors. Therefore, total regional export employment, x_t, may be expressed as

$$x_t = \sum x_i. \qquad (4.7)$$

Critique

Unfortunately, the LQ is an imprecise indicator of the extent of importing and exporting. When the initial assumptions are examined, other explanations for the size of LQs become apparent.

1. When analysts assume that an LQ of 1 implies exact self-sufficiency, they overlook the possibility of cross-hauling. For instance, a General Motors (GM) car may be produced and exported from a region at the same time as other brands are being imported. If cross-hauling existed, an area with an LQ of 1 could be exporting and importing a product simultaneously.

2. If workers in a region are more productive than workers elsewhere, an LQ_i less than 1 might be appropriate for a community, even though the industry was an exporter of the product. Conversely, an unproductive sector could have a high LQ_i, even though it produced only for local consumption. To minimize the problem of worker productivity differences, value added or total output could be used to develop the LQ.

3. If there are significant regional variations in the level of demand, the LQ will not necessarily reflect the extent of exports or imports. For instance, cities in warm climates have had a disproportionate level of employment in air-conditioning maintenance. However, this difference is due to greater local demand compared with the rest of the United States rather than significant exportation of such goods and services.

4. The estimated level of exports depends on the level of industrial detail and product differentiation. As pointed out previously, when broad industrial categories are examined, the LQs tend to be closer to 1 than when more detailed industries are examined. A region could have a low LQ in manufacturing, indicating no exports, but some sectors within manufacturing may be exporters. Similarly, Detroit is a net exporter of automobiles, but it also imports models of cars not made in Detroit due to product differentiation. Because of the existence of cross-hauling, the volume of exports estimated by the LQ technique will be subject to error. Cross-hauling of identical products could even occur under some circumstances. Generally, the more detailed the industrial breakdown, the greater the exporting sector will appear. Thus, the direction of bias due to the failure to disaggregate completely or due to product differentiation is predictable.

5. An LQ of 1 indicates self-sufficiency only in a closed national economy. However, the United States imports products from the rest of the world. Hence, the average community with an LQ of 1 for a particular good or service may still be exporting or importing some of the commodity.

Rebuttal

Most local economic development experts now consider the use of LQs alone to be inadequate for determining the multiplier. They may be useful as a first-cut approximation to determine industries that require further examination, however. Empirical studies indicate that the number of individuals in the export sector is normally underestimated when LQs are used to estimate exports because even an industry with low LQs may be engaged in exporting some of its product even when very similar products are being imported. However, the technique has three important advantages that are responsible for its continued popularity.

First, LQs are an inexpensive way to describe a region's exports because they can be constructed from published data. Second, LQs can help estimate indirect exports. For instance, a city that exports computers may have a high LQ in molded plastic parts because the plastic is embodied in the computer and indirectly exported. Finally, the LQ technique applies equally to commodities and services.

The Minimum-Requirements Technique

Some analysts believe that a more accurate picture of the local export sectors can be obtained by the minimum-requirements technique. Whereas the LQ technique normally uses the entire national economy as a benchmark, the minimum-requirements approach bases the self-sufficient employment level on analysis of similar areas. For instance, suppose you wish to determine the export employment for a region with a population of 100,000. The minimum-requirements approach could involve examination of, say, 10 cities of similar size. The cities might be selected based on other common characteristics such as location or per capita income. The city with the smallest LQ in an industry (i.e., smallest percentage of employment) would be presumed to represent the minimum requirement needed by a city to satisfy its domestic needs. Thus, it represents the self-sufficient level. The minimum-requirements approach normally results in a higher level of estimated exports than the LQ technique. A variant of the minimum-requirements technique might use some other threshold, such as the fifth smallest LQ, as the minimum requirement for self-sufficiency. The threshold depends on the official's justification of the choice. Total export employment would be all employment above the minimum-requirement threshold.

SURVEYS TO DETERMINE EXPORT ACTIVITIES

Distinguishing export from nonbasic activities can be accomplished most accurately by surveying individual businesses in the area and asking the managers (perhaps the sales director) who their customers are and where they are located. If their local customers are themselves exporters, then the researcher must also account for the fact that the intermediate inputs are ultimately exported as well. For instance, a locally made electronic component may be exported when it is included in an airplane manufactured locally but sold outside the area. Even in a small economy, conducting a survey would be costly. When using surveys, the LQ technique may be useful in targeting industries "likely" to be exporters prior to doing the survey.

COEFFICIENTS OF SPECIALIZATION

The coefficient of specialization measures the extent to which a region's structure differs from some standard such as the national industrial structure. The coefficient is a simple measure of the degree to which a region's economic structure is similar to or different from that of the nation as a whole. To calculate the coefficient of specialization, the percentage of local employment in each industry is compared with a comparable national percentage. The sum of the positive differences (or the absolute value of the negative differences) is the coefficient of specialization.

A coefficient of 0 would indicate that the region had exactly the same percentage of employment or other variable from each sector as the nation. The maximum coefficient would approach 100; for instance, residents of a region might receive all their income from sources not available elsewhere in the United States. A coefficient of specialization is high or low by comparison with other areas. The more detailed the industrial structure, the larger the coefficient of specialization.

Like LQs, the coefficient of specialization is a versatile tool. It can be used to examine sales, value-added sales, demographic composition, and so forth.

OCCUPATIONAL STRUCTURE

Industries describe what an area produces, but occupations describe how an area produces. For instance, two regions may both have high LQs in the aerospace industry. However, one place might manufacture airplane, and the other might design airplanes. Hence, the airplane industry in the producing region would have predominately production workers, and the design region would have a concentration of engineers. Policymakers have historically examined a region's industries to understand its economic structure. More recently, information about local industries has been supplemented by information about occupational structure to allow "cross-hair" targeting (Thompson & Thompson, 1985) and indicate future regional growth and location patterns (Riefler, 2007).

Markusen (2004) described some ways in which occupational structure can assist in development planning.

1. A region's export competencies may be reflected in the skills of the labor force rather than the types of industries or natural resources. An area may manufacture medical devices, but whether the area's strength is in low-cost production or precision tool making may be revealed only by considering the occupation.

2. Some occupations have a propensity for generating new business, and so they might be a key factor in business formation. A preponderance of some occupations may explain why some areas have high rates of innovation and business start-ups.

3. An understanding of the occupational structure may inform labor force development efforts. Firms are increasingly concerned with the quality and availability of key local labor skills.

4. Occupational concentrations may occur even in the absence of a concentration of employers. For some occupations, the location of the employer and the location of the workplace spans significant distances.

5. The presence of some occupations such as "artists" or "educators" may attract other business in seemingly unrelated fields.

Markusen (2004) suggested that regional development officials may play an important role in attracting certain types of occupations based on the types of public infrastructure, supporting institutions, and quality of life available locally. Accordingly, policies may influence occupational structure.

Other Aspects of Regional Structure

An industrial focus, including the distinction between export and nonbasic activities, is the traditional way to understand a local economy. Concern with occupational characteristics is emerging. However, the structure of a local economy includes more than its industrial and occupational composition. A detailed understanding of an area's structure might include demographic, ownership, market, political, and social factors as well. All these factors may influence the course of economic development.

Summary

Economic development officials need to understand existing linkages between firms and industries within a local economy so that they can strengthen existing linkages and help build new ones. This chapter examines the cohesive forces that tend to link firms within a region and the quantitative tools that can be used to understand local economic structure.

Agglomeration economies result in cost reductions due to spatial concentration of activity. Internal agglomeration economies are attributed to an increase in one firm's activities in a single place. Firms that trade with each other often benefit from locating in proximity. Localization economies accrue to firms in a particular industry. Localization economies have been attributable to development of a qualified labor pool, specialized equipment, imitation/modification/innovation, and comparison shopping. Urbanization economies are the most diffuse type of agglomeration economy resulting from an expansion in overall economic activity in an area. Shared infrastructure and economies from averaging of random variations are sources of urbanization economies.

Economic clusters view local interdependencies from a broader and more dynamic perspective. Clusters build on the concept of competitive advantage.

The NAICS is a widely used system of organizing information about industries. Industries nest into categories that are increasingly detailed.

LQs are a popular technique for comparing the size of a local industry with that of the industry's importance in the national economy. The LQ formula is

$$LQ = \frac{\text{Percentage of local employment in industry } i}{\text{Percentage of national employment in industry } i} \qquad (4.8)$$

LQs may be used with sales, value added, or other measures of activity in addition to employment.

An LQ greater than 1 indicates that the industry is more dominant in the local economy than nationally. Given a set of very strict assumptions, the LQ has been used to estimate export employment. Although LQs are an imperfect tool for describing a local economy and estimating exports, they are widely used because they are an inexpensive technique, they reflect indirect exports, and they apply to both goods and services.

All employment above the level necessary to set an industry's LQ to equal 1 can be considered export employment. Alternatively, the minimum-requirements technique uses the minimum LQ from a group of similar cities as a benchmark. All employment above the level for the benchmark LQ is considered export.

The coefficient of specialization shows the extent to which an area's industrial structure differs from that of the nation or some other point of comparison.

This chapter was primarily concerned with industrial structure. However, economic development analysts should be aware that other types of structure can influence an area's economic future.

5

Regional Growth
and Development

Previous chapters addressed issues of economic growth indirectly. The implications of various models for urban and regional growth have been very near the surface. Local growth is affected by location decisions of firms, the area's place in the system of cities, and its economic structure. This chapter presents fundamental theories of urban and regional growth.

Stages of Growth

Wilbur Thompson (1968) and Jane Jacobs (1969) both observed that cities pass through stages as they develop. Although there are differences in their terminologies, emphasis, and details, the similarities between their descriptions are striking. Table 5.1 summarizes the stages of growth described by Thompson and Jacobs.

Both descriptions indicate that metropolitan areas initially export one or a few products. The export becomes the foundation for additional activities. During the second state, export activities become more indirect in the sense that an intermediate product may be embedded in the export of a near-final product. The next stage may be termed import substitution. Goods previously imported are produced locally. Increases in the number and complexity of linkages are emphasized in the fourth stage of each model. Thompson (1968) emphasized the connections with other cities, and Jacobs (1969) emphasized agglomeration and cluster economies. In the fifth stage, as cities grow, they hone their ability to improve what and how they produce, including the ability to copy what others have done. Thompson emphasized the ability to maintain leadership in specific industries. Jacobs focused on the ability to create new things. In both models, innovative and imitative ability contributes to further growth in the fifth stage.

Table 5.1   Stages of Urban Growth

Thompson's (1968) Stages of Growth	Jacobs' (1969) Stages of Growth
1. Export specialization: "The local economy is the lengthened shadow of a single, dominant industry" (p. 15).	1. Expanding market for a few exports and suppliers of the exports.
2. Export complex: "Local production broadens and/or depends by extending forward or backward" (p. 15).	2. Suppliers begin exporting directly.
3. Economic maturation: "The principal expansion is in the direction of replacing imports" (p. 16).	3. Goods initially imported into the area are produced and sold locally.
4. Regional metropolis: "The local economy becomes a node connecting and controlling neighboring cities" (p. 16).	4. The city's enlarged and diversified local economy becomes a potential source of exports. The exports increase the volume of imports.
5. Technical-professional virtuosity: "National eminence in some specialized economic function is achieved" (p. 16).	5. New work is constantly developed. An "economic reciprocating system" results in new skill or businesses.

Once an area reaches a critical mass, the local economy has sufficient resources to develop new work. Thompson (1968) referred to an "urban size ratchet." He believed that once a threshold was reached, urban areas could muster the resources—public and private—to maintain their local economies:

> If the growth of an urban area persists long enough to raise the area to some critical size, power, huge fixed investments, a rich local market, and a steady supply of industrial leadership may almost ensure its continued growth and fully ensure against absolute decline. (p. 24)

Thompson (1968) may have overstated the strengths of the size ratchet. In periods of rapid economic change, even well-established metropolitan areas can experience decline although economic size and complexity improve an area's ability to develop new growth generators.

INDUSTRIAL FILTERING (LIFE CYCLE MODEL)

The theory of industrial filtering helps explain the necessity for metropolitan areas to generate new exports. Figure 8.2 provides a graphic representation of the life cycle of a typical product. The fast-growth stage is early in the product's life. Metropolitan areas have a critical role in the product development process. Larger urban areas tend to be the location of firms when their industries are in the early stages of development. During the early stages of industrial development, firms often require advanced technical skills, support of other businesses, and production flexibility, so they need an urban location. Later, after the production process has become more routine, the need for skills, business support, and flexibility decreases. The product becomes commoditized, and pressures to cut costs become intense. Firms engaged in routine work may relocate or expand in less urban areas in search of lower production costs. Thus, urban areas are on a treadmill, developing new economic activities as old activities filter down to areas with lower production costs. Also, larger metropolitan areas may retain control of research and development functions within an industry even as the routine functions are dispersed to a low-production-cost site.

ADDING NEW WORK TO OLD

Jacobs (1969) used the phrase "adding new work to old" to describe a key element in the movement of cities through the developmental stages. Metropolises do not grow by simply doing more of what they have done previously, because these activities seek low-cost locations. Economies expand by developing new kinds of work. New work is usually an extension or modification of previous activities. Development of new work normally springs from the numerous, diverse linkages that characterize a large metropolis. The process of adding new work to old is so pervasive that it is often overlooked—as when a day-care center offers a "sick-child-care service" in addition to normal service. The cumulative impact of such activities is vital to development. New work often increases the specialization of labor. A manufacturer of kitchen equipment, a delicatessen, a cheese importer, and a night club might all have resulted from new work being added to an original restaurant. Creating new work also helps conserve old work. As a product spins off from an old activity, the new product may be a supplier or a purchaser supporting the "mother" activity.

Jacobs (1969) indicated that larger areas have an edge in the ability to add new work to old:

> The greater the sheer numbers and varieties of division of labor already achieved in an economy, the greater the economy's inherent capacity for adding still more

kinds of goods and services. Also, the possibilities increase for combining the existing divisions of labor. (p. 59)

Many instances of service duplication and congestion that urban critics claim are the inefficiencies of large places are defended by Jacobs (1969), because she believed that they contribute to the innovative climate that encourages new products and processes. Her analysis of how new work develops has contributed to our understanding of the process of urban innovation.

HOW DO CITIES MOVE FROM ONE STATE TO THE NEXT?

Theories regarding stages of growth (including the theories of Jacobs, 1969; Thompson, 1968) often fail to explain why some places progress from one stage to the next while other places do not. Thompson suggested that the momentum gained during an early stage of development may help propel an area to the next stage. At each stage, the growth stimulus, including linkages to external growth generators, must be sufficient to lift an area so that additional products can be developed and produced locally.

The momentum explanation is not particularly satisfying. For one thing, it does not explain why one place has momentum or why momentum is maintained in some places and not in others. It further glosses over the variety of situations localities face. Finally, some places may do well without progressing to higher stages. Getting bigger is not a goal embraced everywhere.

The stages perspective provides economic development officials with a framework for policy development. It suggests that policymakers should consider how to set the groundwork for future stages. But knowing how to apply the framework requires an in-depth understanding of an area's locational strengths, interurban linkages, industrial structure, values, and so forth.

Circular Flow Diagram

A circular flow diagram is presented in Figure 5.1. Circular flow is not a theory of *how* a region grows, because it implies no causal relationships. Rather, it is a stylized picture of some important linkages and money flows. It is the basis for several important theories of growth discussed later.

ELEMENTS OF THE CIRCULAR FLOW MODEL

Money flows in a local economy are essential to the economic development process. These flows are shown in a simple circular flow model. The economy is divided into households and businesses. The two categories are conceptually

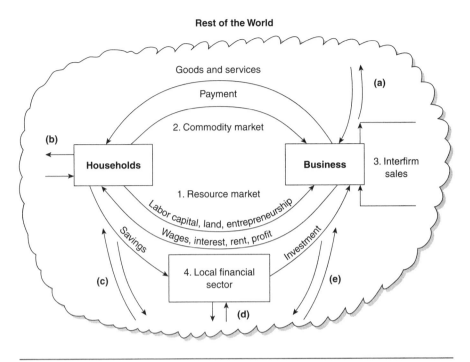

Figure 5.1   A Local Circular Flow Model

NOTE: The circular flow diagram shows major sectors of an economy and how they interact. The main difference between the nation and a regional economy is the importance of monetary inflows (exports) and outflows (imports).

distinct, but the same person can be in the household category while also fulfilling a business role. For instance, a person may own a business and purchase factors of production through that business and also be in a household when purchasing goods and services.

There are five important types of markets in the circular flow model.

Resource Market

The upper portion of the diagram, the resource market, shows that businesses purchase factors of production from households. In return for the factors of production, households receive wages, rents, interests, and profits. Notice that profits are not retained by businesses in this model. If none of the households earn income outside the community, the sum of payments received by households from area businesses would equal the total regional income.

Commodity Market

The local commodity market is the second market. Here, households purchase goods and services from local businesses. If we assume that there are no nonlocal customers, local household spending will account for the net (excluding local firms selling to each other) business receipts.

Interfirm Sales

Interfirm sales are an important category of local transactions. Establishments within an area sell intermediate goods and services to each other. Such transactions are an important part of the growth process.

Local Financial Sectors

The fourth set of transactions occurs within the local financial sector. Some local household savings flow into the local financial sector. In Figure 5.1, all savings is by households, implying that businesses do not retain earnings. This simplification keeps the diagram from becoming too cluttered. Household savings take two forms. A part of the local savings is invested locally. Other savings flow out of the area and are presumably deposited in outside financial institutions or invested directly in outside business ventures by local households. Savings invested outside the area are treated as monetary outflows.

Exchanges With the Rest of the World

The fifth set of transactions is necessary because of the region's interaction with the rest of the world. Exchanges with the rest of the world—other localities both in and out of the country—are important to the local economies. While exports and imports are important for nations, they are even more important for local economies. Normally, the smaller the region, the more open the economy is and the more important money inflows and outflows are. Note that households, businesses, and the local financial sector are all shown to interact with the rest of the world. These interactions result in monetary inflows and outflows.

Figure 5.1a represents business sales to nonresidents that result in a counterflow of money into the area. Businesses also make purchases outside the area. Figure 5.1b represents household transactions outside the area. Direct exports of labor, as when someone is working outside the area, would be included in this flow. Figure 5.1c represents direct investment placed outside the area. The return on such investments constitutes a counterflow. Figure 5.1d represents financial exchanges with the rest of the world that flow through the local financial institutions. Outside investments made directly to local businesses and the return on such investments are represented by Figure 5.1e.

Money flows into a region for a variety of reasons: gifts from relatives, payments for services performed for nonresidents, payment for goods sold to nonresidents, governmental transfer payments, interest on investments made outside the area, and so forth. A portion of the monetary inflows would go directly to households, immediately increasing household income. Another portion accrues to households through businesses that sell goods and services to nonresidents. Businesses also receive money inflows when nonresidents make investments in local businesses.

Money inflows that accrue to local business may become income to households as businesses pay the households for the factors of production used in producing the goods and services.[1] However, only a portion of business sales becomes income to local residences. Suppose a nonresident purchased a $3,000 entertainment system from a local business. How much income will accrue to households? If the system were produced entirely within the area, and none of the resource owners lived outside the area, then the entire $3,000 would flow to local households in the form of wages, rents, interest, and profits. But it is unrealistic to suppose that the entire system was produced locally. More realistically, some of the necessary components would have been purchased from other businesses outside the region. In this case, the local firm selling the system might spend a portion of the $3,000 purchase price, say $2,000, to pay for or replenish inventories such as televisions, speakers, and recorders. Only $1,000 would accrue to local households. Local households receive the value added locally, not the total value of exports. Accordingly, the sale of an item for export may be viewed as a net monetary inflow equal to the total value of the product less the cost of the components and factors of production purchased from outside the community.

Monetary outflows represent money that leaves the local economy. They occur when households purchase goods or services from outside the area, pay taxes to nonlocal governments, make interest payments to nonresidents, invest in business outside the area, and so forth. Many consumer imports represented in the monetary outflow stream are indirect. For instance, if a person purchases a car from a local dealership, a portion of that expenditure may be attributed to the import of the automobile. Only the local value added will accrue as household income.

A model is intended to simplify reality. It is tempting to add details in order to make the model more realistic. However, too much added complexity defeats the purpose of a model, which is to highlight key factors. Perhaps Figure 5.1 may already be too complicated. Nevertheless, it is usually a worthwhile exercise to examine what has been excluded from models and to ask whether the simplifications seriously distort the reality the model represents.

EQUILIBRIUM AND CHANGE

The difference between the size of monetary inflows and outflows is critical to local economic growth. Monetary inflows can cause the entire volume of money circulating within an area to increase, increasing incomes and employment.

Payments for goods produced in the area and sold elsewhere are a major source of income for the community. For example, when a Detroit-made automobile is sold to a Chicago resident (or, more accurately, when the Detroit-made automobile is sold to an auto dealer who expects to sell it to a Chicago resident), money flows into Detroit. Monetary inflows increase the ability of residents to command additional goods and services and may attract additional resources to the area or stimulate the use of previously unemployed local resources. Sales of goods and services to nonlocal customers are usually referred to as *exports*. Other nonlocal sources of community income include interest payments from outside corporations, government transfers such as Social Security, gifts received, and investments by nonresidents.

Monetary outflows shrink an area's circular flow and consequently decrease local income and employment. For example, when residents of one area increase their purchases from neighboring regions, the outflow represents foregone income to local business—money that could have been paid to local households in subsequent transactions. Purchases of goods and services from nonlocal sources are called imports. The term *imports* applies to all purchases made outside the city and not just to international transactions. Thus, the resident of Chicago who purchases a car from Detroit causes an outflow of funds from Chicago and an inflow of dollars to Detroit (assuming that auto retailers maintain their inventories by replacing the car they sold).

What is the equilibrium condition of the model represented in Figure 5.1? When monetary outflows equal monetary inflows, the community income level will remain constant. The equilibrium condition can be grasped intuitively by using the bathtub analogy. The amount of water in the tub will remain constant only when the water flowing from the faucet equals the amount that leaves through the drain.

THE MULTIPLIER

To illustrate the multiplier, suppose a business increases its sales by increasing exports to a customer in a nearby state. A portion of the increase will accrue to local households as payment for labor and other services involved in producing the output. Households will spend a fraction of the increased earnings in local establishments, thereby expanding the local consumer market and allowing businesses to purchase additional factors of production locally. However, businesses and households will also purchase from outside the area and cause monetary outflows. Therefore, the process of local spending and responding will not continue indefinitely.

Figure 5.2 illustrates what might happen if a major convention were held in a city. Suppose the convention resulted in increased spending by nonresidents of $227,273. Assume that of the $227,273 in increased spending, $127,273 went to outside suppliers and a corporation that owns the major hotel or other non-local factors of production. Consequently, $100,000 of the initial spending would go to residents who provided services for the conventioneers. Of the $100,000, local residents might spend $80,000 at local establishments. The remainder, $20,000, would flow outside the city as households spent or invested outside the local area. Carrying the process further, of the $80,000 spent at local businesses, $45,000 might be used by local businesses to create nonlocal income (maybe purchases outside the city) and $35,000 may be returned to residents in the form of local wages, rent, interest, and profits. Thus, the $227,273 of new spending resulted in an increase of $100,000 in local income initially and $35,000 of income from a second round of spending. In this instance, because of imports of local businesses, the marginal propensity of households to spend with local businesses would be .8 (80000/100000). In addition, when households spend at local businesses, another type of monetary outflow occurs. They spend outside the area through an intermediary—other local businesses. This flow is an indirect import. Thus, the initial $100,000 of income resulted in leakages of $20,000 directly and $45,000 indirectly, so the complete marginal propensity to import is .65. The marginal propensity to consume locally is .35 ([100000 − 20000 − 45000]/100000). The original $100,000 would eventually leak out of the community in the form of business and consumer spending. Because of successive rounds of local spending, about $53,846 of household income would be created in addition to the initial $100,000 of income.[2] The larger the leakages per transaction, the smaller the total increase in household income.

The multiplier has a different effect if the monetary inflow occurs in a single period compared with a permanent increase in income. To distinguish between temporary and permanent increases in exports, assume that local convention business increased permanently by $227,273 annually. An extra $100,000 would be earned by households every period. Community income would be increased by $135,000 in the second period—the $35,000 second-round increase shown in Figure 5.2 plus the extra $100,000 earnings from the first round of spending in the second year. In the third period, total income would rise to the sum of (1) first-round, Year 3 spending; (2) second-round, Year 2 spending; and (3) third-round, Year 1 spending—or $147,250 (100000 + 35000 + 12250). Eventually, the permanent increase in inflows would cause annual community income to rise permanently by $153,846. Figure 5.3 compares the income effects of a temporary and a permanent increase in monetary inflows.

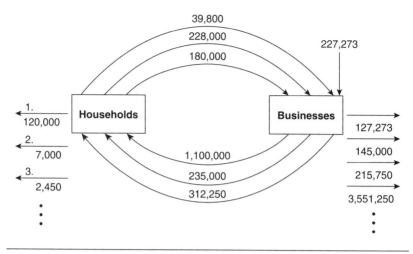

Figure 5.2   A Community Income/Expenditure Pattern

NOTE: Impacts from an initial monetary inflow of $227,273.

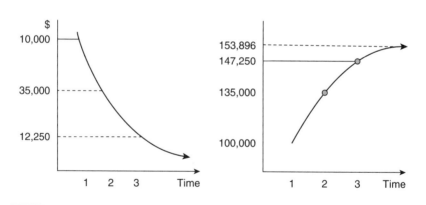

Figure 5.3   Income Paths From Temporary and Permanent Increases in
Monetary Inflows

NOTE: A temporary increase in monetary inflows will increase income by successively smaller amounts. A permanent increase in monetary inflows will permanently increase income by a multiple of the original increase.

The fact that households receive only temporary increases in income from "one-shot" money inflows has important implications. Many public construction projects and other temporary infusions cannot be the source of a long-run equilibrium increase in incomes unless the project changes the money flows permanently. Of course, even a temporary increase in income is nice. However, a change that permanently increases exports will increase community income to a new, higher equilibrium. Thus, local development officials may prefer a project that promises a continuous inflow of funds to the one-shot injection associated with many public works.

The Export Base Theory of Growth

The export base theory of growth is grounded in the idea that a local economy must increase its monetary inflows to grow and the principal way to increase monetary inflow is to increase exports.

Tiebout (1962) described the fundamental relationships posed by the export base theory:

> Export markets are considered the prime movers of the local economy. If employment serving this market rises or falls, employment serving the local market is presumed to move in the same direction. When the factory (export) closes, retail merchants (local) feel the impact as laid-off factory workers have less to spend. Because of the prime mover role, export employment is considered as "basic." Employment which serves the local market is considered adaptive and is titled "non-basic." (p. 10)

The export base theory may be expressed in terms of either income or employment:

$$\Delta T = k * \Delta B \tag{5.1}$$

or

$$\Delta y = k * \Delta E, \tag{5.1'}$$

where T is total employment, y is total income, B is basic (export) employment, E refers to export earnings, k is the export base multiplier, and Δ represents change.

The key concept of the economic base theory is that the export activity is the engine of growth. Income originally earned by the export sector is spent and respent locally, creating additional income through the multiplier. A portion of the export-earned dollars is spent locally by the export workers, creating nonbasic jobs. Employees in the nonbasic sector, in turn, spend much of their earning locally, thus supporting additional jobs. The size of the multiplier depends on the propensity of individuals to spend money in the local economy rather than spending it outside the local area.

At one time, economists considered mining, agriculture, and manufacturing as basic activities and other activities as service. Increasingly, services are recognized as a possible source of export earnings and, therefore, a part of the region's basic activities. Services can be exported from the region either when local residents travel outside the area to provide the service or when nonresidents come from outside the area to purchase local services. Services play several important economic development functions. They (1) serve as exports, (2) substitute for existing imports, and (3) provide services to local residents (Gillis, 1987).

Studies have shown the extent to which service activities can be important export earners. Ashton and Sternal (1978) found that 20% of New England's service-producing industries export more than half their sales to individuals outside the region. Tourism, which primarily involves providing services such as lodging, food, and recreation to nonresidents, is an economic development path throughout the world and key to South African development strategy (Miriam, 2006). Specialization in knowledge-intensive services is driving economic development throughout European cities (Kratke, 2007), and Chinese students are now the largest export market for Australian education services.

Proponents of the export base theory recognize that many businesses serve both local customers and nonresidents. However, in practice it can be difficult to distinguish between the two because many industries serve both the export and the local markets. The use of location quotients and other techniques to determine the export and service sectors was discussed in Chapter 4.

THE FORMAL INCOME MODEL

The export base theory can be derived from the circular flow model. Income rather than employment is usually the focus of formal presentations of the export base theory. Income may be expressed as

$$Y = C + MI - MO. \tag{5.2}$$

where Y is total local income, MI represents monetary inflows, C is consumption spending by local residents, and MO represents monetary outflows.

Equation 5.2 states that income of local residents is equal to consumption (C) plus net monetary inflows. Note that consumption of goods or services purchased from outside the area would increase C and MO by equal amounts, so Y would not be changed when local residents spend outside the region.

Consumption

Consumption has two components. Some consumption is unrelated to income, as suggested by the A term in the equation below. But most consumption depends on the level of income. The marginal propensity to consume is a fraction of an increase in income that is spent. If the marginal propensity to consume is .80, then 80 cents of each dollar increase in income will be spent. Thus,

$$C = A + bY, \qquad (5.3)$$

where A is consumption that is unrelated to income and b is the marginal propensity to consume.

Monetary Inflows

Proponents of the export base theory argue that exports are the primary source of monetary inflow and that exports are determined by outside demand for goods and services produced in the region. Since the extent of outside demand is beyond the area's control, it is considered "exogenous." (Some development officials attempt to increase the demand for products of a particular area. For instance, individuals may be encouraged to vacation in New Orleans. Thus, outside demand is not totally exogenous.) Accordingly, exports are considered the only source of monetary inflows. Therefore,

$$MI = E_0, \qquad (5.4)$$

where E_0 is the exogenously determined export income.

Monetary Outflows

Monetary outflows result when residents send money outside the area, either directly or indirectly. As local incomes increase, spending outside the area will increase. Purchases of goods and services from nonresidents, imports, are the primary source of monetary outflows. Savings that are not reinvested in the local economy are another form of leakage. The greater the saving, the lower will be the marginal propensity to consume, b. However, to avoid complicating the model, the role of financial institutions in the recycling of savings will not be addressed directly. For simplicity, assume that all money outflows are related to the level of income. Thus,

$$MO = iY, \qquad (5.5)$$

where i is the marginal propensity to import (create monetary outflows). Imports may be either direct or embedded in products purchased from local sellers.

The Unified Model

Equations 5.3 to 5.5 can be inserted into Equation 5.2

$$Y = A + bY + E_0 - iY. \tag{5.6}$$

or

$$Y = (A + E_0) [1/(1 - b + i)]. \tag{5.7}$$

Based on Equation 5.7, the factors that determine regional income can be summarized. The first term represents spending sources independent of local income. The second term reflects the tendency for dollars to recirculate within the circular flow. The larger the marginal propensity to consume, b, and the smaller the marginal propensity to import, i, the larger income will be for a given level of autonomous spending. Therefore, according to the logic of the strict export base model, income will increase only if exports, E_0, change.

Setting ΔA to 0 and allowing the change in exports to equal ΔE_0, the change in income is[3]

$$\Delta Y = (1/(1 - (b - i)) * \Delta E_0 \tag{5.8}$$

Equation 5.8 indicates that a change in export income will change total income by $(1/(1 - (b - i))$ times ΔE_0. Note that $(b - i)$ is the marginal propensity to spend locally—the marginal propensity to consume minus the propensity to consume from outside the area, both directly and indirectly. Thus, the export base multiplier is conceptually similar to the Keynesian multiplier used in macroeconomic analysis. The multiplier effect occurs because the initial increase in export income is spent and respent, thus creating additional income. However, some of the additional spending "leaks" from the circular flow in the form of monetary outflow.

HOW TO OPERATIONALIZE
THE EXPORT BASE APPROACH

Estimating the multiplier is key to operationalizing the export base approach. Surveys of local spending habits can be made to determine the propensity to spend locally. The ratio of value added to total sales has been used to measure indirect imports (Olfert & Stabler, 1994). But such surveys are expensive and difficult to design. A survey would have to determine both consumer and business spending patterns in order to be a complete measure of import tendencies. To avoid the need for surveys, practitioners have developed a technique to estimate the local multiplier using readily available employment data. Thus, while the formal model was concerned with income, employment can be used to operationalize the model. On the basis of location quotients, surveys, or other techniques, local employment can be split into the number of workers producing for export and the number producing for local consumption.

Two assumptions are useful in operationalizing the export base model. The first assumption is that income is proportional to employment. Therefore, nonbasic income as a proportion of total income will equal nonbasic employment divided by total employment. This assumption is important because it supports the use of employment changes as a measure of income changes. In the short run, it is likely that incomes could increase without employment increasing. In this case, per capita income would increase. However, it is reasonable to suppose that higher incomes would attract additional workers to the area. Hence, the link between income and employment can be supported by the movement of labor from lower- to higher-wage areas. The second assumption is that the ratio of export employment to total employment is constant. Each new export job creates the same number of nonbasic jobs. This assumption implies that as the number of export workers (income) increases, the number of nonbasic employees (income) will increase in the same proportion as the existing export to total employment ratio. The assumption is important because when combined with the first assumption, it allows the estimation of $(b - i)$. With reference to Equation 5.7, $(b - i)$ is the proportion of an income increase spent locally. Given the assumptions, $(b - i)$ will be the same as the nonbasic employment to total employment ratio (the portion of total employment serving local residents). Accordingly, the export base multiplier (Equation 5.1) can be expressed as

$$k = 1/1 - (b - i) = 1/1 - (NB/T)$$
$$= 1/(B/T)$$
$$= T/B, \qquad (5.9)$$

where T is total employment, B is export (or basic) employment, and NB is nonbasic employment (serving the local market).

Therefore, Equation 5.1 may be expressed as

$$\Delta T = (T/B) * \Delta B \qquad (5.10)$$

or

$$\Delta T = k(\Delta B), \qquad (5.11)$$

where Δ represents change, T is total employment, B is basic employment, and k is the multiplier.

Given an understanding of the theory that underlies the export base approach, the multiplier can be easily calculated. If total employment is 2,000 and export employment is determined to be 1,000, then the employment multiplier would be 2. The export base model emphasizes (1) the change in exports and (2) the multiplier effects that exports have in determining local economic growth.

There are other, more complicated techniques for estimating local multipliers, such as regressions or input-output models. These are described further in Chapter 6. Advanced analysis has generated "sectoral" multipliers. Rather than showing the relationship between total employment and export employment, a sectoral multiplier might show how a change in the automobile sector would change income or employment in all other sectors or even particular sectors such as "retail trade." When using sectoral multipliers, Equation 5.10 might be reconceptualized as

$$\Delta T_i = (k_{ji})(\Delta B_j), \tag{5.12}$$

where ΔT_i is change in employment in sector i, DB_j is change in employment in industry j, and k_{ji} is the multiplier showing the impact of industry j on sector i.

IMPACT STUDIES AND EXPORT BASE FORECASTS

Export base studies are used for a variety of purposes, tailored to specific circumstances. The export base approach is often applied to local forecasting and impact analysis. Export base studies tend to have similar structures.

1. The first step in an export base study is to determine the appropriate geographic area for study. The appropriate area is sometimes a compromise between the area relevant for the purpose of the study and the area for which data are available. A neighborhood or small town may be too small an area for a successful study because data on such areas are often not available. Furthermore, small neighborhoods or suburban communities have extremely high degrees of interdependence within the larger metropolitan economy. Such subareas do not have a sufficiently integrated internal circular flow, so the export base concepts may have less meaning in such a very small area. While the appropriate area depends on the purpose of the study, cities, counties, or metropolitan statistical areas are generally chosen for analysis because such areas are integrated economies, export similar items, and are affected by the same trends.

2. The second step is to describe the local economy and determine the sources of export employment. This step may set the stage for deriving the multiplier. A table showing the location quotients for each industry is useful

for identifying export sectors. The method shown in Chapter 4 is one technique that can be used to calculate export (basic) employment.

3. The third step in an export base study is to determine k, the local multiplier. The question to be answered is "If basic employment increases by a given amount, how many additional jobs will be created in the region as a whole?" As explained above, the multiplier may be expressed as the change in total employment divided by the change in export employment. The multiplier may be estimated using a variety of techniques, including using location quotients to estimate export and nonbasic employment, econometric models, surveys, and input-output analysis.

4. The fourth step is to forecast exogenous changes in the local export sector. A frequently employed estimating technique is to apply national trends to key export sectors. The knowledge of the local environment could be used to modify national growth projections. Opinions of experts could be used to estimate the possibilities of development of new export sectors. This step can be quite complicated. However, the end result will be an estimate of the change in export employment (ΔB in Equation 5.1).

5. Once the export employment has been forecast, the multiplier can be used to determine total employment changes. For instance, if the multiplier is 2, and the export sector is estimated to increase by 75 jobs, then the total estimated increase in employment would be 150.

If it is assumed that employment is proportional to income, the same multiplier can be used to estimate the change in total income given an initial change in export income.

The forecasting process need not stop at Step 5. The projected level of employment may be used as information to forecast other variables such as income, population, housing demand, and traffic congestion.

Urban and regional economists are occasionally asked to estimate the impact of a known or anticipated single event, such as the opening of a new plant or the closing of a military base. For instance, an analyst may be required to estimate the total impact on the economy if a local firm were to close. The initial change in export employment could be multiplied by the multiplier to estimate the total employment impact. In addition to employment change, the impacts of a major event may be wide-ranging, including impacts on local fiscal capacity and cultural opportunities.

Many observers are skeptical of impact studies because sponsors often exaggerate the size of the impact, often by exaggerating the size of the local multiplier. By exaggerating an activity's importance, institutions may strengthen their influence or enhance their ability to seek government assistance. Multipliers for a small city that is integrated into a national economy will seldom be more than 2.

Critique of the Export Base Approach

The criticisms of the export base approach suggest significant limits. In general, objections can be divided into those that concern theory and those that concern technique when conducting an export base study.

PRIMACY OF EXPORTS

Critics contend that the export base theory places too much emphasis on exports and overlooks other important factors that can lead to growth. In addition to exports, regions may experience increases in income through increases in the productivity of resources, through increases in investment from outside the region, or by substituting domestic production for goods and services that were previously imported.

Reductionism is an attempt to reduce a complex situation to one cause or to one explanation. The export base approach is a reductionist analysis. Are exports the only source of monetary inflows? No.

IMPORT SUBSTITUTION

Import substitution is an alternative development strategy. Rather than increasing exports, it may be useful to produce locally what otherwise would have been imported. Such a strategy would result in fewer leakages; each dollar that enters the circular flow would create more income. A successful import substitution strategy would increase the multiplier and the overall size of the local economy.

An advantage of import substitution is that many products currently being imported into the area can be identified easily. If those products could be produced locally, they might have a cost advantage in the local market compared with similar imported products due to lower transportation costs. Both Thompson (1968) and Jacobs (1969) emphasized the role of import replacement in a region's evolution (see Table 5.1). Persky, Ranney, and Wiewel (1993) suggested that local development officials could implement an import substitution by examining the location quotients of industries that supply major businesses and by redirecting purchases of local governments to targeted industries. Import substitution will not succeed if the local community cannot produce the targeted products economically (Shafaeddin, 2005).

PRODUCTIVITY

Improving labor productivity can also increase the level of income without increasing the level of exports. Suppose productivity increases in the nonbasic or service sector of the economy. The level of real income in the community could increase, while the level of exports remains the same. Productivity increases in the export sector could also result in more exports. In this case, the increased exports would not be due to changes in outside demand (exogenous) but due to forces inside the region.

EXPORTS NOT ALWAYS EXOGENOUS

The export base theory includes the implicit assumption that the demand for exports originates outside the area. Several analysts believe that the ability to develop and produce exports may in fact rest with the quality of local services within the economy. For instance, a particular financial institution may provide the capital needed to start an export business, a local university may provide an idea that results in an innovation, or a land developer may create an attractive industrial park. Collectively, the service sector may provide an overall environment conducive to export development. Most large cities have development organizations that include bankers, real estate developers, brokers, university officials, and public utility planners. These individuals represent the nonbasic sector, but they play major roles in encouraging the location and growth of export firms.

In a related vein, Chinitz (1961) asked why some areas are able to rebound after losing their export base while other cities experience long periods of stagnation when they lose their base. He concluded that resilience depended on the structure of the local economy, especially the availability of intermediate services. Chinitz's analysis, which has been supported by Carlino (1980), contributed to the development of the supply-side approach, discussed in the next section.

SMALL VERSUS LARGE REGIONS

The export base theory may be more applicable to small regions, such as metropolitan statistical areas, than to large regions, such as state or multistate areas. As the size of the community increases, opportunities to increase income by internal developments increase. The world, a region in the cosmic scheme, has grown without exports. Clearly, the scope for growth through internal production is greater the larger the region. Thus, the larger the region, the less important exports are and the less adequate the export base theory will be in describing growth.

FEEDBACKS AMONG REGIONS

Feedbacks occur when one region's actions cause another region to increase its purchases from the subject region. For instance, when a major region, such as the European Economic Community (EEC), increases its purchases from the United States, incomes in the exporting region (the United States) will increase. Therefore, the United States may in turn increase its imports from the EEC, a major trading partner. Thus, one reason for the EEC exports is the extent of their imports. Feedback effects are usually not accounted for in the simple export base model. When the region is small or has weak linkages, these feedbacks can be ignored because income increases in a small region will have only negligible feedbacks.

NONBASIC ACTIVITIES MAY NOT INCREASE

The export base multiplier is predicated on the assumption that when the export sector expands, (1) the demand for local nonbasic activities will increase and (2) and the demand increase will be sufficient to bring forth an increase in supply of nonbasic activities. However, some nonbasic activities may not be easily expanded. If an activity requires large capital investment, highly skilled labor, innovative entrepreneurship, or other local resources, the increased demand for local services may not bring about an increase in supply. If exports increase (decrease) but the nonbasic sector does not increase (decrease), then the multiplier will not magnify the impacts.

LONG-RUN INSTABILITY OF THE MULTIPLIER

In the long run, most of the "other things being equal" assumptions that underlie most economic models will change. With regard to the export base approach, changes in the fundamental economic relationships will alter the impact of the export sectors on the nonbasic sectors. Hence, the multiplier will change over time.

The marginal propensity to import, and consequently the multiplier, is particularly sensitive to three variables: (1) the size of the economy, (2) per capita income, and (3) the degree of spatial isolation. The smaller the economy of the region, the fewer the opportunities to purchase goods locally. For example, if you live in a small town and want a meal in a four-star restaurant, the service would have to be "imported," thus increasing the leakages. Higher-income individuals have a greater propensity to purchase specialized goods that need to be imported. So, as per capita income increases, the marginal propensity to import increases. Finally, proximity to other communities will increase competition for local customers. Residents will have a greater tendency to shop outside the community. Thus, towns within metropolitan areas will have smaller ratios of total employment to basic employment than isolated towns.

EXCESSIVE AGGREGATION

The assumption that the impact of all exports is the same is embedded in the use of some export base studies, although some approaches recognize that some exports may have a greater impact on the economy than other exports. Thus, the greater the extent to which unique individual businesses or groups of businesses are aggregated into one sector, the less accurate will be an export-base-oriented study.

Supply-Side Approaches

Supply-side theories of economic development are an outgrowth of criticisms of demand-dominated approaches, such as the export base theory. The heart of regional supply-side growth theories is the idea that regions grow because the supply of local resources increases or existing resources are used more effectively. Current economic activities "explain" the development of local factors of production. The local factors of production, in turn, shape the future businesses that will locate in the area.

Regional policymakers have done a better job in developing hypotheses about what factors might affect the local supply of productive resources than they have in developing workable ways to stimulate the supply side. A sketch of some potentially important determinants of supply would include intermediate inputs as well as the primary factors of production—land, labor, capital, and entrepreneurship.

INTERMEDIATE INPUTS

The availability of intermediate inputs is an important supply factor. Some observers believe that local economics dominated by large, vertically integrated firms have fewer intermediate inputs for sale. In contrast, communities with many small, interdependent firms may provide a rich market of intermediate goods and services as local firms are more likely to buy or sell from each other. The greater variety of intermediate inputs provides localities with more economic flexibility and resilience. It will be much easier to start a new business in an environment where intermediate inputs are available than otherwise.

ENTREPRENEURSHIP

Almost every development economist has stressed the importance of the entrepreneur in risk taking and bringing the factors of production together. Storey and Johnson (1987) attributed regional differences in the rates of new business formation to differences in entrepreneurship. Long waves of regional decline have been attributed to the absence of entrepreneurial activity (Booth, 1986). The founders of new firms are almost always local residents. There are few documented instances of entrepreneurs who relocate to a new community to start a business (Allen & Hayward, 1990, p. 56).

In spite of the generally recognized importance of entrepreneurship, economists know very little about factors that contribute to the development of entrepreneurship. The importance of risk taking, creativity, the presence of role models, family background, and national culture are among the factors that have been mentioned in the diverse and multidisciplinary literature that has attempted to understand entrepreneurship (Harper, 2003).

The interest in entrepreneurship has been spiked by findings that firms employing fewer that 20 people account for a large percentage of all new jobs created. Small firms have more entrepreneurship per employee than large firms and are often associated with the early stage of a product's life cycle, when percentage of growth is rapid. Thus, entrepreneurship has been seen as key to developing fast-growth firms.

CAPITAL

Capital is often considered the most mobile factor of production because of the existence of national and international capital markets. As a result, capital is available on roughly equal terms (adjusted for risk) in different regions. For instance, an automobile loan may be secured in Chicago or Phoenix on approximately the same terms. Large corporations borrow in the international capital markets, so the availability of capital to major firms is not significantly influenced by location. Capital may not be equally available everywhere for small firms or for unique local purposes.

Micro banking, involving very small loans of a few hundred dollars or less, has become an important economic development tool. Individuals are important sources of capital, especially equity capital, for small and start-up businesses. Through various types of joint ventures, wealthy residents may provide funds for new enterprises. Venture capitalists specialize in identifying small, high-growth-potential companies and providing them with funds for projects that commercial banks and other traditional lenders consider too risky or unorthodox. The venture capitalists normally take an equity position in a company (i.e., they earn a share of the profits) and often provide business advice as well as money. Government and quasi-government agencies such as community development corporations have recognized the need that small firms have for capital and have developed programs to increase the supply of funds to smaller companies.

LAND (ENVIRONMENTAL RESOURCES)

Land includes all naturally endowed factors of production. They are major immobile factors of production. If nonland factors of production were perfectly mobile, land would be the only resource that would differentiate areas.

Historically, analysis of land resources has centered around specific attributes such as topography, land fertility, mineral deposits, and so forth. Land was not considered to be an important contributor to urban development like other supply factors. More recently, the concept of land has expanded to include important aspects of the environment. Consequently, it has become a more important supply factor.

A "good" climate contributes toward regional economic growth. Certainly, climate is important in many tourist-oriented development and retirement plans. Econometric models have included variables such as average temperature and sunny days as independent variables influencing employment growth.

Water resources are an element of land that is limiting urban growth in many cities in the developed world. The desert climate that attracted residents is being checked by water needs. Of greater concern is lack of water in poor regions where drought has limited the ability to produce even subsistence living standards and has contributed to disease.

The ability of the environment to absorb pollution associated with population and production growth is a serious challenge. Economists view the environment as imposing constraints on the development of regions. However, regions may benefit from a clean environment. In addition, firms seeking to develop and export green production techniques may locate in the area (Ricci, 2007).

LABOR

The strength of the labor force is more difficult to define than its size. Quality is probably more important than size in determining an area's growth or revitalization prospects.

Past industrial activities and education/training resources are two factors that shape the skills of the current workforce. Work habits and attitudes may be transmitted through the culture of the region.

Supply- and Demand-Side Approaches: A Synthesis

Both supply and demand are necessary for local economic development. Sometimes lack of demand for the region's products or for the region's factors of production may hinder development. At other times, lack of productive resources may prevent development. Demand-side strategies focus on increasing the demand for a region's products and resources. Attracting or strengthening export activities exemplifies this approach. Supply-side strategies seek to improve the quantity and/or quality of an area's resources. Job-training programs, entrepreneurship development, or venture capital efforts are examples.

Demand-side strategies are most appropriate when local resources are unemployed or when the supply of resources is immobile. Thus, an increase in external demand will result in employment of unemployed resources and an increase in production. Supply-side approaches are appropriate when existing demand is sufficient to absorb additional factors of production or when the lack of local resources is a constraint on expanding output. Accordingly, improvements in the quantity or quality of local resources can result in increased output.

It is usually appropriate to pursue supply- and demand-side strategies simultaneously depending on the circumstances in various submarkets. Some parts of a local economy may be constrained from growing due to lack of demand for output, whereas other sectors may lack appropriate factors of production.

Summary

Whether dealing with isolated villages or global centers, it is helpful to understand where a community is in the development process and to have a theory about what drives a local economy. Stage theories describe the key stages that cities pass through as they develop. Thompson (1968) and Jacobs (1969) have similar theories of growth stages. Initially, a region may export one or only a few products. As regions develop, they achieve the ability to replace imports and generate new products for exports. Thompson's model emphasized the importance of industrial filtering. Jacobs emphasized the process of "adding new work to old" in the innovation process.

The circular flow diagram is a simplified model of how an economy operates. Five important subsectors of a local economy are (1) the resource market, (2) the local consumer market, (3) interfirm sales, (4) the local financial sector, and (5) the import and export sector. The circular flow model can be used to illustrate equilibrium—when monetary inflows equal monetary outflows—and the local multiplier.

The export base theory of growth states that exports are the dominant source of monetary inflows and, hence, the main source of growth. The export base theory may be summarized thus: The total change in employment or income equals the multiplier times the change in export employment or income. The export base approach has straightforward policy implications and is relatively easy to operationalize.

There are several criticisms of the export base theory. First, it may place too much emphasis on exports. Import substitution is an alternative development strategy. Second, improvement in productivity is another source of growth. Third, exports may not always be exogenous, particularly in the long run. The theory may have more explanatory power for small regions than for large regions. Fifth, it ignores interregional feedback. Sixth, the export base theory implies that additional local services will respond only to an increase in local demand. Seventh, the value of the export base multiplier will change over time. Finally, the assumption that all exports affect the local economy alike is an oversimplification. In spite of numerous criticisms, the export base theory remains a dominant theory of regional growth.

Supply-side theories emphasize the availability of inputs as principal growth determinants. The presence of intermediate inputs as well as the primary factors of production—land, labor, capital, and entrepreneurship—contributes to the ability of a region to produce. Supply-side factors may also account for the ability of a region to generate new sources of exports. Although demand- and supply-side approaches are sometimes presented as alternative theories, economists recognize that both supply and demand are necessary for profitable production and economic growth.

Both supply of resources and export demand are potential constraints on growth. At any given time, one of the two factors may be a more important constraint. For instance, if a region has substantial unemployment, the constraint on growth is likely to be demand. If the economy is at or near full employment, the constraint is likely to be supply.

Notes

1. The payments may accrue to households before the export sale or investment is actually made if the business increases production in anticipation of export sales.

2. For reasons explained more thoroughly later, this figure was derived by using a multiplier of about 1.54. This was derived as $1/1 - $ (marginal propensity to consume locally) $= 1/(1 - .35) = 1.54$. The initial \$100,000 of locally created income was multiplied by 1.54. Allow for rounding.

3. Let a new level of exports equal $(E_0 + (\Delta E_0))$ and the resulting level of income equal $Y + (\Delta Y)$. Hence, the new income level will be

$$Y + \Delta Y = (1/(1 - b + i)) * (A + E_0 + \Delta E).$$

Subtracting Equation 5.7 from the new income level results in Equation 5.8.

6

*Additional Tools
for Regional Analysis*

The previous chapter provided an introduction to urban and regional growth, emphasizing demand- and supply-side approaches. However, except for some very broad distinctions such as the basic-nonbasic categories or the various factors of production, Chapter 5 did not explore the relationships among specific subcomponents of an area's economy. This chapter extends the analysis begun in Chapter 5 by presenting perspectives and tools that view local economies in a more disaggregated fashion.

Shift-and-Share Analysis

Shift-and-share analysis provides a retrospective view of the causes of growth. It is a technique for dividing an area's growth into three components. First, part of an area's growth can be attributed to national economic growth. Growth at the national average rate is termed the national growth component. If a locality grew at the national average, it would have maintained its share of national employment, hence the *share* term of shift-and-share analysis. Second, an area may grow faster (slower) than the national average if it has a disproportionate level of employment in industries that grew fast (slow) nationwide. For instance, financial services were a fast-growth activity during the 1980s. One would expect that if an area had a large employment base in financial services, it would have grown more rapidly than the national average. Growth that differs from the national average because of the initial employment composition of an area is termed *the mix component*. Third, an area may have a competitive advantage (disadvantage) compared with other areas because its environment is conducive (an impediment) to the growth of particular industries. Growth differentials due to the nature of the local environment are

115

termed *the competitive component*. The mix and competitive components account for regional growth that differs from the national level.

The formula for calculating the shift and share components for a single industry can be expressed as

$$\Delta e_i = e_i[(US^*/US) - 1] + e_i[(US_i^*/US_i) - (US^*/US)]$$
$$+ e_i[(e_i^*/e_i) - (US_i^*/US_i)], \qquad (6.1)$$

where Δe_i is the change in local employment in industry i, e_i is the local employment in industry i at the beginning of the period, e_i^* is the local employment in industry i at the end of the period, US^* is the total U.S. employment at the end of the period, US is the total U.S. employment at the beginning of the period, and subscript i indicates industry i.

The first term indicates the growth that would occur if local industry i grew at the national average rate. The second term indicates extra (reduced) growth because a particular industry grew more (less) rapidly than the overall national average growth rate. The third term indicates that local industry grew more (less) rapidly than the national rate for industry i. The shift and share components for individual local industries can be summarized to provide an overall description of growth components. Table 6.1 shows the data and the results of a shift-and-share analysis for a local economy.

AN APPLICATION

How would an economic planner or analyst interpret the findings shown in Table 6.1? Star City had a total employment increase of 100 workers during the 10-year period. If Star City had grown as rapidly as the nation as a whole, 123 jobs would have been added. Agriculture, manufacturing, and services would have added 16, 41, and 66 jobs, respectively, totaling 123.[1] Therefore, there was a loss of 23 jobs in Star City's share of national employment. This negative shift of 23 jobs can be accounted for by the negative mix component. If Star City had an industrial base proportionate to the rest of the United States, the mix component would have been zero. In the example, agriculture and manufacturing grew faster than the U.S. average, and Star City had some employment in these nationally fast-growing industries. Thus, the mix of components for these sectors was positive. However, the service sector was a slow-growth industry nationwide, and Star City had a strongly disproportionate concentration of employment in that slow-growth sector. Therefore, the mix component for service was −99, and the overall mix effect for Star City was −81 jobs.

The actual shift was 23 jobs—Star City had 23 fewer jobs than "anticipated" based on overall national performance. The mix component by itself would have resulted in a shift of −81 jobs, but Star City appeared to be a particularly good competitive environment for agriculture and services. Both activities

Table 6.1   Shift-and-Share Analysis

a. Data

	Star City		United States (in 1,000,000)	
Sector	1970	1980	1970	1980
Agriculture	50	100	7	10.5
Manufacturing	125	175	4	5.6
Service	200	200	3	2.5
Total	375	475	14	18.6

b. Shift-and-share results

		Components		
	Share National		Shift	
Sector		Mix	Competitive
Agriculture	16.42	8.56	25
Manufacturing	41.06	8.91	0
Service	65.7	−99.07	33.33
Total[a]	123	−81	59
Actual change = 100			

[a.] Some totals may not equal due to rounding.

grew more rapidly in Star City than they did nationwide. Manufacturing grew at the same rate in Star City as it did in the nation. Thus, the region recorded a positive competitive component of 59.

The actual employment change was equal to the sum of the share (123), mix (−81), and competitive (59) components.

The positive competitive components in agriculture and services may indicate a potential building block for future growth. For instance, a development official might try to determine exactly why local service firms maintained their employment levels while service employment declined nationwide. If one or two favorable aspects of the local environment could be identified, they could be used to help market the community to other service firms that might consider locating in the area. The shift-and-share approach can also be used to help spot weaknesses in the competitive environment that may require corrections.

CRITIQUE

Shift-and-share analysis is used by planners and economic development officials to help them understand economic performance and support development strategies (Rubin, 2005). It is relatively easy to use and understand. The data required to perform the analysis are not excessive. However, the technique has some legitimate criticisms.

First, the components are frequently misinterpreted. Some critics have charged that shift-and-share analysis implies that industries should grow at the aggregate national rate. The national growth rate is used as a point of comparison, but there is no theoretical reason to believe that local employment growth should match the national rate. Likewise, the mix component should not be interpreted as implying that local industries "should" expand at the same rate as their nationwide counterparts. The national and mix components serve only as comparative benchmarks. Accordingly, geographic areas other than a nation may be used as benchmarks.

A second criticism is that the shift and share components may change depending on the level of industrial detail. If industries were greatly disaggregated so that, at the extreme, each plant constituted its own industry, the competitive component would be zero. The plant's growth would equal the national industry growth rate. Defenders of shift-and-share analysis recognize this problem but reply that selecting the appropriate level of industrial detail is a problem common to most industry studies.

Third, although the competitive component may be useful in explaining what has happened, its ability to predict the future course of development has been questioned. Critics claim that the competitive component changes too frequently and rapidly in response to a variety of forces such as local taxes, resource availability, technology, and so forth. Therefore, a competitive component for one historical period may be a poor guide to future competitive components for the same sector.

Finally, although the competitive component can be an indicator of where to look for local strengths and weaknesses, it does not identify *why* a particular sector may have a positive or negative competitive component. In fact, the competitive component is a residual and may not necessarily reflect what most of us envision when we talk of a good competitive environment. Thus, analysts must go beyond the model to explain positive or negative competitive effects. More in-depth local study will be required to understand the competitive component.

Econometric and Simulation Models

Econometric models combine statistical techniques and economic theory to estimate relationships among variables. Simulation models answer "what if" questions. For instance, a simulation model may be used to forecast government revenue if local employment increased by 2,000. Simulation models use econometric techniques to calibrate the degree to which variables are related. Both econometric and simulation models have a variety of uses, although this section focuses on how they are used to understand the growth process.

ECONOMETRIC MODELS

Econometric models are perhaps the most widely used tool for analyzing regional growth. While changes in output or employment are the primary outcomes of input-output forecasts, econometric models can include equations to estimate changes in other variables such as prices, tax revenues, infrastructure needs, and other important urban or regional outcomes. Also, econometric models can be modified if unanticipated questions arise. New equations may be added to the core model. For instance, if a city official wanted to know how a change in federal tax policies will affect the local economy, new equations could be estimated that feed into the core model.

Good econometric models are informed by economic theory. Theory normally specifies what variables are important and the causal relationship among them. Three major uses of econometric models are to (1) test the validity of theoretical relationships, (2) specify the magnitude of relationships, and (3) assist in forecasting. For instance, theory might indicate that migration into an area occurs when the local employment rate is less than the nation's. Statistical analysis might confirm the proposition and demonstrate that migration increases by, say, 3% a year for each percentage point difference between the national and local unemployment rates. Hypothesis testing is an important academic use of econometric models. A planner then might apply the quantitative relationship between unemployment and migration to help forecast the future population.

There are three important components in econometric models. Independent variables are not estimated by the model; they are taken as "given." The value of dependent variables can be predicated by the model. Often, independent variables can be thought of as a "cause" and dependent variables as the "effects." Parameters are the third important component of econometric models. They show the magnitude of the relationship between the dependent and independent variables. For instance, suppose a $120,000 increase (decrease) in regional exports resulted in an employment increase of 1 person. This relationship could be described by the following equation

$$LE = 25,000 + 120E, \qquad (6.2)$$

where LE is local employment and E refers to local exports in thousands.

Statistical techniques, specifically regressions, are used to determine how much confidence can be placed in the relationship. The relationship between an independent and dependent variable may be estimated using cross-sectional data or time-series data. Cross-sectional studies examine relationships that exist based on a variety of observations at a single time. Time-series studies show relationships within a particular set of variables during various periods of time.

An Export Base Example

Weiss and Gooding (1969) used an econometric equation to examine growth in the Portsmouth area. They postulated that local service employment should grow when export employment grows. However, one shortcoming of some export base applications is that they lump together all export sectors, even though changes in some sectors may have a bigger impact than changes in others. Accordingly, a theoretical model was specified that divided the export sector into three categories reflecting the employment patterns in Portsmouth

$$S = Q + b_1X_1 + b_2X_2 + b_3X_3, \tag{6.3}$$

where S is service employment, X_1 is private export employment, X_2 is civilian employment at Portsmouth shipyard, and X_3 is employment at Pease Air Force Base.

Q and b_i are parameters that can be estimated statistically using multiple regression. A time-series data set was collected for each of the independent variables and their relationship to service employment estimated.

The statistical results yielded the following equation

$$S = -12,905 + .78X_1 + .55X_2 + .35X_3 .$$
$$\underset{(t=2.5)}{} \quad \underset{(t=2.4)}{} \quad \underset{(t=2.5)}{}$$
$$\tag{6.4}$$

$R^2 = .78.$

Statistical tests were performed to provide a confidence level in the findings. The R^2 of .78 indicates that 78% of the variance in service employment (the dependent variable) was accounted for by the independent variables, X_1, X_2, and X_3. The "t" values indicate that the coefficients for each dependent variable are statistically different from 0.

The econometric findings can be used to simulate the impact of a change in employment in one of the three export sectors. Suppose, for example, that employment at Pease Air Force Base (X_3) was projected to increase during the next year by 100 employees. What would be the total impact on the economy? Assuming that all other variables remained unchanged, the change in service employment would be

$$S = .35X_3 = .35(100) = 35. \qquad (6.5)$$

Since the change in service employment is 35 and the change in export employment is 100, the total employment change due to the increase in export employment is 135. The multiplier for X_3 is 1.35 (i.e., 135/100).

The econometric model depends on the export base theory that the increase in export jobs caused an increase in service jobs. If, for instance, an observer believed that service employment significantly influenced private export employment, then causation runs both ways: S determines X_1 and X_1 determines S. In this case, a simultaneity bias would exist. Consequently, the estimate of b_1, the parameter that links service and private employment, would probably be inaccurate. Regression tests whether variables are related by a mathematical pattern, while theory supports causation.

More Complicated Models

The model described had only one equation, and there was only one "outcome"—service employment. Urban econometric models are usually much more complex, including hundreds of equations. The relationships are usually linear or "straight line," but new computational techniques now help model builders construct more complicated relationships among variables.

Once a model is established, it may be extended or modified to address other questions. Suppose that the developers of the model described above later wanted to estimate total regional income. Using similar econometric techniques, an additional equation could have been developed relating total income to employment in the service sector and the three export sectors. After estimating the parameters, the income equation might be

$$Y = a + 20175S + 22546X_1 + 27159X_2 + 25445X_3 \qquad (6.6)$$

Notice how the outcome of the original model, service employment, feeds into the determination of total income. The model might be further expanded by including an equation relating both income and employment to changes in construction and another equation showing the link between the federal defense budget and employment in Sectors X_2 and X_3. (Thus, X_2 and X_3 will no longer be exogenous [taken as a given] to the econometric model, although they will still be independent variables in the local employment equation.)

Time lags could also be introduced so that the model's predictions for one period "feedback" and determine outcomes in later periods. For instance, a statistical relationship might be established between expenditures (E) in period (t) and taxes (T) in period ($t + 1$); $T_{t+1} = a(E_T)$, where a is a parameter. By (1) determining how key economic variables are linked theoretically and then (2) using statistical techniques (primarily regressions) to quantify the relationships, large and complicated models containing hundreds of equations may be constructed. Some consulting firms specialize in building and applying models to communities to answer "what if" questions.

CAVEATS

Econometric models are an established part of the regional economist's tool kit. However, they are limited because the values of parameters are based on past observations. Relationships among variables may change in such a way that a model that worked well in the past can no longer serve as a good predictor of the future. This is particularly likely to happen when large or abrupt changes occur. For instance, many economists believe that globalization has rendered previously estimated relationships inaccurate. Econometric models are much better at "predicting" the past than the future. The "other things being equal" assumption is necessary to believe that previously estimated statistical relationships remain valid. In this regard, Klaassen and Pawlowski (1982) pointed out that models that predict the future on the basis of current trends are bound to fail, because current trends will change.

Two general types of limitations are measurement errors and specification errors. Measurement problem involves data requirements. Even the best data collected from well-established sources may be subject to significant measurement errors, and often the errors are not randomly distributed. (Officials in many cities believed that the Census of Population underestimates the number of city residents by failing to account for the homeless, families that were doubled up, the large portion of transients living in parts of major cities, and illegal immigrants. Since many intergovernmental funding programs are linked to population, the issue is vital to the size of urban grants.)

Many governmental statistics are published first as estimates and revised later for better accuracy. Consequently, model builders sometimes must choose between using the most recent data and using older, but more accurate, data. Furthermore, data for large, comprehensive econometric models are seldom available from published sources, so "proxy" variables are often required. The use of changes in employment to reflect changes in output is an example of the use of proxy variables. Sometimes the use of proxy variables is benign, but sometimes the practice can reduce the accuracy of the model.

Specification errors arise from theoretical misunderstandings or deliberate simplification. Suppose that a regression model attempted to show that the local unemployment rate was a function of job growth. Since other factors such as labor skills and migration patterns are also important determinants of the unemployment rate, such a model is likely to exclude theoretically important variables and, hence, be misspecified. Often, models are knowingly misspecified, while sometimes inaccurate theoretical understanding of the process being modeled results in misspecifications. Economists tend to assume that relationships among variables are linear or some other easy-to-model shape when the true relationship is more complicated.

Both measurement and specification errors can be compounded when equations have multiplicative or exponential forms. If there were a ±10% error in measuring X, the problem would be greater if the equation to estimate Y were $Y = X^2$ than if the equation were $Y = 2x$ or $Y = 12 + x$. An additional type of error compounding can arise when long chains of logic are employed. If a logical chain has four steps from beginning to end (if A, then B, then C, then D) and if each step is 80% certain, then the certainty of the conclusion would be less than 50%. This type of problem arises when the results of one equation feed into another, and it is common to both econometric models and other models such as input-output.

A healthy dose of skepticism about large-scale econometric models is justified. Computers have facilitated the testing of very complicated relationships among variables. This flexibility creates the danger that tenuous relationships might appear reliable when in fact they are due to chance. One in 10 random variables will be found to be statistically significant at the 10% confidence level by chance, so the more the experimentation the greater the probability of spurious findings.

Many models, particularly those developed by consultants, have "black-box" characteristics (Mills, 1993). They are either too complicated for officials (let alone citizens) to understand or the details are not revealed. Furthermore, very few models are reexamined to determine the accuracy of their forecasts. One of the weaknesses of academic research is that "negative findings" are much less likely to be published than "statistically significant" findings. Thus, if one professor finds that water quality is associated with economic growth, the results are more likely to be published than a finding that the association is not statistically significant.

Local economists have less choice in building an index of leading economic indicators than economists engaged in similar activity at the national level because they have fewer time-series data (Kozlowski, 1987). Washington State generates local economic indicators for individual counties. The choice of indicators for each locality is based on individual characteristics. However, the six important indicators are

1. nonfarm employment,

2. building permits,

3. initial unemployment insurance claims,

4. tax collections,

5. drivers' licenses, and

6. in-migration.

In addition, seasonal and trend factors are included.

Importance-Strength Analysis

An importance-strength survey can be useful in assessing the attributes needed to foster growth of an industry in an area. It is intended to determine simultaneously how important locational attributes are and how the local environment compares with competitor environments. Since the importance of location factors differs depending on the industry, the importance-strength analysis of locational environments should be industry specific rather than an amalgamation for all economic activities in general.

To conduct a survey that does not simply "average ignorance," it is necessary to seek the cooperation of individuals who have knowledge of (1) the area's locational attributes, (2) attributes of competitor regions, and (3) the importance of locational attributes to the industry being studied. The best respondents are local executives in the industry under consideration. Local executives normally will have knowledge of both the industry and the local environment, regions that may compete with the locality for industry growth. The opinions of about 10 well-informed executives will probably be more useful than the opinions of hundreds of random citizens.

Once a group of local executives has agreed to participate, they should be asked to rank a list of locational attributes on two criteria: (1) importance of the locational attribute and (2) relative (compared with other areas) strength of the locational attribute in the community. Both importance and strength may be rated on a 1 to 10 scale.

The survey can be conducted either in a round-table format or by a conversational-style telephone interview. By using an open-ended approach, the interviewer will gather unanticipated, useful information. An additional advantage of using an interactive format is that the nature of location factors or the reasons for the region's relative advantage or disadvantage can be better understood. Such information can be used to devise developmental strategies.

Location factors that are important and for which the region is strongly competitive could be promoted. Important locational characteristics in which the region is relatively weak could be targets for improvement, or at least efforts to improve perceptions. A region may find that it is not competitive over a wide range of important location factors. In such a case, it may be wise to focus development efforts on other industries. Furthermore, if locational matrixes are developed for a variety of industries, then common strengths and weaknesses may be uncovered. Such commonalities may help local officials decide which improvements will enhance the locational environment for more than one industry. By finding locational commonalities, development officials may develop clusters of industries that may be a focus for development policies.

Input-Output Analysis

Input-output analysis is a versatile tool, because it enables us to examine linkages among sectors. Input-output tables may be used to simply describe a regional economy or to analyze and forecast. First, we show how input-output analysis can contribute to understanding interindustry linkages and regional structures. Next, the model's usefulness in understanding the growth process is presented.

THE TRANSACTIONS TABLE

The first step in understanding input-output analysis is to understand the transactions table. It shows sales and purchases for each sector in a regional economy during a year (see Table 6.2). The interpretation of the transactions table is straightforward. Reading across each row shows the annual dollar value of output each sector listed along the left hand sold to each of the sectors shown on the top. For instance, Table 6.2 indicates that agriculture sold $300 of output to itself, $350 to firms in the manufacturing sector, $300 to firms in the service sector, $1,000 directly to local households, and $700 to businesses and households in the rest of the world as exports.

Reading down the columns shows where the sectors at the top purchased their inputs. In this example, local manufacturing firms purchased $350 from agriculture, $150 from each other, $800 from local service firms, $300 from local households (factors of production, especially labor), and $1,200 in the form of imports from individuals and businesses outside the area.

In addition to the interindustry sales, two final demand sectors are shown in Table 6.2. The household column reflects purchases of residents of the region, and the export column reflects goods and services that are sold to nonresidents. Two primary supply sectors are also shown—household and imports. Households provide labor, entrepreneurship, capital, and land as inputs, and the values in each cell of the household row reflect compensation for these services. The import row shows the dollar value of all commodities imported during the year. From Table 6.2, it can be seen that the manufacturing sector was the largest importer. It imported $1,200 worth of goods from outside the region.

Table 6.2   The Transaction Table

		Sales ($) to		Final Demand ($)			Total Gross Output ($)
	Sales From	Agriculture	Manufacturing	Service	Household	Exports	
Primary supply	Agriculture	300	350	300	1,000	700	2,650
	Manufacturing	50	150	600	600	1,400	2,800
	Service	500	800	800	700	1050	3,850
	Households	1,100	300	100	30	20	2,450
	Imports	700	1,200	115	120	0	3,170
	Total	2,650	2,800	1,915	2,450	3,170	14,920

The basic transactions table provides detailed information about the local economic structure. However, the transactions table can be rearranged to show the linkages between sectors more directly. A table of direct coefficients can be constructed to show the amount each sector listed across the top will purchase from the sectors listed down the left, per dollar of output of each sector listed across the top.

THE TABLE OF DIRECT COEFFICIENTS

Table 6.3 is a table of direct coefficients. It was derived by dividing the amount that each sector purchased from each of the economy's subcomponents by the total gross output of each of the three producing sectors and the household sector. For instance, the manufacturing sector purchased $800 of inputs from the service sector to produce $2,800 of total gross output (see the transaction table). Thus, for each dollar of output, the manufacturing firms purchased $0.286 (800/2800) from firms in the service sector. The direct coefficient for the manufacturing column and service row is the strongest linkage among the three industries in the model economy. Agriculture requires the most resources from local households; $0.415 of household inputs is required for each dollar of agricultural output.

The table of direct coefficients implies a "fixed input production function." In other words, there is only one "recipe" for producing the output of each sector; inputs cannot be substituted. If the price of a commodity increased or decreased, the total amount spent on the commodity per dollar of output would remain constant. In reality, most production processes allow for some substitution, such as substituting capital for labor if the price of labor increases.

Table 6.3   Table of Direct Coefficients (Purchases per Dollar of Output)

Sales From	Sales to			
	Agriculture	Manufacturing	Service	Households
Agriculture	.113	.125	.078	.408
Manufacturing	.019	.053	.156	.245
Service	.189	.286	.208	.286
Households	.415	.107	.259	.012
Imports	.264	.429	.299	.048

The table of direct coefficients illustrates interindustry linkage. For instance, if the agricultural sector were to produce an extra dollar of output, using the *same input proportions* that were used when the input-output table was constructed, it would need to purchase $0.113 directly from other agriculture producers (i.e., when a hog producer purchases corn or feed), $0.019 from the manufacturing sector, and $0.189 from services. In addition, $0.415 would go to households to pay for inputs such as labor, and $0.264 would be spent on imported inputs of all types. All manufacturing goods, services, agricultural products, and direct inputs from households that are purchased outside the region are included in the $0.264 of imports.

THE TABLE OF DIRECT AND INDIRECT COEFFICIENTS

Regional multipliers can be obtained from the table of direct coefficients. The table of direct coefficients shows only partial multipliers because they account for only first-round spending effects. Sectors providing inputs by manipulating manufacturing will require additional output from their suppliers; suppliers of suppliers will purchase more from their suppliers and so forth. For instance, from Table 6.3, it can be seen that if the manufacturing sector increases its output by $1, $0.1250 of additional output will be required from the local agricultural sector. But if agriculture is to increase its output by $0.125, agricultural firms must purchase $0.0166 (0.1332 × $0.1250) from other agricultural firms, $0.0024 (0.0189 × $0.1250) from manufacturing firms, and $0.0236 (0.1886 × $0.1250) from service firms. Household income will increase by $0.0134 ($0.125 × 0.107) because of the primary factors of production needed to produce the extra output required by manufacturing. But household income will also increase because of the increases in agricultural and service output created by the initial increase in manufacturing output. The household income will be spent according to the coefficients in the household column of Table 6.4 if consumption patterns remain constant. Obviously, we can only scratch the surface of the various feedbacks before the calculations become very awkward.

In theory, these ripples would continue forever. However, each round of spending results in successively smaller amounts of induced output. The cumulative size of the various rounds of spending can be calculated mathematically.[2] The results are shown in Table 6.4. It shows the total dollar amount of output that would be required from each sector on the left to accommodate a dollar's increase in output from each sector listed at the top. In other words, if manufacturing increased its output by $1, the total effect on the agricultural sector would be to increase output by $0.5354. The total effect is the sum of the following:

1. *Direct effects:* The first-round increase shown in the table of direct coefficients

2. *Indirect effects:* The interindustry effects as local industries purchase from one another

3. *Induced effects:* The additional increases in output due to household spending and the indirect effects of household responding

INPUT-OUTPUT APPLICATIONS

This section shows how input-output tables can be used to (1) assess local economic structure, (2) estimate imports, (3) inform locational decisions and industrial targeting, (4) forecast and determine economic impacts, and (5) simulate technological change.

Assessing Regional Structure

Comparing a region's direct and indirect coefficients with those of another place may provide a useful perspective on its internal structure. Small and

Table 6.4   Table of Direct and Indirect Coefficients

	Agriculture	Manufacturing	Service	Households
Agriculture	1.570	0.373	0.255	0.815
Manufacturing	0.342	1.250	0.298	0.538
Service	0.757	0.651	1.490	0.907
Households	0.717	0.310	0.179	1.440

underdeveloped regions normally have few internal interindustry linkages. The interindustry coefficients will be small or zero. The lack of internal linkages can be an impediment to development because if one firm increases its output, few of the benefits will ripple through the rest of the economy; the local multiplier would be smaller.

Estimating Imports

It is also useful to evaluate local input-output coefficients to estimate imports. Suppose that nationally the electrical machinery sector sells 0.10 cents to the motor vehicles sector per dollar of motor vehicle output. Furthermore, suppose the corresponding coefficient for a locality is 0.04 cents, as indicated by a local table of direct coefficients. Also, assume that (1) the national economy is closed, so there is no international trade, and (2) the production technology locally is the same as at the national level. The difference in coefficients implies that for every dollar of output by the regional motor vehicle sector, 0.06 cents worth of electrical machinery is imported. If the motor vehicles sector is large, the dollar value of imported electronic equipment may be large. The total value of the imports of electrical machinery for motor vehicles could be calculated by multiplying 0.06 times the value of automobile output. Consequently, a development planner may wish to determine whether there was potential for growth in the electrical machinery sector based on the potential for import substitution. Of course, there are other locational requirements besides the presence of a buyer that a community must satisfy if an area is to attract electrical machinery producers. However, the structural perspective given by examining local interindustry linkages can be a useful starting point for analysis.

Informing Location and Targeting Decisions

The identification of imports from examining regional coefficients can assist in location decisions. A firm may wish to locate near potential customers or suppliers. A firm located near its customers may be able to undersell competitors because of lower transportation costs, provide better service, or cultivate contacts that could enhance future sales. Hence, some firms may choose to seek locations where imports of their product are substantial.

Since input-output tables indicate how each sector affects every other sector and households, they can be very useful in industrial targeting. Urban and regional planners may wish to recruit industries that strengthen interindustry linkages to build a more substantial agglomeration in a particular industrial cluster. This strategy may involve attempting to attract buyers of products already produced in the region or sellers of products that local industries purchase. Another development strategy might be to target high-value-added industries, activities that purchase a large portion of inputs directly from households.

Conducting Impact Studies

Economic development officials frequently seek to determine the impact of events such as building a sports stadium, location of a new plant, or closure of a military base. Multipliers generated by input-output analysis are widely used for these purposes. An input-output forecast would normally first require an estimate of final demand (export levels) for each sector. Final demand is considered exogenous, so estimates of final demand must come from outside the input-output model. The changes in final demand can then be multiplied by specific multipliers for each industry that will be affected. The result is an estimate of economic impacts on individual local industries. The use of input-output models to perform impact studies is facilitated by multipliers for each county and metropolitan area in the United States produced by the Bureau of Economic Analysis (1993). They use multipliers that are customized for local areas. To estimate the multipliers, national input-output multipliers are adjusted downward to reflect greater imports in a local economy than the national economy. The extent of local employment in different industries is the basis for the adjustment.

Examining Technological Change

Input-output analysis has also been used to simulate technological change. Suppose a panel of engineering experts reported that new technology would reduce the dependence of manufacturing on the agricultural sector by 10%. In economic terms, the impact could be expressed as "for each dollar of manufacturing productions, manufacturing firms will purchase 10% less from agriculture." But if less per dollar of output is spent on agriculture, another sector's sales to manufacturing will have to increase, because the value of total output must equal the value of the inputs. Perhaps, the household sector would "sell" more entrepreneurial services to manufacturing on the assumption that the lower agricultural requirement would flow to households in the form of higher profits. A new set of direct input requirements reflecting the most likely repercussions of technological change can be developed showing new economic dependencies.

Summary

There are several important empirical tools that are used to understand the power of local economic development. Practitioners should understand the strengths and weaknesses of these tools. Shift-and-share analysis is a technique for dividing an area's growth into three components. First, the share component of growth is equal to the national average growth rate. Second, an area may grow differently from the national average due to its mix of industries. Third, an area may have a favorable or unfavorable growth environment. Shift-and-share analysis has been criticized because the components are frequently misinterpreted and because the competitive component is a residual that can be attributed to a variety of other factors.

Economic models use statistical techniques and economic theory to estimate relationships among variables. Good econometric models are informed by economic theory. The export base model can serve as the theoretical foundation for an econometric model, with changes in export employment serving as the independent variable. Nonbasic or service employment would be a dependent variable. Econometric models have important weaknesses, including the following: (1) relationships among variables may change, so models that worked well in the past might not do so in the future, and (2) variable data are often lacking. Simulation models answer "what if" questions, such as how key social indicators would change if a particular policy were implemented. Many simulation models use econometric techniques, such as regression, to establish relationships among variables.

Leading economic indicators are designed to anticipate the turning points in economic activity. Housing permits are an example of a leading indicator. A sharp increase in housing permits suggests an increase in economic activity several months in the future.

An importance-strength analysis allows policymakers to identify local attributes on two scales simultaneously: (1) importance and (2) the locality's strength in terms of the attribute. Policies may be developed to strengthen important, weak attributes. Important attributes in which the area exhibits strengths can be promoted.

Input-output analysis can be used to determine the impact that an increase in the output of one sector will have on other sectors of the economy. The total impact is the result of direct, indirect, and induced effects. Input-output analysis has several uses, including assessing regional structure, estimating imports, assisting in targeting decisions, conducting impact studies, and examining structural change. One of the major advantages of input-output analysis is that the results provide substantial industrial detail. The most noticeable difficulties of the input-output approach include the high cost of data collection and the static nature of the model.

Notes

1. These figures were obtained by multiplying the national average growth rate of 32.8% by the initial year employment in each section.

2. The table of direct and indirect coefficients is the $[I-A]^{-1}$, where A is the matrix of direct coefficients and I is an identity matrix of equal dimensions.

7

Institutionalist Perspectives on Local Development

Previous chapters described theories and tools used to analyze local development. Economic development officials must use theories and empirical evidence to formulate action plans and implementation policy. They do so within an institutional and social framework that establishes recognized ways of doing things. This chapter examines issues that local development planners confront when developing and implementing policies. Issues regarding the distribution of benefits from economic development, interjurisdictional competition, and the social context of LED are analyzed.

External Benefits From Economic Development

The external benefits local residents receive from new economic activity are the major incentive for local development programs. When economic growth occurs, a wide variety of individuals will benefit both directly and indirectly. Although the objectives of economic development programs are not always explicitly stated, most communities have three objectives: (1) job creation, (2) fiscal improvement, and (3) physical improvements. Residents who improve their employment are usually the most direct beneficiaries of the external benefits accruing from development. Property owners may also realize gains through higher property values and rents. Other residents may benefit from lower taxes, agglomeration economies, and so forth. In addition to public objectives, public officials and private investors engaged in economic development efforts have their own aspirations for success, recognition, and wealth.

JOB AND INCOME CREATION

Communities with loose labor markets are characterized by high unemployment, low wages, discouraged workers, and underemployment. Most economists regard job creation as a primary purpose of local economic development (LED) strategies. Many state and federal grant programs employ job creation as an explicit program goal along with other important grant selection criteria. Indicators of labor market problems are also criteria used by state and federal officials to decide which areas should receive LED assistance. Job creation is closely associated with improvements in real incomes. However, planners must distinguish between per capita income growth, which will benefit current residents, and increases in total incomes, which could occur primarily because new residents moved to the area to secure existing jobs.

FISCAL IMPROVEMENT

Many municipalities encourage economic development in the expectation that new businesses will contribute more in tax revenues compared with the extra cost of municipal services. Generally, land uses devoted to commerce and manufacturing generate net revenues for the city, whereas middle- and lower-income residential properties tend to cause public service costs to increase more than the tax revenues generated. Thus, communities seeking to strengthen their fiscal positions will usually attempt to attract either upper-income residential housing or businesses.

Fiscal objectives often result in competition among localities within a metropolitan region. In the absence of tax-sharing agreements among neighboring communities, only the locality where a business actually locates will receive increased property tax revenues. The job creation benefits of a new or expanded business will be more diffused throughout the metropolitan area than the fiscal benefits. New jobs may be obtained by residents throughout a metropolitan area regardless of whether or not they live in the municipality in which the business located.

PHYSICAL IMPROVEMENTS

Finally, many urban officials view economic development as a way to achieve physical improvements in their community. For instance, public officials may want to attract a new business at a particular corner of the downtown area to remove an existing eyesore or because too much vacant land in the downtown area creates an image of lack of progress. This motive is a remnant of the urban renewal period of economic development, when physical change was the principal criterion used to evaluate the success of economic development predictions. Today, many neighborhood economic development efforts empha-size physical improvements, partly because of a tendency for blight to spread to other areas.

Who Benefits From Growth?

The formal goals of economic development should not mask the fact that there are often some groups that will benefit from growth more than others do and some groups that lose. Although the beneficiaries of growth vary dramatically depending on the type of growth, some generalizations are possible.

The demand for the output of the export sector is not likely to be altered by growth of the local economy because the demand for exports is determined outside the area. However, local growth will increase the demand for products and services that are normally considered part of the nonbasic, or service, sectors, such as brokerage services, groceries, retail activities, and newspapers. Increased demand for local services will in turn tend to increase the prices of resources, including labor, used to produce nonbasic goods. Hence, owners of resources who produce for local consumption, eventually, may experience increases in income as a result of regional growth.

The permanence of the gains from growth depends on how quickly resources move into the sectors experiencing an increase in demand. If resources from out-side the area move quickly into a growing local economy, resource supplies will tend to be elastic. The increased factor payments for the original resource own-ers will be short-lived. The elasticity of resource supply will depend on (1) how easily additional resources can be brought into the area and (2) the ability of resources to shift from other local sectors to the sector experiencing a demand increase. The longer the time period, the greater the likelihood is that resources can be brought from outside the area. Therefore, the size of the annual benefits from growth will diminish in the long run for owners of resources. The rapidity of the adjustment depends on the elasticity of supply.

Figure 7.1 illustrates three possible resource supply situations. In the first case, the supply of the resources to the local economy is perfectly elastic. Thus, an increase in demand for the resource will not cause the price of the resource to increase. This case may approximate the actual situation for many factors of production in the long run or for regionally mobile factors of production even in the short run. Figure 7.1b represents a situation where some new resources enter the industry but not sufficiently to bring the price down to the original level. Figure 7.1c illustrates a perfectly inelastic supply. The total impact of the demand increase is absorbed in the form of a higher price. Figure 7.1c could represent a resource for which increased compensation does not bring forth any additional supply.

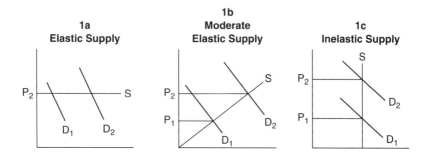

Figure 7.1   The Elasticity of Supply Determines the Extent to Which the Price of a Resource Will Increase Due to a Demand Increase. The More Inelastic the Supply, the Higher the Price Increase Will Be. The Same Logic Applies in Reverse When Demand Falls

CHARACTERISTICS OF RESOURCE SUPPLY

The supply of money capital to most sectors of local economies is very elastic. If the expected rate of return on newly invested capital increases, investment from outside will flow very quickly into the area, thus reducing the interest disparity. Banks and other financial institutions are connected to national and international money markets. However, owners of capital embodied in real assets invested prior to local economic growth may earn above-normal rates of return for an extended period. Individuals who purchased buildings may find that their rents have increased due to local growth. Therefore, the rate of return on real assets may be greater than would have been anticipated. Similarly, owners of local service businesses may experience increased rates of return. The ability to maintain above-normal profit rates due to economic growth depends on the speed at which new competitors enter the industry.

Labor resources tend to be modestly elastic over an intermediate period, but there may be substantial variation depending on the type of labor. Some members of the labor force may also earn income increases due to local growth. Imagine an automobile salesperson whose income increased because of increased sales attributed to a stronger local economy. Thus, the salesperson could be a beneficiary of local growth. However, the salesperson's increased compensation is likely to be only temporary. The owner of the dealership may realize that the income of the sales staff has increased and cut commission rates. Alternatively, other dealerships may enter the area, thus reducing sales at the original dealership. In general, the mobility of labor will cause some gains from growth to dissipate over time. However, even temporary gains are beneficial, and *temporary* may mean several years in some cases.

Other workers may have their incomes tied to state or national labor markets. A federal government employee will not experience a significant wage increase due to *local* economic growth. In fact, someone with a fixed income may experience high costs as an area grows. Thus, their net welfare may diminish.

Unemployed workers have opportunities to benefit from the increased jobs associated with growth. In fact, an expanding facility is likely to directly and indirectly create jobs that will be filled by unemployed residents. Those unemployed who capture new jobs may benefit in both the short and the long run. However, in the long run, growth may attract unemployed workers from elsewhere into the local area or slow the rate of out-migration. The previous unemployment rate may be reestablished. Some of the original residents may have obtained permanent employment or better jobs as the economy grew. Bartik (1991) estimated that 80% of jobs created in a metropolitan area are likely to go to in-migrants in the long run—over a period of 5 years or more.

Owners of local monopoly resources are likely to benefit from growth, even in the long run. Landowners do not have to worry about an increased supply of land coming into the area. Since the supply of land is fixed and each site has slight monopoly power, landowners will maintain benefit from growth even in the long run. It is not surprising that individuals involved in land development are usually prominent local progrowth advocates. Similarly, some franchise owners may have been granted licenses to serve a region, and they can maintain that "monopoly" as the region grows.

The lumpy nature of much economic activity can contribute to the perpetuation of monopolies or quasi monopolies. Suppose a shoe repair shop requires a population of at least 10,000 to provide sufficient demand to earn normal profits. If an area grows from 10,000 to 15,000 people, the owner of the shoe repair store could earn above-normal profits because of the 50% increase in the market size. Yet there would not be room for another competitor. A second shop would face the possibility of splitting a 15,000-person market. (A new store might not even be able to capture half the market.) Therefore, a 15,000 population would not be large enough to support two stores.

New firms may enter a region that has experienced a demand increase only after substantial time lags. Even after a new enterprise enters an area, it may take a long time for it to get established to the point where it is a strong competitor with existing businesses. The original enterprises will have established customers, locations, and reputations that can provide an advantage for generations. The lumpy nature of economic activity and the time lags that characterize new business formation help explain why small retailers tend to be progrowth advocates. If economic growth is accompanied by increased amenities, shopping choices, and other opportunities that will become available as their community grows, benefits will be further diffused. Hence, not all the indirect effects of growth are monetary. Winners from economic growth include both direct and indirect beneficiaries, but that is not the whole story.

OPPONENTS OF GROWTH

Growth may also affect an area negatively. Many individuals oppose growth because they believe it makes their area less attractive. Higher prices, particularly in resource inelastic sectors, are a cost of growth that may be imposed on many residents. For instance, growth will probably affect housing rents. An individual living on a fixed income may be disadvantaged due to the higher prices that may accompany growth. Furthermore, additional production tends to be associated with more pollution, and population growth is associated with greater congestion. Individuals who do not receive substantial growth benefits may feel that they are losers from growth. The extent of negative growth spillovers and the inability of everyone to share fully in the benefits of growth explain why some communities have instituted "no-growth" campaigns.

States and regions differ in their receptiveness to growth. Slow-/no-growth advocates have substantial influence in some communities. However, most regional communities realize that some economic growth is necessary to provide jobs for current residents and their children. If no new jobs are being created, some out-migration will occur simply due to natural population increases.

Particularly strong antigrowth coalitions tend to emerge in suburbs or neighborhoods of metropolitan areas. Many individuals seek to protect their immediate neighborhood from negative growth consequences (the "NIMBY" or "Not in My Backyard" phenomenon), while they hope to benefit from growth in other parts of the metropolitan area. The prevalence of such attitudes often brings suburbs in conflict with each other and hinders metropolitan competitions.

Subsidies, Competition, and Economic Development

As cities have increased their efforts to attract businesses or to encourage expansion, they have become competitors in a "market for jobs" (Blair, Fichtenbaum, & Swaney, 1984). LED policies may be thought of as attempts to purchase jobs and the related benefits associated with economic growth by offering businesses a wide variety of subsidies. The market for jobs seldom operates so explicitly that a community would, say, offer $10,000 per job created. Rather, communities offer indirect inducements in an almost endless combination of direct and indirect forms. Table 7.1 lists some of the subsidy techniques used by local communities. An important skill of an economic development official is combining these subsidies into a package that will appeal to businesses without costing the community too much.

The purpose of this section is to discuss some of the problems and issues that occur as communities attempt to use public funds to encourage economic development.

Table 7.1   Common Direct Economic Development Subsidies

Type of Subsidy	Description
1. Tax abatements	A reduction of tax liability either permanently or for a period of time; most types of taxes can be abated
2. Low-interest loans	Can help reduce costs as well as provide seed money to help start-up companies that may be high risk
3. Infrastructure and site assistance	These subsidies include providing land at reduced costs, construction of buildings, and providing public infrastructure such as roads and sewers; "incubation" programs include site assistance
4. Labor force training	Communities may finance the training of workers, including selection; wage subsidies may be included
5. Regulatory relief	Firms may be exempted from environmental, safety, or other state and local regulations; can be part of "cutting the red tape"
6. Sale-leaseback	A firm may sell its building to a community and lease it back at a nominal rate, thus providing an infusion of capital
7. Technical assistance	Economic development agencies may provide technical assistance in the areas of finance, marketing, exporting, technology transfer, and so forth

IS LOCAL ECONOMIC DEVELOPMENT A ZERO-SUM GAME?

One of the criticisms of LED activities is that cities compete with each other over the location of jobs without increasing the total number of jobs available. Consequently, whatever one community gains, another community loses. An example of a zero-sum game occurs when a company announces that it will establish a facility in one of three cities and suggests that the ultimate site will depend on the size of the local incentive package. Zero-sum games are particularly likely to occur when communities within a particular metropolitan area compete for jobs because the firm has probably already decided to locate somewhere in the area. The *President's National Urban Policy Report* (1988) expressed concern over the zero-sum-game aspect of economic development:

> At the federal level place specific economic development policies often do nothing more than tax one place to improve conditions in another. The wealth of both places is not greater and may actually be less than it might have been. (p. II-2)

Although economic development efforts can result in zero- and even negative-sum outcomes, they need not necessarily do so. Three examples of economic development activities that result in positive-sum benefits follow: First, the economic development incentives offered by localities may have greater value to businesses than they cost local governments. For instance, a city may build an industrial park costing $1 million. If it provides benefits to existing and potential firms of $2 million, the value creation constitutes a positive-sum outcome. Because one local government project benefits many firms simultaneously, the value of a single project may be significant even if each business receives only moderate benefits.

Second, economic development efforts may cause a firm to locate in an area of high external benefits rather than in an area of low external benefits. For instance, assume that City A has full employment and possibly heavy congestion. Perhaps individuals who might get the new jobs will have to move into the area, thus expending resources in relocation. Consequently, current residents will receive few external benefits from new economic development activity. Suppose, however, that there is significant unemployment and unused infrastructure in City B. The external benefits from job growth will be significant. If economic development efforts encourage job creation in City B rather than City A, the country as a whole will experience positive gains. Even though the level of economic activity would be the same if the firm located in A or B, the benefits are greater at B. Thus, redistributing a fixed level of economic activity can increase the net benefits from economic development.

Third, LED efforts can help create jobs. Imagine a firm that could generate significant external benefits to the community if it started operations. However, the expected profits are not quite large enough to justify opening the firm. In this case, a small economic development subsidy would make the firm profitable. If the economic development incentive was less than the value of the external benefits the subsidy made possible, a positive-sum game would result.

INEFFICIENCY AND OVERSUBSIDIZATION

The existence of potential gains from local jobs is a necessary, although not sufficient, condition for efficient local job creation programs. If economic development officials knew better the nature of the community benefits their community might receive from particular types of economic development, they would be better able to operate efficiently in the job creation process. If community officials offered the firm more than the minimum subsidy necessary to attract it or to induce it to expand, oversubsidization would occur. There are at least four important reasons why the market for jobs tends to be inefficient: (1) problems of collective action, (2) information asymmetry, (3) unspecified property rights, (4) the operation of federal economic development programs, and (5) differences in the cost and value of subsidies.

Collective Action

The ability of local governments to operate efficient incentive programs depends on how well the political process operates to reflect the interest of citizens. There are two potential problems. (1) A small group of highly interested persons can influence government more than a large group of moderately interested persons. The small group has an incentive to bear the costs of influencing governmental action. (2) It is less costly for individuals represented by existing organizations to influence policy than it is for unorganized individuals.

Organizations representing small, organized groups of people with money interests are likely to be very influential in LED policy development compared with politically unorganized groups. Thus, redevelopment projects that enhance the interests of major property owners and retail businesses are more likely to receive assistance than are projects lacking influential beneficiaries. Also, existing establishments that threaten to reduce their workforce are in a strong position to mobilize political support to secure a public subsidy since they are likely to already have a local political presence. In contrast, small firms are less likely to muster the support needed to receive special incentives. The economic development incentives are also likely to be affected by the strength or weakness of local politicians. Because the costs of an industrial location are generally paid in the politically distant future, a weak officeholder may have an incentive to overpay for a major industrial location.

Information Asymmetry

Information asymmetry arises when the circumstances surrounding a transaction are known better by one party but not by the other participating party. Such a situation can arise when one party deliberately provides distorted information to other parties.

Typically, private parties involved in economic development negotiations have incentives to provide selective or distorted information when seeking government assistance. For example, a firm may make it appear that it needs a greater subsidy than is really necessary to locate in an area. This advantage provides the private company a considerable advantage when negotiating with local governments.

Vaguely Defined Product

A third deterrent to efficient market operations is the poorly defined nature of the good (a "job" or "economic development") or poorly defined property rights. Although most negotiations over industrial location include corporate estimates of the number of jobs that will be created, firms usually do not guarantee specific numbers of job characteristics in exchange for locational grants. Often, temporary (i.e., construction) employment is included in the job estimates, and seasonal low-paying jobs are not distinguished from better jobs. Projections by grantees tend to overstate the number of jobs that would be created by businesses receiving subsidies. Cities seldom attempt to elicit guarantees that a particular number of jobs will be provided for current residents, partly because job creation is difficult to forecast. However, many communities are inserting "clawback" clauses when they provide economic development incentives. The clause requires firms to repay part of the benefits they received if jobs or other external benefits fall below a certain level.

Federal Subsidies

A fourth factor that may reduce efficiency is federal programs that encourage cities to offer more for jobs than the benefits received or that subsidize cities competing against each other for the same jobs. Of course, federal assistance is appropriate when the federal interest in job creation transcends local interests, perhaps because of externalities received by other local areas in addition to the area that captures the firm. But to be efficient, federal programs must be carefully structured to avoid situations in which one city bids against another in a zero-sum game with federal dollars.

Subsidy Cost Versus Value

How much of a subsidy actually reaches the intended party compared with the taxpayers' cost? Two types of problems can cause the value of economic development incentives to the firm to be less than the cost to taxpayers: (1) the subsidy program may provide costly goods and services that are not highly valued by the locating firm (similar to a gift that is expensive but not appreciated by the receiver) and (2) unintended parties may capture some of the benefits.

The most obvious instance of a poorly targeted subsidy is when a local community provides a service or infrastructure improvements that cost taxpayers more than they are valued by the firm the community is trying to attract. For example, suppose a region spends millions of dollars to beautify an industrial park. The better looks undoubtedly would be a plus in attracting firms and jobs. But would firms value the beautification efforts enough to warrant the community's cost? (Of course, beautification programs provide benefits to residents as well, so one could argue that the marginal benefits to the community outweigh the costs.) However, if the community has a narrow goal of attracting a particular firm, the more directly the benefits are tailored to the firm, the greater the firm is likely to value the benefits.

Suppose a property owner had a parcel of land that he wished to develop as an industrial park and he convinced the city council that a tax abatement would be necessary to attract firms. Consequently, the city agreed to provide a tax abatement for any employer building a new facility in the industrial park. Prior to the availability of the tax abatement, the landowner might have asked $10,000 an acre. Because of the availability of the abatement, the demand for the land in the industrial park will increase. The owner may raise the price of the land to $15,000. Thus, the landowner may capture part or all of the value of the tax abatement. In this case, the landowner will capture $5,000 of the development incentive. Not all of the abatement's value will accrue to the industrial firm that locates in the area.

Subsidy programs have been compared with carrying water in a leaky bucket. Some of the water will leak out on the way from the well to the destination just as some of the subsidy often goes to unintended parties.

What Does a Job Cost?

One indication of an inefficient market is the presence of large variations in the product's price. Of course, the price of a job could vary even in an efficient market, owing to variations in job quality and the externalities associated with jobs. Nevertheless, the cost of a job varies so much even within a local area that there can be little doubt that the market is inefficient.

Data on the cost of a job are fragmented and difficult to obtain. Lack of cost data is itself an indication of an imperfect market because well-functioning markets are characterized by buyers and sellers who know the prevailing price. However, the scattered evidence from various economic development programs shows that costs per job range from over $300,000 per job created to as little as $5,000. Most jobs involved no direct subsidies. (The cost of a job is the subsidy per job, not the capital-labor ratio.) The conclusion that there are wide cost variations is clear. The variation in the cost of jobs is accentuated because jobs created in small retail and service establishments receive no direct subsidy. Hence, the cost of an unsubsidized job is zero.

DISCRETIONARY VERSUS ENTITLEMENT SUBSIDIES

Discretionary policies provide local development officials with choices regarding the type or size of an incentive they may wish to extend to a particular business. Benefits from entitlement programs are due to any firm that meets a set of stipulated requirements.

The advantage of discretionary programs is that governments may avoid paying unnecessary subsidies or tax expenditures. The disadvantage of discretionary programs is that government officials must make decisions regarding the business potential of firms seeking subsidies. Can the firm succeed? How much of a subsidy is necessary? Government bureaucrats may not be able to make such decisions accurately. Discretionary programs also carry potential for petty and

large corruptions. Entitlement programs create a business climate that all quali-
fying businesses can potentially exploit. Once the framework is established, government officials need not be directly involved in business decisions. This
approach can benefit firms that do not need incentives in the first place.

COST MINIMIZATION VERSUS HUMAN CAPITAL STRATEGIES

The majority of economic development tools are designed to reduce business costs and, hence, attract new industries to an area. Business cost reduction
approaches have been criticized for three reasons. First, cost minimization
approaches may tend to attract branch plants of mature industries; yet most
growth is generated internally by local businesses. Second, it is extremely difficult for most regions in advanced countries to compete with locations in less
developed countries on the basis of cost. Large multiplant companies are in a
position to consider locations throughout the world. Third, LED strategies
should attempt to increase local living standards, not just the number of jobs.
A cost minimization strategy might actually lead to lower per capita incomes
for residents if low-paying jobs are created.

In contrast, human capital strategies, such as education attempts, provide
businesses with a high-quality labor force. The labor force will appeal to activities that perform nonroutine operations such as corporate headquarters,
skilled operations, and technologically oriented activities. Advocates of the
human capital approach contend that local residents will be better served by
stimulating growth in these better-paying occupations. However, there is a
danger that low-skilled populations could be left out of a development plan
that valued only high-paying, high-skill jobs.

The major problem with labor force development programs is that there are
insufficient jobs for all individuals qualified to be trained. Training programs
are successful in placing their students, but they may simply bump someone
with equal or superior skills. Thus, a particular program may seem to be successful from the perspective of the persons in the program, but from the perspective of the larger community, it is a zero-sum game. Job training works best
in a job growth environment or when an employer needs workers with skills
that are not available among other unemployed persons in the community. In
an atmosphere of slow growth and high local unemployment, training programs may have difficulty placing clients or simply influencing who is hired.

Warner (1989) conducted an empirical test to determine whether improvement in the variables associated with cost minimization or variables associated
with human capital improvement best explained the changes in per capita
income among urban regions between 1977 and 1984. He concluded that the
human capital approach is more effective in increasing average incomes.
Although the specifics of Warner's empirical tests may be questioned, they

indicate that regional development officials should not overemphasize cost reduction programs at the expense of the human capital strategy.

Social Capital and Economic Development

Social capital is networks of individuals bound together by attitudes of trust, norms of reciprocity, and shared values. Both bonding and bridging social capital have been identified. Bonding social capital unites individuals within a group or network. Bridging capital is reflected in the ability to form coalitions. Social capital can also overcome the vertical barriers that make it difficult for individuals and groups with unequal social status or power to work together.

Economic development practitioners routinely, almost instinctively, rely on social capital to achieve their ends. Because of its importance, local officials may wish to regard the use and management of social capital as at least an important ancillary activity in addition to direct economic development projects.

GENERIC ECONOMIC PROBLEMS AND SOCIAL CAPITAL

Social capital transforms many generic local problems involving externalities and collective action. Negative externalities (costs imposed on third parties to transactions) may diminish and positive externalities increase in social-capital-rich environments. First, individuals are likely to be more reluctant to impose costs on others (or more willing to provide benefits) because the presence of dense social networks also reduces their anonymity. A "retaliation" cost to persons imposing externalities may be imposed if they are known. Also, individuals will be more apt to psychologically internalize some of the costs (or benefits) when they are operating in a social network with others they regard. In other words, the importance of narrow self-interest may be reduced when operating in social-capital-rich environments.

Similarly, social capital can transform collective-choice situations such as the free-rider problem or the problem of the commons. In addition to the factors described above, an individual making a decision within a social network bound by trust and reciprocity will be more likely to believe that others will cooperate. While the strict maximizing agent will still see the advantage of not cooperating regardless of what others do, many people will make small sacrifices when they believe it is a part of a shared community effort. Also, a cooperative outcome is more likely to emerge from repetitive games when individuals believe that others will follow a "tit-for-tat" strategy if the game is repeated. In reality, identical games are seldom repeated, but individuals will face similar situations, so there is advantage in establishing a cooperative reputation within a network characterized by reciprocity.

AMBIGUOUS RECEPTION OF SOCIAL CAPITAL

Social capital concepts do not fit traditional economic paradigms and consequently have not been integrated into the economic development literature. Reasons for the reluctant acceptance include its reliance on the work of noneconomists. Also, (1) it is difficult to quantify; (2) social capital is both a resource and an end in itself; and (3) once created, social capital cannot be easily transferred.

SOCIAL CAPITAL AND LOCAL DEVELOPMENT STRATEGIES

Economic development strategies can be enhanced when practitioners use social capital as part of program implementation. Practical applications can be facilitated by an appreciation of how social capital contributes to specific development strategies. This section describes some popular economic development approaches and shows how social capital can be part of these approaches.

Innovation

Serendipitous as well as calculated linkages of ideas and practices from a variety of fields combine to create innovations. These connections are more likely to be discovered when social networks are dense.

Quality of Life

The various networks that a person belongs to are important in determining the quality of his or her life. An area's quality of life probably exerts a stronger influence toward maintaining existing residents in an area than attracting new residents to the area. An area's social capital may not be evident to someone considering in-migration but is appreciated by people already integrated into those networks. Social capital also contributes indirectly to the local quality of life because community cohesion helps mobilize resources to create cultural, recreational, and other amenities.

Micro Credit

Social capital makes micro credit lending feasible. Micro credit practices emphasize making loans to individuals with inadequate resources to justify a loan given normal lending practices. Social capital can be thought of as the loan's collateral (Reinke, 1998).

Globalization

Social capital can help regions maintain location advantages, particularly among knowledge-based firms in the global economy. The value of physical plants may decline rapidly, leaving companies little incentive to remain in the area. Social capital may anchor knowledge-based companies because knowledge employees are not interchangeable parts and those employees who are critical to business success might not be willing to transfer because they value their local networks.

The Informal Sector

The informal economy includes activities that are not fully accounted for in the formal sector, such as day care services, lawn work, and many new start-up businesses. Many of these businesses use informal arrangements to evade taxes. Agreements tend to be sealed with a handshake rather than a formal contract. Consequently, values and attitudes of trust and reciprocity (social capital) are important to successful operations. Many businesses in the informal economy are able to operate successfully because of how they use social capital.

The Social Economy

Economic development strategies should include the social economy— organizations that have significant economic functions but are not primarily profit oriented. Contributions of the social economy include supporting the safety net, as many church-based organizations do, and enhancing household income through activities such as community gardens, local currency plans, and human capital development. Among these groups, social capital is necessary to carry out their activities, in part, because they have relatively fewer monetary resources. Leaders of organizations in the social economy often have great skill at using social capital because they depend on volunteer labor and teamwork to get things done.

USING SOCIAL CAPITAL TO MITIGATE ECONOMIC DEVELOPMENT CONFLICTS

The economic development process generates conflicts between various groups. Sometimes these conflicts harm economic development by generating gridlock, involving costly reconciliation processes, or resulting in missed opportunities. When these conflicts arise, they are sometimes resolved based on "what's good for the community."

Social capital can be used to mediate economic development conflicts. First, an organization's social capital can be used to support a forum for dialogue and compromise. Second, and more subtle, social capital can be used to construct a community vision or "metanarrative" that can frame unanticipated conflicts that may arise in the future (Lejano & Wesse, 2006). When specific conflicts can be evaluated in terms of widely shared visions, solutions can be considered within the context of community interest in much the way land-use plans reduce some conflicts. However, even when consensus is struck around abstract metanarratives, there will still be disagreements and the need for compromises.

The concept of social capital can also be used to unify the practice of economic and community development. Traditionally, economic development focused on a set of variables that are business oriented, while community development workers concerned themselves with neighborhoods and service programs for disadvantaged groups. These orientations frequently conflict. The recognition that social capital is both a consumption good and a contributor to business development will help bridge the gap between these areas.

Social Network Analysis: Getting the Right People to the Table

Economic development practitioners depend on networks to collect current information, develop consensuses, disseminate information, and implement policies. Accordingly, a knowledge of local networks—who speaks for which groups and who controls which resources—is an important part of an LED official's tool kit.

Social network analysis (SNA) is a simple tool that helps identify key people and key organizations in a development project. SNA provides a visual map of the relationships in a group and a mathematical measure of the group's properties, such as its size, connectedness, and complexity. The nodes in the network are the people and organizations, while the links show relationships or flows between the nodes.

To understand networks and their participants, SNA examines the relationships between network components. Measuring the location of individuals within groups gives an idea of a member's centrality. These measures give us insight into the various roles and groupings in a network—who are the connectors, leaders, bridges, and isolates; where are the clusters and who is in them; who is in the core of the network; and who is on the periphery.

Understanding how networks operate is critical to community mobilization, where extensive cooperation and collaboration are necessary. It is imperative to have the right people at the table. Having the wrong people or an incomplete group is frustrating and wastes time and money.

For example, in Figure 7.2, Persons 1 and 2 form the only link between the two groups. Therefore, if it is advantageous to have access to the members of each group, you must include Persons 1 or 2 as they are the connectors in the network. The more influential they are, the more advantageous their participation may be.

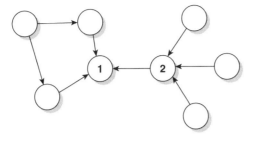

Figure 7.2   A Small Social Network Linked by Members 1 and 2

The importance of individuals and groups depends on specific issues. LED officials are more effective when they have sufficient knowledge of their community to know who the key individuals for particular issues are. However, it is often difficult to know who the key players are because it is difficult to see beyond your own network. You may believe you have the right people only to discover 6 months into a policy development process that an important constituency has been overlooked. It may be useful to conduct a formal SNA analysis that involves a formal survey and quantitative analysis of the results. Several computer programs can generate substantial information about local networks.

Whether doing a meticulous quantitative study, or a "back-of-the-envelope" list, important characteristics to consider when organizing a group include (1) the number of contacts an individual has, (2) the relevance of those contacts to the task at hand, (3) the individual's ability to monitor relevant events, (4) the strength of participants' connections within and among groups, (5) overall knowledge of the community, (6) willingness to contribute to the effort, and (7) the ability to bring other resources to the task.

Targeting Development Efforts

In his analysis of attitudes of LED officials, Rubin (1988) suggested that they "shoot anything that flies and claim anything that falls." His analysis highlights an important tendency. Officials often fail to target activities and, therefore, perform their duties without a strong strategic framework. Lacking a strategic framework, economic development officials tend to become procedurally oriented rather than outcome oriented. They respond to requests, hold meetings, make contacts, and so forth. When they are evaluated they can report on activities. "I provided 400 potential businesses with information, conducted business development roundtables . . . " Naturally, they will take credit for good things that fall from the sky, too.

Many LED officials are attempting to target their efforts so as to focus on certain types of activities. Advantages of targeting include a better use of resources. Each business contact has an opportunity cost, and a good targeting strategy may avoid effort in trying to attract or develop businesses that are unlikely to locate in the area. Also, targeting strategies can focus on businesses that have good community fit. Some areas might seek only nonpolluting industries, for example.

There are also drawbacks to strict targeting strategies. First, opportunities that are not within the community targets may be overlooked. Small industries are likely to be ignored in favor of targeting larger groups. In particular, new innovative industries may not even be recognized when the targets are selected. Second, the current state of LED theory and practice is insufficient for effective targeting in most circumstances. Certainly it makes sense to target industries where the extra benefits from success adjusted for the probability of attracting that activity is greatest. But that formulation is too vague to be useful. Theory says nothing about whether officials should target underrepresented activities or activities that are already attracted to the area. Finally, unexpected opportunities may arise to attract businesses that are not preselected targets. Few communities can pass on unanticipated activities, which might happen in a strict targeting regime.

Most communities target particular industries. However, it has been suggested that focusing on industries only may not be a detailed enough target because within any industry, there are many functions and there is a type of local environment that is best for each function. For instance, within the automobile industry, there are research, sales, production, and headquarters, and numerous other functions. A "crosshair" targeting has been suggested whereby policymakers target particular functions within a closely related group of industries. Thus, there are two targets: industry (what is produced) and activity (what processes are involved).

Thompson and Thompson (1987) suggested five types of activities that communities may use in targeting economic development efforts: (1) routine operations, (2) precision operations, (3) research and development, (4) central administration, and (5) entrepreneurship. Each of these "paths" requires different locational attributes. A development official may wish to analyze which type of activity fits the community's existing resource base and its aspirations. These paths are not mutually exclusive. Finally, choosing regional development paths should be linked to state public policy. The state affects economic development when it allocates funds for university research, higher education, transportation, infrastructure repair, airports, and so on. Although the economic development impacts are often unintentional, they will affect the state settlements patterns for years to come.

CLUSTER-BASED ECONOMIC DEVELOPMENT

Cluster-based economic development (CBED) is a popular targeting strategy. It is an extension of agglomeration economics. The neo-Marshalian definition currently in vogue was offered by Michael Porter (1998b):[1]

> Clusters are geographic concentrations of interconnected companies, suppliers, service providers, firms in related industries, and associated institutions (for example universities, standards agencies, and trade associations) in particular fields that compete but also co-operate. (p. 197)

CBED seeks to build groups of dependent businesses that are strengthened by proximate location. Unfortunately, the concept of a cluster has expanded and taken on multiple meanings. The term is no longer limited to external economies. It now is used to describe a wide variety of firm behavioral characteristics and policy prescriptions. Martin and Sunley (2003) offer a list of 10 distinct definitions that have appeared in the economics, policy, and geography literatures. The term *cluster* has tended to morph with the presupposition that clusters create innovations, represent "learning regions," and increase the transference of knowledge simply because the firms are colocated. Often, little or no thought is given to the enabling institutions that underpin clustered firms. Also, and particularly disturbing to institutionalists, unequal power relationships between firms are ignored. "Issues of inter-firm subordination, exploitation and control have dropped out of the cluster lexicon" (Taylor & Plummer, 2003, p. 240).

As the cluster concept lost its rigor, its popularity as a development tool has grown. Practitioners rushed to identify local clusters and target them as growth poles. It is not uncommon to see clusters being built around nothing more than a locality's aspiration. So if they want to be like Silicon Valley, they identify groups of businesses and refer to them as an "IT cluster." The increasing misuse of cluster development programs has prompted Martin and Sunley (2003) to suggest that the "cluster concept should carry a public policy health warning" (p. 5).

Successful cluster programs usually include more than an analysis of which industries attract one another. If a region is to enjoy economic vitality, the local firms must be engaged in the region's development strategy. Without this active participation of local enterprises, CBED policy will never reach its full potential. As new firms develop in a region, they still need to be integrated into the existing industrial web. Even branch plants that produce components for a parent company rely on local social and economic networks for operation.

In short, the colocation of firms in a cluster presents an opportunity for external economies, but it is the depth of social capital that enables the supradevelopment activity. An important characteristic of a successful cluster is the emphasis on social networks. Operational clusters have formal and informal networks that operate for the economic benefit of the cluster participants and the region. An efficient cluster strategy ensures that economic activity is embedded in the social fabric of the region.

A comprehensive CBED strategy is a network-driven approach that stresses communication and cooperation between firms in the cluster core industry; the core's local supply chain; and local government and support institutions such as universities, think tanks, and development agencies. It works with existing market forces, anticipating and exploiting business opportunities to promote growth faster and more completely than in the absence of a cluster strategy. CBED starts with a rigorous examination of the local economic structure and identifies opportunities for mutual gain from collaboration.

CBED is an *active* development strategy rather than a grouping of industries. It will not reach its full potential without support from the local public sector, regional economic development agencies, and the existing private sector. Developing the necessary social capital is a challenge in implementing a CBED policy. The *real gain is not from changing market forces but in reinforcing them and accelerating change beyond what would be possible without the cluster policy.* The cluster process is summarized in Figure 7.3.

CBED did not enjoy the necessary refinements of a thorough academic debate. The evaluation of cluster-based development is an example of how "faddish" words or ideas have captured the attention of economic development officials and academics. Yet, as with most fads, the idea has some merit. The word has been applied willy-nilly to many development problems regardless of

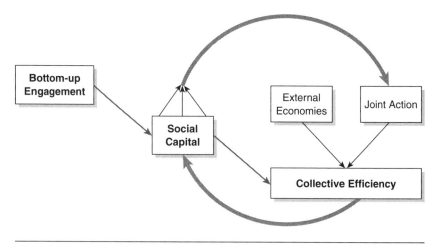

Figure 7.3   Dynamics of a Development Cluster

social circumstances, in a feeble attempt to turn CBED into a "one-size-fits-all" policy (Taylor, 2005). Consequently, it has been very easy to criticize most CBED efforts as lacking substance or being less than effective (Martin & Sunley, 2003). In truth, CBED has been properly applied in only a handful of cases. Furthermore, most of the recent academic literature has focused on the technical aspects of identifying clusters (Feser & Sweeney, 2002) and not on the philosophical underpinnings of economic clustering.

Summary

LED takes place within a web of institutions and social practices. Most economic development projects have three primary goals—job creation, fiscal improvement, and physical improvement. This chapter examines several contextual issues within which these goals are pursued.

While economic development promises substantial benefits to communities, the benefits are seldom distributed evenly across the population. When the local economy expands, the demand for exports likely will be unaffected because it is determined predominantly by forces outside the area. However, the demand for nonbasic goods and services will increase. Hence, the demand for some local resources will increase. The permanence of the increase in the value of local resources will depend on the elasticity of supply. However, growth may also harm some individuals. Higher prices, congestion, and other quality-of-life issues underlie many antigrowth coalitions.

Communities provide a variety of subsidies and incentives as they compete with one another in a "market for jobs." In this competition there is potential for zero-sum outcomes—either one city may gain at the others' loss or the benefits from growth may be taken from taxpayers and given to businesses. However, LED can generate net (positive) benefits for the locality and the nation. Whether a positive-sum outcome occurs depends, in part, on the external benefits that may be generated.

While local competition for jobs may be beneficial, it can be inefficient and businesses may receive excessive subsidies. There are at least five important reasons why the market for jobs tends to be inefficient: (1) problems of collective action, (2) information asymmetry, (3) poorly defined property rights or outcomes, (4) operations of federal programs, and (5) cost/value differences. These problems can be minimized by well-designed economic development programs.

There is disagreement regarding whether economic development strategies should emphasize discretionary or entitlement subsidies. Discretionary programs rely on skills of economic development officials in avoiding oversubsidization. There is also disagreement regarding whether development strategies should focus predominantly on cutting business costs through subsidies and tax cuts or strategies that emphasize investment in human capital through education and training.

Social capital can be a positive resource toward local development if managed properly. Social network analysis can be a useful tool in understanding the nature of social capital and in getting the right people to the table.

There are pressures on LED officials to explore all possible opportunities. Yet such a shotgun approach may waste resources. Targeting economic development toward highly promising opportunities may be useful, yet the theory of targeting is not fully developed. Cluster-based development is a promising approach to LED targeting.

Note

1. The 1998 book was not Porter's first discussion of clusters. There were a number of his works that dealt with clustering that predate this piece. The most famous would be his 1990 book, *The Competitive Advantage of Nations.*

8

Local Economic Development in a Flattening World

Today, local economic development strategies are seldom without some global influence. Many site selection decisions involve at least one offshore location; labor markets are truly global as firms outsource pieces of their operation; and advances in transportation and communications have reduced the costs of multinational operations. In short, to use Thomas Friedman's (2005) words, the "world is getting flatter."

The "flattening" is simply a broad reference to the fact that economies of the world have become more open or globally integrated. Barriers to economic flows across political boundaries have been reduced, but furthermore, there has been a leveling of political and economic relationships, away from vertical authority structures to horizontal, negotiated agreements. Friedman (2005) points out that this global change, mandated by technological and political economic forces, offers great opportunities but also great challenges. Opportunities are present to increase economic welfare and reduce uneven development. Challenges arise in managing the pace of change within the institutional capacity to absorb it and making the necessary institutional adjustments to reduce uneven development and not allow it to persist, albeit along remodeled contours.

This flattened world is not a new concept. Regional economists have traditionally assumed that most resources were free to move among regions within a nation. In contrast, international trade theorists developed models in which capital and labor were considered immobile between countries but commodities were mobile. In more recent analyses, nations have been studied as regions in a larger global economy. Therefore, the theoretical distinction between regional and international development has become blurred. In practice, the distinction has also faded as groups of nations have formed multinational economic units in which both resources and commodities have relatively free movement. The European Economic Community is a prominent example of a region where economic relationships among countries are becoming more like linkages between regions in a single country. Urban policy makers recognize that local economies can be influenced significantly by trade patterns and resources flows.

Models of Trade and Resource Flows

Two simple models of regional interaction are developed in this section. The first assumes that resources cannot move from region to region but that commodities can. The movement of commodities will equalize wages. The second model is built on the assumption of perfect resource mobility. In this case, worker mobility will equalize wages.

COMPARATIVE ADVANTAGE

The theory of comparative advantage was developed to show that countries can benefit from trade. The principle of comparative advantage states that if factors of production cannot move between areas, then residents should specialize in commodities they can make relatively cheaply compared with other countries. Relative cost is determined in terms of opportunity cost—the number of units of a commodity (or service) that must be foregone to produce another product. If countries produce goods and services in which they have a comparative or relative advantage and then trade with other countries for other goods, the specialization and trade can potentially benefit both countries. The theory of comparative advantage is the basic reason U.S. policy seeks to expand free trade and why we have sought to reduce trade barriers through agreements such as the North American Free Trade Agreement.

Heckscher-Ohlin Theorem

Heckscher and Ohlin hypothesized that if a country had a relative abundance of a particular factor of production, it would have a comparative advantage in the production of goods that require large amounts of the abundant factor. For instance, a region with abundant topsoil and rain could be expected to have a comparative advantage in agricultural products, which could be exported. Thus, although factors of production may be immobile, Heckscher and Ohlin envisioned a mechanism whereby the abundant factors of production would be mobilized as they become embodied in the dominant exports.

The commodity flows will affect not only commodity prices but resource prices as well. A country with abundant labor will tend to have low wages (relative to the rest of the world) prior to trade. Export of labor-intensive products will increase the demand for labor and, hence, the wage. Labor-short countries will import labor-intensive products, thus taking pressure off labor demand, which in turn, tends to lower wages for their workers. One reason why labor unions favor some tariffs on goods from labor-abundant countries is that domestic wages and employment can suffer from the inflow of cheaper products. In a world of perfect knowledge and commodity mobility, the Heckscher-Ohlin theorem leads to the conclusion that commodity movements will result in equalization of factor prices. In this sense, commodity movements can be a substitute for resource movements.

Comparative Advantage Reconsidered

The theory of comparative advantage and its complement, the Heckscher-Ohlin theorem, have been challenged on four grounds: First, empirical studies to determine whether countries export products that require a large portion of abundant inputs and import products that require resources that are scarce locally have not found the expected pattern of trade (Bowen et al., 1987). Second, areas may not specialize in their comparative advantage because the mechanisms and institutions necessary for specialization may not exist. Third, comparative advantage is a static theory. Some analysts believe that nations should produce goods and services in which they may have a comparative cost disadvantage in the short run to develop a comparative advantage. Finally, while free trade may potentially enrich both trading blocks, it may not enrich everyone within both nations. For instance, trade with low-wage countries may depress wages among certain groups in the United States. Consequently, free trade raises issues of equity.

RESOURCE MOBILITY

The theory of comparative advantage was developed on the assumption that resources were immobile. While some resources may be regionally immobile, urban economists consider most resources to be fairly mobile among regions. Certainly, there are fewer impediments to the movement of labor and capital between regions in the same country than to factor movement between countries. In a world of perfect information and no relocation costs, factors of production would move to the region where compensation is highest. Figure 8.1 can be used to analyze resource mobility. Assume that there are two regions and that compensation for labor (or any other) resources is initially $2 per unit greater in Region J than in Region I. The differential would induce migration from Region I to Region J. As labor leaves Region I, the supply of labor will decrease and wages will increase; as the supply of labor in region increases, wages will fall. When the compensation of the factor of production is equal for the two regions, migration will stop.

Next, consider how relocation costs will affect adjustment. In this case, a move would be worthwhile if the present value of future earnings in the destination region minus the relocation costs exceeds the present value of future earnings in the region of original residence. To provide a sufficient incentive to relocate, relocation costs must be less than the present value of future extra returns that the factor could earn in J compared with I.

Figure 8.1 shows the labor supply curves shifting so as to eventually equalize factor prices because of the assumption of costless mobility. If relocation of resources were costly, then the present value of the difference in compensation over the life of the factor of production would equal the relocation costs in equilibrium.

The adjustment process is not instantaneous and may slow as the wage gap in the two areas narrows.

The model represented by Figure 8.1 does not show a demand response. In reality, a low resource price in one region could induce users of the low-cost resource to move into the area. Hence, movements in demand may also help eliminate price differentials. For example, suppose labor and capital are the principal factors of production. Labor may relocate from a low-wage to a high-wage

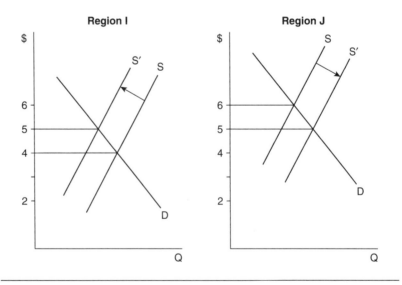

Figure 8.1   A Model of Resource Mobility

NOTE: The resources in Region I are initially priced below the same resources in Region J. Therefore, resources move from Region I to J, decreasing supply and increasing the price in Region I. The supply increases and the price falls in Region J.

region. But simultaneously, capital may flow to the low-wage region to take advantage of the low-cost complementary input and increase the demand for labor in the process.

Evidence of factor mobility raises an interesting question for manpower and development officials. Efforts to increase wages for local residents could be futile if when local wages increased, other workers moved into the area, creating a countertendency to reduce wages to the level of nearby regions or the nation as a whole. Even if wages did not fall, new entrants could capture some of the newly created jobs. Consequently, many local officials have decided that it is preferable to spend economic development dollars to train current residents so that they can command higher wages due to unusual skills.

Economics of Migration

When development officials consider migration in and out of an area, they may wish to understand the causes of population and labor movements. Economic models provide some important insights that planners may find useful.

Figure 8.1 illustrated migration based solely on wage differentials. When the two markets were in equilibrium, the migration would stop according to the model.

Migration can occur even when regional factor markets are in equilibrium. Lifestyle changes at key periods of life—at graduation, at marriage, before and after military service, after the birth of children, at retirement, and after the death of a spouse—are not always motivated by wages. At each of these "passages," the motive for relocating may be quite different.

NONWAGE FACTORS

Most empirical studies indicate that labor tends to migrate to high-wage or employment-growth areas, but nonwage factors also help explain migration. First, fringe benefits as well as the basic wage rate should be recognized. Many migrants are interested in the total compensation package, not just wages. Second, cost of living might have to be accounted for to reflect the fact that individuals desire a higher real compensation, not just a higher money wage. Both fringe benefits and differences in costs of living are relatively concrete concepts. More complex factors must also be considered, such as the quality of life, future pay and promotion prospects, and so forth.

"Equalizing differentials" refer to compensation differentials that will persist over time even if labor were perfectly mobile. For instance, an individual may be willing to accept 25 cents per hour less to enjoy the climate, quality of life, and future opportunities.

The costs of relocation also enter the individual migrant's decision in a way that is more complicated than may appear. In a simple model, the relocation cost might simply be the cost of transporting one's possessions from one place to another. However, other monetary costs include the cost of selling a house and transaction costs of closing accounts, purchasing new license plates, and so forth. Nonmonetary costs include hassles, loss of proximity to friends and relatives, taking the children out of school, and lifestyle changes. In many cases, these factors may be more important than monetary costs. Uncertain prospects are another type of cost likely to be considered very significant by risk-adverse individuals.

GRAVITY MODELS

Migration flows are frequently estimated with a gravity model. Gravity models assume that migration between two regions increases in relation to the population of the region and decreases with the distance between them. In the basic model, population represents the likelihood of a random individual leaving or migrating to an area. Distance is the main impediment. The following is an example of a simple gravity model:

$$M_{ab} = P_a P_b / (D^x_{ab}), \tag{8.1}$$

where M_{ab} is migration from A to B; P_a and P_b represent the populations of A and B, respectively; D_{ab} is the distance between A and B; and x is a parameter.

The most obvious problem with the simple gravity model is that migration between the places would always net to zero. To avoid this outcome, other variables have been included to reflect opportunity differences. Differences in wage, income, and unemployment rates have been the most frequently used measures of opportunity differentials.

Another criticism of gravity models is that they are poorly specified because distance does not adequately measure difficulty of journey, particularly in an era of modern transportation. To address this problem, travel time has been substituted for distance in some models. Social and political barriers, as well as uncertainty, are more important. These factors are poorly correlated with distance. For instance, it is probably easier for a Texan to migrate to Oregon than to Mexico. So although gravity models are used as empirical shortcuts, they do not reflect important theoretical factors that reflect opportunities and difficulty of the journey.

BEATEN-PATH EFFECT AND INTERVENING OPPORTUNITIES

One reason why gravity models are sometimes inaccurate is the beaten-path effect. The beaten-path effect refers to the observed tendency of individuals from a particular area of origin to select the same destination. Often a few "pioneers" from an area will migrate first. Later, others, often relatives, will follow. Most migrants do not consider a shopping list of destinations. They do not ask, "Where among all possible places will I move?" Usually, they consider only one destination—often where their friends or relatives can provide a job, housing information, or other help. Previously settled friends and relatives often also help support new migrants if necessary. Thus, by following a beaten path, migrants can reduce the financial and social costs and the uncertainties of relocating. A recent migration path between retired migrants from the Panama Canal Zone and Dothan, Alabama, illustrates a beaten path. The beaten-path effect also helps explain the concentrations of particular ethnic groups in particular cities. The concentrations of Rwandans in Dayton, Irish in Boston, or Cubans in Miami can be attributed to the beaten path.

In addition to lowering migration costs, the beaten-path effect has two other important implications for economic development officials. First, the flow of migrants may become self-perpetuating as migration costs fall and additional migration is stimulated. Second, the beaten path can be traveled both ways, so there is often a noticeable return migration. If economic prospects dim in the destination area or if migrants otherwise become disenchanted, large numbers may return to the place of origin.

NET AND GROSS MIGRATION

When economists first collected and analyzed data on migration, they were mainly concerned with net migration, the difference between in- and out-migrants. However, net migration patterns mask substantial differences in the level of gross migration because some individuals move into an area at the same time when others move out.

Table 8.1 illustrates four different gross migration patterns: (1) high mobility/high in- and out-migration, (2) high in-migration/low out-migration, (3) low in-migration/high out-migration, and (4) low in-migration/low out-migration. Both the cases of high in-migration/high out-migration and low in-migration/low out-migration could result in low net migration, but for very different reasons. The former instance may indicate a very dynamic economy attracting a highly mobile, opportunity-seeking population. The latter case is characteristic of a stagnate community with an older, less mobile population.

RETIREE-MIGRANT DEVELOPMENT STRATEGY

Fagan and Longino (1993) suggested that migrating retirees may form a solid basis for building an economic development strategy. They pointed out that retirees are mobile and many have substantial incomes. They compared the economic impact of a new manufacturing plant employing 100 persons

Table 8.1   Gross and Net Migration Flows and Local Economic Conditions

		Out-Migration	
		High	Low
In-Migration	High	Low net migration (i.e., footloose population, college or military)	High net migration (i.e., area of expanding opportunities)
	Low	Negative net migration (i.e., area of declining opportunities)	Low net migration (i.e., stable job base, few new opportunities)

with that of 100 in-migrant retiree households. They concluded that the economic impact of the retirees would be nearly four times that of the manufacturing employees.

Retirees tend to be either amenity seeking or dependency seeking. Amenity-seeking migrants are oriented toward natural environments among other things, while dependency-seeking migrants move to be near a caregiver. The beaten-path effect also influences retiree migrants. A community seeking a retirement development path should probably attempt to establish an amenity-rich environment with good health care facilities. Rural areas near areas with metropolitan amenities and medical facilities may be an excellent setting for planners to develop a retirement-oriented development path. Even if development officials do not find it advisable to attempt to attract retirees from elsewhere, an economy may receive a substantial benefit by *retaining* retirees who might otherwise live elsewhere.

Mobility of Capital

Discussions of capital flows are often confused by the various meanings of *capital*. In everyday use, *capital* often means financial capital and real assets that can be converted into money. But economists define capital as produced goods that can be used for further consumption or production. Accordingly, capital includes physical inputs in the production process, such as buildings, machinery, and also human capital. The amount of physical capital is usually expressed in monetary terms ("The machine is worth $100,000"), because money is a measure of value. So the distinction between financial capital and real capital is easily blurred. The value of human capital can be expressed in terms of the increased value of increased earning power. For an individual, the distinction between money and physical capital may not always be important because an individual can convert some types of real capital into money by selling assets. However, an economy as a whole cannot convert between real capital and financial capital.

Financial capital is generally considered to be highly mobile among regions. Individuals and corporations can move accounts and transfer funds from financial institutions in one region to financial institutions in another region in a matter of minutes. Differences of fractions of percentage points trigger massive money capital flows from one region to another.

Economists are generally as concerned with real capital as they are with money accounts because real capital is one of the basic factors of production. Real capital used in production is much less mobile than money. Buildings and some heavy machinery are almost place-bound once created.

In spite of the limited mobility of some real capital, an individual may sell such an asset and transfer the proceeds to another region. So capital may be spatially mobile from the perspective of an individual even if the physical asset is immobile. Furthermore, since real capital is *valued* in money, the amount of capital invested in a region can shift quickly even when the real (physical) capital is not changed in any way. For example, a facility that is operating efficiently may have high value based on the income stream it generates. But if the owner decides to abandon operations because the local environment is no longer suitable, the value of the physical assets could quickly drop to zero. Abandoned facilities may even have negative value if demolition costs are significant. Of course, if an alternative use for an abandoned facility were found, its value could be supported, but experience indicates that alternative uses often cannot be found.

In light of the various definitions of capital, three types of capital mobility can be identified. First, money capital can be transferred from one region to another, either in exchange for goods and services or to finance real investment. Second, physical assets can be transported from one place to another, although the mobility of many physical assets is extremely limited. Finally, the value of physical capital may change, reflecting changes in the economic environment.

Many development officials seek to increase the capital available for investment in their area. While pure theory leads to the conclusion that capital will be employed where it earns the highest return, this is not always the case. Investors often fail to identify excellent investment opportunities, in part because of lack of knowledge. Development officials can play a role in informing investors of opportunities they might otherwise overlook.

The following are hypotheses about factors that limit the flow of capital to its area of highest return:

1. Lenders may be reluctant to extend loans to businesses located in the inner city because they incorrectly perceive high risks of central-city investments. Racial bias against blacks and other minorities is considered to be linked with the failure of institutions to invest in minority-dominated sections of the central city.

2. Rural areas may fail to attract capital because they are underserved by financial institutions. Hence, it is more difficult for businesses to develop in rural areas. Special government programs have been developed to stimulate the supply of capital to rural areas.

3. Firms may have a preference for reinvesting profits internally rather than investing outside the company. The preference for internal investment may be due to better knowledge about in-house opportunities or a psychological preference for control. Hence, distressed cities with few profitable firms have less access to this source of funds.

4. Investors with small amounts of money have difficulty directly lending in distant regions because of high transaction costs. Investors need to be able to assess risks and may, therefore, avoid making loans to less known companies. Such investors may participate in nationally marketed securities, or they may limit their investments to the particular regions they know. This point is reflected in the belief that venture capital is not equally available in all regions.

Local officials may seek to increase the inflow of capital into a region by programs to inform investors of opportunities or by programs to provide investors with higher returns for making investments in perceived high-risk areas.

Innovations and Ideas

Ideas and new ways of doing things are a major source of economic growth. Economic development officials traditionally have been more concerned about innovations than inventions. Innovation is the economic application of a new idea, although the distinction may become blurred when the same person is both the inventor and the innovator. Not only are innovations important to economic growth, but the rate at which innovations are copied, modified, and spread to other sectors of the economy influences economic progress.

At first glance, it may seem reasonable to assume that innovations would spread quickly and uniformly. After all, ideas are weightless, so it is easy to assume that they are costless to transport. As Borts and Stein (1964) said, "A new manufacturing process or a new machine is, under competition, available to all." However, numerous empirical studies have indicated resistance to innovation. The length of time between an invention and its commercial application can span decades, and gaps of several years are common. More important for our purposes, there is a spatial pattern to the spread of ideas and innovations.

SPATIAL DIFFUSION

Innovations tend to originate in large metropolitan areas. The spread of innovations can be complex and differs depending on the production process or the product being developed. In general, innovations tend to spread from large metropolitan areas along a variety of paths.

Metropolitan Origination

There are many related explanations for the dominance of metropolitan areas in the development of new ideas, products, and production processes. Pred (1966), in a historical study of the spread of industrial innovations, used a supply-and-demand framework to explain the predominance of the metropolis in the innovative process. The quantity of innovations is greater in urban areas because both the supply of and the demand for innovations are greater.

On the demand side, urban areas provide greater economic rewards for innovation because markets for new products and processes are more readily available. New products may capture only a small market share initially, so a large local market may be critical to achieving an adequate initial sales level. The demand for process innovation in metropolitan areas is due to the larger agglomeration of producers. A new production process may have applications in a variety of industries.

On the supply side, metropolitan areas have a greater variety of support activities needed for innovations. Skilled engineering consultants, marketing firms, lawyers, intermediate manufacturers, venture capitalists, and other important contributors to the innovative process are all more readily available in metropolitan areas. Urban areas may also be the workplace of innovative elites and other individuals in key national information loops. Recently, policymakers in many urban areas are deliberately perusing strategies to enhance the supply of local innovations by encouraging incubators, inventors, entrepreneurial networks, and research parks.

Diffusion

New products and processes spread from the point of innovation in three distinct ways. First, there is a tendency for consumer-oriented innovations to spread in a radial pattern from the source of the innovation outward. Movement of an idea from the central city to suburban areas is an example of the radical diffusion pattern. Innovations that depend on personal, nonbusiness contacts are likely to have a strong tendency to spread in a radial manner.

Second, innovations move among cities of roughly equal size. For instance, an innovation may appear in Houston and Chicago at the same time. The similarity of environments, including similar supporting services for those who stimulated the original initial innovations in metropolitan areas, makes replication in similar metropolitan areas more likely.

Third, the diffusion of innovations from major metropolitan areas to smaller places in the major area's sphere of influence can be explained by business organization patterns. Thus, the corporate headquarters will tend to be the location of a company's first FAX machine. If the innovation is successful, it may filter down to regional offices and later to local offices. Distribution channels for consumer products and information channels may also follow business organizations.

Another factor in innovation literature is the recent emphasis (Batheldt, Malmber, & Maskell, 2004) on knowledge transfer and learning regions. Some argue that knowledge spreads through informal contacts. In other words, the ideas that are passed in casual conversation may be the seed for new products or innovative application of existing technologies. If this spread of knowledge occurs subconsciously (or not deliberately), then this tacit knowledge is embedded in the culture of a community. Tacit knowledge is then spatially linked to a location. In the previous chapter, we saw the importance of such social capital in the formation of industrial clusters. The social capital of a region is slow or impossible to replicate and therefore may not be easily manipulated by development policy.

IMPLICATIONS FOR REGIONAL DEVELOPMENT

The diffusion process from metropolitan areas to smaller places, coupled with the tendency for products to grow rapidly in the early stages of their life cycle, has been termed industrial filtering. Figure 8.2 illustrates the time path of employment growth in a typical industry. The explanation for the shape of the industrial growth curve centers on the fact that early in an industry's development any absolute increase in output or employment will be a larger percent increase. Furthermore, sales in the early stages include both new purchases and replacements, whereas in later stages, only replacement production is needed.

Metropolitan areas tend to be the site of production early in the life cycle of a product or process. After a process is better understood and is broken into routine steps or after a market has been established for a product, a shift in the site of production to smaller towns often occurs. Firms may relocate to take advantage of the lower costs in smaller, less urban places. The large metropolitan areas have a higher proportion of fast-growth activities, but those activities spin off to smaller places. Accordingly, metropolitan areas will tend to lose a portion of their economic base to lower-cost cities.

Large cities may require a more highly skilled labor force because products in the early stages of development involve non-routine production. The different skill requirements may account for the persistence of higher incomes in urban areas. Strategic investments in education, training, and quality of the environment may help metropolitan areas attract and develop the skilled labor force needed for nonroutine operations. Larger cities may also explore ways to maintain the activities that originate there, and hence slow the filtering process.

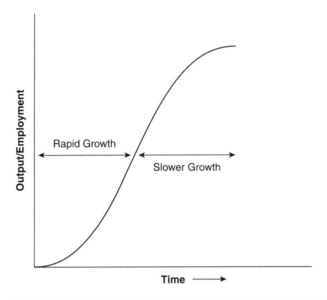

Figure 8.2   Employment Growth Over Industrial Life Cycle

NOTE: More rapid growth occurs during the early stages of an industry's life cycle. As the industry ages, growth slows.

Conversely, smaller cities may consider how to speed up the filtering process so that they can capture industries early in the product life cycle.

Recently, some policy analysts have questioned whether major urban areas can maintain their leadership in innovation if the site of production becomes too remote. Underlying this issue is the concern that if research becomes too distant from the shop floor, researchers will lose their sense of purpose or diminish their knowledge of operations on the production floor. Giese and Testa (1988) examined research and development firms in the Chicago area. They concluded that metropolitan regions can retain their eminence as industrial research and development centers even as the manufacturing activities decline, but this important study has not been replicated.

Mobility and Development Policy

Many policy areas involve mobility issues. Economists generally believe that the economy operates more efficiently when resources are mobile, so removing unnecessary barriers to mobility is often viewed as a way to improve performance.

JOBS-TO-PEOPLE VERSUS PEOPLE-TO-JOBS

One of the perennial regional development issues is whether government policy should encourage job creation in high-unemployment areas or whether individuals should be encouraged to move to places where jobs already exist. Both moving jobs to people and moving people to jobs have been suggested as partial solutions to the problem of poverty. The issue presupposes the existence of a geographic mismatch between available jobs and workers. Table 8.2 provides a comparison of the two approaches.

Supporters of the jobs-to-people approach generally believe that people are so reluctant to move that the inducements—both the carrot and the stick— would have to be substantial before they would move. They also point out that push factors, such as high unemployment rates and low incomes, are poor predictors of out-migration. Therefore, "natural" market forces will not necessarily result in the efficient movement of people to jobs. Jobs-to-people advocates also contend that job-creating activities can be induced to locate to areas of high unemployment at a low cost or with little or no loss of aggregate national output. In addition, Clark (1983) argued that only a jobs-to-people approach can support the stable communities and the social relationships that *community* implies.

The jobs-to-people approach has been criticized because it appears to place the welfare of places over the welfare of people. "We must do something to help Dallas," an advocate of place prosperity might say. However, jobs-to-people strategies are really designed to help people where they live, not places per se.

The people-to-jobs approach assumes that the market allocates investments efficiently among cities and regions, so the government should not attempt to alter the pattern. Individuals are assumed to be highly mobile, and jobs are not easily transferred from one region to another. Furthermore, advocates of the people-to-jobs approach suggest that even if the government attempted to stimulate development in declining regions, the efforts would probably fail because the governmental resources available for regional development are small compared with private investment.

IMMIGRATION AND URBAN DEVELOPMENT

Urban development officials often find it difficult to address the issue of immigration because of conflicting domestic interests. A simple supply-and-demand model of immigration can clarify conflicting interests regarding the migration issue. Suppose U.S. residents were divided into capital owners and laborers. As additional foreign workers enter the country, labor compensation would drop due to the increased labor supply. Because of the potential for lowering the wage rate of current workers, many labor representatives tend to favor restrictive immigration policies. The competition between low-skilled

Table 8.2   The People-Versus-Places Controversy

Issue	People Prosperity	Place Prosperity
Rationale	Only individuals matter; individual welfare is relatively independent of the condition of the place	Places also matter; the welfare of individuals is relatively dependent on the condition of the place
Presumed efficiency	Not certain; might increase GNP by improving the quality of the labor force nationally	Inefficient; lowers GNP effects if the orthodox view is correct
Effects on interarea migration	Probably accelerates it	Retards it
Strategy	Bottom up; may take a "worst-case-first" approach	Too down; may focus on places with the most development potential (within the eligible area)
Benefits to the nonpoor	Undoubtedly some; probably not as many as in other cases	Clear and substantial benefits to the nonpoor
Most obvious drawback	Does little to mitigate the social and psychological costs of economically forced migration; may do little to aid the survival of dying places	As a strategy to aid the long-term poor, it is at least partly defeated by mobility and elasticity of the labor force
Political support	Relatively weak, particularly if programs bypass the local political structure	Very strong support from the political establishment of eligible areas
Relation to recent locational trends	No necessary conflict	Definitely swimming against the tide

SOURCE: Levy (1985).

native and foreign workers often results in conflict, particularly when economic competition is combined with cultural or racial differences. Bloomberg and Sandoval (1982) contrast the tensions along the California-Mexico border with the border shared by Detroit and Windsor, Ontario, in Canada. Whereas the potential for conflict has led to strains and racial divisions in

California, the commonality of interests and/or cultures has resulted in economic integration between Detroit and Windsor "almost as fully as if they were the same nation" (p. 120).

If capital and labor are complementary inputs (i.e., increased labor enhances capital productivity), then capital owners would welcome additional immigrant labor, because the larger number of workers would tend to enhance the productivity of capital and depress wages. Undoubtedly, many employers recognize that they benefit from an increase in labor supply. The simple model helps explain why some employers and trade associations favor allowing large numbers of migrants into the United States and oppose sanctions on employers who hire illegal aliens. Many industries in the Southwest and the Farm Belt and some unorganized urban manufacturers are dependent on labor from abroad.

Complications

There are several complications that limit the relatively static labor-supply-and-demand approach. First, consumers may also benefit from high levels of immigration, particularly consumers of products whose manufacturers attract immigrant labor. The lower wage rates may translate into lower prices. Since workers are also consumers, it is necessary to balance these two effects to determine the net benefits from migration for a particular labor group.

Second, labor is not homogeneous. Since there are, in fact, many types of labor, the impact of immigration on wages and employment depends on the type of labor that enters the country and on whether labor markets are linked or segmented. If labor markets are linked, wages of employees in sectors with few immigrant workers may be depressed because of the possibility of substitution among types of labor. However, many economists believe that labor markets are segmented. If labor markets were completely segmented, each market segment would be unaffected by events in other markets. In this case, only the domestic workers who compete directly with immigrant workers would be adversely affected by immigration. Borjas (1987) presented empirical evidence indicating that immigrants are a substitute for some types of U.S. labor but a complement to other types. Consequently, the overall effect of immigrant labor on the earnings of the native-born worker is small.

Evidence indicates that even if markets are segmented, the skills of migrants are so varied that few labor markets are unaffected by migration. About 40% of U.S. legal migrants are managerial or professional workers, and about 30% are operators, fabricators, and laborers. Consequently, there are no major labor groups protected from competition due to migration. However, the immigration mix is changing. The proportion of unskilled and semiskilled immigrants is increasing. If illegal immigrants were included in the statistical estimates, the number of unskilled laborers would increase significantly.

Even if most immigrants were initially low-skilled workers, the longer migrants are in the country, the more likely they will be to acquire the skills necessary to qualify for higher-skilled jobs. Therefore, skilled workers will not necessarily be protected from competition from initially unskilled immigrants in the long run. (The potential for skill changes is even greater from an intergenerational perspective.)

Furthermore, not all migrants are poor or unskilled. Many bring substantial capital and skills into the country when they migrate. In fact, most countries have immigration policies that make it much easier to gain entrance if the applicants have assets. British Columbia experienced a boom in economic development due to the relocation of wealthy Chinese from Hong Kong. Thus, the stereotype of the impoverished immigrant with no way to earn a living but by selling labor is inaccurate. Finally, the static supply-and-demand model ignores important dynamics. Immigrants can bring new ideas, contacts, and customs that help areas compete in global markets. A region that welcomes foreigners is more likely to attract world-class talent and foreign direct investment.

Foreign Ownership

Tolchin and Tolchin (1987) suggested that foreign ownership of key industrial sectors threatens to dilute the political sovereignty of the United States. Foreign ownership, they contended, may undermine the ability of the host country to control its own fate and defend its status as an economic power. The same argument can be applied at the regional level. Other observers have expressed the fear that the situation will degenerate to a point where important economic decisions are made abroad and U.S. workers become relegated to low-paying, routine jobs. However, most economic development planners view foreign investment as an opportunity to improve regional welfare.

Foreign investment has contributed to the economies of many regions. For instance, many areas in California have greatly benefited from Asian investments. South-central Ohio has developed based on Japanese automobile investment. Not only have the Japanese helped create jobs, but they have also contributed to the emergence of new management and production techniques on the part of domestic producers. The total quality management (TQM) movement was based on principles first employed in Japanese firms.

Local economic development officials are increasingly seeking to attract foreign investors because they believe the benefits in terms of local economic expansion far outweigh the costs. States and localities are organizing overseas trips for local officials in an effort to encourage foreign investment as well as open export markets for local goods. Because of the increasing importance of foreign investment, many analysts have questioned whether location factors that are important for American companies are important to foreign "transplants."

Extrapolating from studies of location requirements of foreign firms, it appears that most factors important to domestic companies apply. In addition, foreign firms seek (1) government cooperation (cemented by personal association), (2) proximity to home country cultural events, (3) flexible labor environments, and (4) good international communications and transportation facilities (Doeringer & Terkla, 1992; Blair & Premus, 1987).

Summary

Local economic development efforts take place in an increasingly "flattening" world. Traditional economic borders are being reduced at an astonishing rate. Business operations are being spread throughout the world. To makes sense of this process, it is useful to develop a polar model. On the one hand, if resources are immobile but commodities are mobile, then regions will benefit by producing and exporting the product in which they have a comparative advantage. Commodity trade can be a substitute for factor mobility; regions will export products that require a high proportion of the abundant factor of production. On the other hand, if resources are perfectly mobile, they will tend to flow from the low-return to the high-return area. If compensation reflects productivity, then the resource flow will increase total output in the combined regions.

Migration is the result of push factors in the place of origin and pull factors in the destination area. Most empirical studies indicate that labor tends to migrate to high-wage areas, but wages alone are inadequate to explain migration determinants. Migration will tend to equalize wages unless there are equalizing differences.

Gravity models assume that migration between two regions increases in relation to population and decreases with distance between places. A major criticism of gravity models is that they are poorly specified because they fail to reflect all the factors that contribute to migration. The beaten path effect illustrates how knowing individuals who have already migrated to an area may encourage additional migration.

Many communities have successfully implemented retiree migration strategies. Such a strategy offers promise for amenity-rich areas in particular.

Capital is generally considered to be a mobile factor of production, although there are numerous obstacles to capital movement. In light of the various definitions of capital, three types of mobility can be identified. First, money capital can be transferred. Second, physical assets can be moved. Third, the value of physical capital may change.

Patterns in the movement of innovations and ideas also affect economic development. Innovations tend to originate in metropolitan areas. The spread of innovations occurs (1) across and down the urban hierarchy and (2) away from the innovative center in a radial pattern.

Interregional resource flows play an important role in policy questions. The issue of whether jobs should move to high-unemployment areas or whether people should move to where the jobs are may hinge on the relative mobility of labor and capital. Immigration policy aims at restricting international labor mobility without imposing an undue burden on the United States.

9

Land Use

L and-use patterns contribute to a city's productivity and quality of life. The ability to influence land-use decisions is an important economic development lever. Consequently, economic development officials are active participants in real estate development and land-use decisions.

What Gives Land Value?

In economic terminology, "land" is a natural factor of production, and therefore, the supply of land is unaffected by price. Real estate analysts are careful to distinguish between *land* and *property*. A property is land and improvements such as buildings. Properties are valued based on the flow of benefits they generate. This section starts by examining land in the absence of capital improvements to understand what kinds of capital or structures are combined with land.

LAND RENTS AND VALUE

Land rent can be thought of as a flow of income. The value of that income flow should equal the value of the land. However, since dollars received today are worth more to investors than dollars received in the future, in 10 years, for example, future dollars must be discounted to reflect the value differences of dollars received in different time periods. The sum of the discounted present values of the future rents equals the land value. In a perfectly functioning economy (where, among other things, investors have perfect information), the present value of future returns would also equal the sale price of the land.

If land were expected to provide a constant return in perpetuity, the formula for determining value would be

$$V = R/d, \tag{9.1}$$

175

where V is the land value, R is the periodic return (net of other costs such as property taxes), and d is the appropriate discount rate. The discount rate is similar to an interest rate and will rise and fall depending on the conditions of the economy.

The logic of Equation 9.1 is that if the value of the land were exchanged for cash and invested in a comparable investment, it could command return of d. Thus, $Vd = R$, the cash value of the land if placed in an equally risky investment (V) should earn an annual cash return (R) equal to the return from the land.

Equation 9.1 has two limitations. First, it applies only to assets that generate a return in perpetuity. In practice, even agricultural land will not generate a constant return forever. Most agricultural land benefits from numerous capital improvements that have a limited life. For instance, the soil can be depleted. Second, the assumption of a constant return year after year is unrealistic. Equation 9.2, developed later in this chapter, addresses these two problems in a more flexible but complicated model.

THE NATURE OF RENT, PRODUCTIVITY, AND ACCESS

The return to land is a residual—what is left after all other resources have been paid their market-determined price. Since labor, capital, and entrepreneurship can move to where their compensation is highest, these factors must be paid competitive rates. Whatever is left after paying the mobile factors of production is the residual to land—rent.

Ricardo (1821) concluded that sites receive different rents because of varying productivity. The productivity of the land was attributed to its fertility and its proximity to markets. For instance, suppose the most productive use of a site is to produce $3,000 of corn at a cost of $2,500 for nonland inputs. The return to land would be $500. Thus, $500 would equal the rent. Accordingly, the return to land is a residual. The value of the land is the present value of the residuals.

Ricardo's analysis also showed that the more productive land would be used more intensively. For instance, fertile land might be worked by four employees while low-productivity land might be worked by one person. In general, valuable resources tend to be used more intensively.

Ricardo's analysis was expressed in the context of agricultural land, where fertility was the dominant factor in determining productivity. In an urban setting, access to urban goods and protection from urban bads are the most important factors in determining productivity. Of course, aspects of access that are valuable depend on the types of land use. For instance, a fast-food restaurant would value access to mealtime traffic, a law firm might value access to courts and documents, and households might value access to good schools or protection from crime.

To understand the relationship between productivity and access, imagine that a site that provides the best access combination for a retail clothing store and other uses would generate a smaller residual to land. A clothing store located at the site could earn gross revenues of, say, $3,000 per year. Suppose that after deducting capital costs (including construction of the store), labor, and normal profits, $1,800 is left. Competition among other clothing retailers or potential clothing retailers would drive rents to $1,800.

Proximity and access are not the same thing. Often, access is limited by social, political, and geographical barriers, in addition to distance. For example, in most suburban areas, it is the school districts that create access. Political access explains why property values jump thousands of dollars from one side of a street to the other.

Time and convenience are important determinants of access. Modern transportation networks have made access as much a function of urban infrastructure—type of roads, availability of mass transportation, and so on—as of simple physical distance. There are also social dimensions to the accessibility concept. Fear of crime, for example, has caused many individuals to feel that areas in the central city were not accessible to them.

HIGHEST AND BEST USE

One of the first questions developers ask is "What is the most profitable use of a site?" The most profitable, legal use of land is called the highest and best use. The most profitable use will also be the use that provides the greatest residual to land. Clearly, the residual to land depends on how it is used. The residual to land will differ if the site is used as a parking lot or a grocery.

The highest and best use is not necessarily the most socially desirable use because land uses have considerable positive and negative spillovers. Construction of a supermarket in the middle of a rare downtown open space may be the most profitable legal use, but some might argue that it is not the "best" in a social or ethical sense. Therefore, development officials should be aware of third parties who may be helped or harmed when making zoning or other land-use decisions. However, there is a link between the most profitable use and the most socially beneficial use. The profitability of a particular land use is usually due to the fact that consumers are willing and able to pay higher prices (or larger quantities) for goods sold at a favorable location. Therefore, the market for land usually reflects societal demand for products at particular sites.

The most profitable use of land is seldom the most intensive or most highly developed use. For instance, a high-rise apartment (land and capital) is usually more valuable than a single-family house, but it will not necessarily be more profitable to construct high-rises rather than single-family houses on vacant land. The residual to land will decrease if the greater value of property due to improvements is offset by additional capital and labor costs in construction and operation. The key question in highest and best use determination is "What use will provide the greatest return to land (residual) after construction and operating costs have been subtracted?"

Table 9.1 shows a hypothetical relationship between intensity of development cost and the return to land. Economies of vertical construction are illustrated by the lower per-story cost of the second level. However, construction costs per story start to increase after the second level because it is increasingly expensive to construct additional stories. At the same time, the present value of the property increases at a decreasing rate, reflecting the fact that per-unit property rents might fall due to increased vacancies or the need to lower rents in order to avoid increased vacancies. The combined result of these forces causes the present value of land's residual to fall after the second floor. The present value of the return to the land is maximized at three stories. Hence, a building of two stories is the highest and best use.

Table 9.1 illustrated the highest and best use principle by examining different heights of a residential building. The same method applies to the choice among types of land uses. For example, to determine whether a bakery or a two-story apartment would be the highest and best use, a similar calculation of the residual to land could be made.

Table 9.1   Highest and Best Use Determination

Intensity of Use (Stories)	Present Value of Income ($)[a]	Present Value of Nonland Inputs ($)	Value Residual to Land ($)
1	2,000,000	1,000,000	1,000,000
2	4,000,000	1,075,000	2,925,000
3	5,075,000	3,000,000	2,075,000
4	7,050,000	5,025,000	2,025,000
5	9,000,000	7,075,000	1,925,000
6	10,000,000	12,500,000	−2,500,000

[a.] Present value of income net of operating costs.

Market Mechanisms

Market processes reinforce the tendency of land to be employed to its highest and best use. Suppose an individual owns a parcel of land for which the most profitable use requires construction of a two-story apartment building

(Use 2 in Table 9.1). However, the owner of the land intends to build a one-story building (Use 1 in Table 9.1). Perhaps the landowner doesn't know a multistory structure is the highest and best use, or perhaps the owner lacks the financial or other technical skills necessary to develop a two-story apartment. In a competitive market, the land would probably still be developed according to its highest and best use. Another developer might notice the vacant parcel (developers actively seek out such properties) and after analysis determine that a two-story apartment would be optimal. The developer could offer to buy the land for a maximum of $2,925,000. Since the residual to land is only $1,000,000 as a single-story building, there is an ample bargaining range in which the two parties may reach a mutually satisfactory deal. Perhaps the original owner will sell the land and use the proceeds to purchase a property elsewhere on which a one-story building would be the highest and best use. If the owner knows the initial market value of the property, he would find it more profitable to sell the land and buy another lot rather than develop it as a one-story building.

If the real estate market were operating with perfect knowledge, there would be many potential buyers willing to pay a maximum of $2,925,000. Under normal assumptions of the competitive model, competition would drive the price to exactly $2,925,000.

Existing Structures

The highest and best use discussion has been about use of land prior to development. The highest and best use principle also applies to changing existing structures. The use that will provide the greatest residual after additional capital costs such as remodeling or demolition have been subtracted from the total value of the renovated property is the highest and best use. This approach implicitly assumes that existing construction costs ("sunk" costs) must be paid even if the building is demolished. Like land, the preexisting structure is immobile and, hence, is treated like land. In this case, the residual is attributed to land and the preexisting building. Table 9.2 illustrates how the owner of a gas station should analyze the modification of a property to either add a convenience grocery or convert to a body shop. The addition of a convenience grocery would cost more than the increase in the present value of the income generated by the improvements. Consequently, the gas station/grocery would not be a profitable land-use change. The conversion to a body shop is feasible because the present value of the increased income is greater than the cost of the improvements.

The Land Development Process

This section builds on land-use theory by showing the type of analysis that land developers use to determine the highest and best use in a world where

Table 9.2   Highest and Best Use of a Developed Property

Land Conversion	Present Value of Income Change ($)	Conversion Cost ($)	Residual to Existing Property ($)
Gas station	0	0	80,000
Body shop	525,000	200,000	325,000
Gas/grocery	100,000	150,000	−50,000

information is costly and imperfect. It shows in greater detail how the hypothetical figures in Tables 9.1 and 9.2 can be derived.

The amount of effort that goes into a land-use study depends on the scope of the project and the value of the land. It would not be cost-effective to evaluate every possible land use for a particular site. Some decisions are based only on hunches. For instance, a retailer may open a store simply because it is believed to be a good area and space is available. However, major decisions are usually based on careful analysis. Figure 9.1 summarizes the steps in a typical land-use study.

DEVELOPER GOALS

The developer normally initiates the land development process. Think of the developer as the entrepreneur of the process. The developer's objective may be approximated by the desire to maximize profits, but routes to profit maximization include maximizing current cash flow, sheltering income from taxes, appreciation, personal use, and other factors. Income generation might be the goal of a retired investor, while a younger person might want to emphasize appreciation. Thus, developers normally determine their appropriate mix of objectives before focusing on particular real estate investments. During the early planning stages, a developer may have a site and wish to determine a use for it or have a general development concept such as a motel on the east side of a city and seek an appropriate site. Preliminary architectural sketches may be drawn to illustrate the proposed concept, but the ideas are very tentative at this stage.

THE MARKET STUDY

After a development concept has been identified, the analysis proceeds to the market study phase. The market study will help determine whether there is a market for the space under consideration, the likely income generation, and

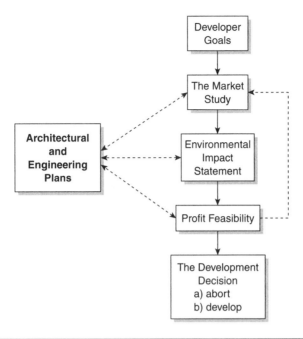

Figure 9.1   The Land Development Process

NOTE: The land development process starts with developers goals and proceeds to increasingly complex stages. There is interaction between financial and engineering analysis.

what potential impediments exist. The market study may also help the developer secure a loan; attract investors; or argue for public support, such as zoning changes or development incentives.

The concepts of supply and demand are useful in real estate market analysis even though supply and demand curves are almost never estimated. Researchers may initially assume that existing rents for similar projects, perhaps adjusted for inflation, reflect anticipated prices for the new development. This view would be reasonable if existing market conditions reflected equilibrium, but property development often occurs in disequilibrium markets. In considering the existing market, a researcher may develop a grid showing characteristics of existing properties in the area, including rents, occupancy rates, location, and amenities. This information will give developers an idea of whether there is a current demand for additional space, the rental ranges that can be expected, and the features a project should include.

While the comparison grid may reflect current conditions of supply and demand, conditions constantly change the price at which the project will be sold in the future. The demand side will be examined to provide an indication of how demand will change. Population and employment growth are good indicators of demand increases for residential and retail space. Demand for industrial and office space can be estimated by examining manufacturing or office employment forecasts. All planned development depends on changes in future market conditions.

Construction costs are an important supply determinant. Land-use policies also influence the ability to impose limits on the market. Building permits may be examined to determine whether an increase in supply is already being planned. Often a tight real estate market is accompanied by numerous construction plans and other plans to capitalize on high rents and low vacancies. Because time lags in construction, tight markets have become glutted when new projects are completed.

ENVIRONMENTAL IMPACT STATEMENTS

Environmental impact statements (EISs) are required by a variety of governmental units, particularly when some form of governmental support is part of the development. Most large development projects require considerable analysis to minimize the adverse impact on surrounding areas. EISs focus on social, economic, and congestion impacts as well as the consequences for the natural environment. Thus, a project's impact on crime, poverty, and employment may be as much a part of EIS as the effect on birds and water quality.

A quick low-cost environmental scan early in the planning process can identify potential conflicts that might be either insurmountable or very costly obstacles that prevent project completion. If identified early in the planning process, some issues can be managed to avoid strong political conflicts later.

Some governmental agencies provide guidance regarding what to include in an EIS and appropriate methodologies. In general, the EIS should reflect the size of the development. However, many observers believe that an objective EIS is illusory.

PROFIT FEASIBILITY

The market study and EIS should help the developer decide whether a project can be sold or rented within the target price range and whether it is environmentally and politically workable. It does not, however, assess whether the project will be profitable. This will be done in the profit feasibility analysis. To determine the profitability, the present value of returns must be compared with the present value of the costs. The returns will normally be spread over the economic life of the property, say 20 years. Most of the costs will be incurred in the year of construction, although maintenance and utilities, taxes, and possibly financing charges will be future costs. Income tax factors may also be incorporated in the feasibility analysis.

The general formula for estimating the value of a property with a limited economic life and fluctuating returns is

$$V = \text{NOI}_0 + \frac{\text{NOI}_1}{(1+d)} + \frac{\text{NOI}_2}{(1+d)^2} + \cdots + \frac{\text{NOI}_n}{(1+d)^n}, \qquad (9.2)$$

where V is the property value, d is the appropriate discount rate, and NOI is the net operating income. Subscripts indicate years in the future, with 0 indicating now.

Although the formula for converting future returns to the present value is straightforward, this is usually complicated and can seldom be applied mechanically. Net operating income is income minus operating expenses. Operating expenses for a typical urban property include utilities, property taxes, management fees, maintenance, insurance, and so forth. Clearly, the higher the net operating income, the greater is the value of the property. Thus, if future or expected rents from a property increase while expenses remain constant, the value will increase, assuming everything else remains the same.

There are complicated controversies surrounding the way the discount rate should be calculated. For our purposes, d can be considered as representing the return to capital, such as an interest rate plus a rate to account for the return of capital. By application of Equation 9.2, you can see that the higher the discount rate, the lower the value of the property will be, other things being equal.

As a general rule, if the present value of the projected NOI discounted at the appropriate rate is greater than the costs of the development (including land and capital costs), the project is feasible. If the present value is less than the construction costs, the project is not feasible because the developer cannot earn the required rate of return. Why is there less real estate development when interest rates are highest? The higher discount rates make for lower property values of proposed projects.

A profit analysis indicating that the present value of the revenues exceeds the costs is a necessary, but not sufficient, condition for implementation. Each potential land use will "bid" for the site, and the profit feasibility analysis determines the maximum amount that can be bid.

Usually, the initial economic analysis will be based on "quick and dirty" assumptions. A pro forma statement, for instance, may show a static picture with NOI and reflecting a "typical" year. The static picture ignores variations in cost and revenue patterns that may occur over time. If initial pro forma calculations indicate that the project could be profitable, more thorough analysis will be undertaken. The final cash flow analysis will account for the timing of cash expenditures and receipts during construction and throughout the project's life as well as possible lower occupancy during the start-up phase.

Suppose at some stage the feasibility study indicated that the project was not profitable. Rather than immediately abandoning the idea, the project may be rethought. The developer might redesign architectural features to reduce costs. Perhaps some features of the project could be cut—the number of rest rooms in an office complex could be decreased or gingerbread removed from a facade. Attempts to increase revenues will also be explored. Perhaps space could be rearranged to provide more rentable area. Interaction between the architectural and economic aspects of the plan will continue until a decision is made to abort or proceed with the project.

If the present value of the returns is equal to or greater than the present value of the construction and operating costs, the developer will earn or exceed the rate of return given by the discount or target rate, and the project will continue toward development. Table 9.3 is a simplified cash flow analysis of a project based on Equation 9.2. Although many of the details of a large-scale model are missing, the basic elements are present. It is based on the assumption that the project is built in Year 0 at a cost of $1.3 million. The immediate costs include land ($300,000) and building ($1,000,000). Income in the first year is projected to be $300,000, and property rents are assumed to increase 4% annually throughout the 20-year life of the project. Expenses are 45% of rents, so expenses also increase with inflation. Line 3 is the net operating income discussed in conjunction with Equation 9.2. Although property taxes have been deducted from gross income to calculate NOI, additional calculations are necessary to account for income taxes. Depreciation, an important tax shelter item, is $50,000 annually, creating a taxable income of $115,000. The developer is in the 30% marginal tax bracket, and so the after-tax income ($130,500) will differ from the before-tax income. The seventh row shows the present value of the future after-tax income.

The discounted value of the income flow is shown in Row 8. The inventor's discount rate or target rate is 10%. Accordingly, the present value of the $130,500 after-tax income in Year 1 is $118,636 ($130,500/1.10), and for Year 2 it is $111,669 ($135,120/1.10^2). Row 9 is simply the sum of the present values for the current year and all succeeding years.

After 20 years, the sum of the present values of the income is $1,425,738. (The initial construction cost was not discounted since it occurred in the first year. A more complete analysis could show monthly expenses appropriately discounted). The present value of the future net income discounted at 10% is greater than the project cost, which was assumed to be $1,300,000 so the project would be profitable. If the discount rate were to increase to 15%, the present value of the projects net would be insufficient to justify the project. Because of the discounting process, early year cost and revenue projections will

Table 9.3   A Simple Cash Flow Analysis

	Year		
	1	2	20
1 Income ($)	300,000	312,000	632,055
2 −Operating expenses ($)	135,000	140,400	284,425
3 =Net operating income ($)	165,000	171,600	347,630
4 −Cost recovery ($)	50,000	50,000	50,000
5 =Taxable income ($)	115,000	121,600	297,630
6 Change in taxes ($)	34,500	36.480	89,289
7 Cash flow after taxes ($)	130,500	135,120	258,341
8 PV cash flow after taxes ($)	118,636	111,669	38,401
9 Sum PV on investment ($)	$118,636	$230,306	$1,425,738

NOTE: Explanations by row:

1. Increasing at 4% per year.
2. Equal to 45% of Row 1.
3. Row 1 minus Row 2.
4. Depreciation at $50,000 annually.
5. Net operating income less cost recovery.
6. Taxable income times 0.30.
7. Row 3 less increases in taxes.
8. Row 7 discounted at 10%.
9. Running total of Row 9.

have a much bigger impact on profitability than in later years. This observation is comforting since errors are more likely to occur in out-year estimates.

The value of land is the residual value after accounting for other, mobile factors of production used in the construction of the project. Since capital costs were assumed to be $1,000,000, the residual to land suggests a land value of $425,738, the original $300,000 paid for the site plus the $125,738 excess. Alternatively, the land value may be calculated as the value of the project ($1,425,738) less the capital costs ($1,000,000). If the developer purchased the land for $300,000, as was initially assumed, he or she would have gotten a good deal and the market would not have been fully efficient. If other developers recognized that the present value of the returns indicated that substantial profits were attainable, they might have been interested in the site, driving the price up and decreasing above-normal profits. If, on the other hand, preliminary feasibility analysis indicated that the present value of the returns were less than the present value of the costs (including estimated land costs), the developer would be in a strong position to negotiate the land price downward.

The focus on "the numbers" gives the impression that property development is a more objective process than it really is. During the study process, a favorable group-think mentality sometimes develops. Most of the people involved in a project want it to be successful. Consequently, numerous, unanalyzed, implicit assumptions that may tilt in favor of moving the project to the next stage became embedded in the projections.

Key questions in analyzing a profit-feasibility statement include the following: Are the revenue estimates realistic? Has the market been properly identified? Are there any hidden costs or unanticipated problems? Will the public be receptive? Is the discount rate appropriate? How will the policy influence prospects? And so forth.

THE DEVELOPMENT DECISION

After examining the market and profit feasibility analysis, the developer will be in a position to determine how to proceed. If it is decided to go forward with the project, the market and profit feasibility study may serve as a basis for securing a loan or attracting other equity investors. On the other hand, the investor may determine that the project is not feasible and abort the development. Other options include waiting until market conditions change or selling the plans to a developer who is interested in proceeding with the project.

IMPLICATIONS OF FINANCIAL ANALYSIS FOR LED OFFICIALS

Development officials are frequently asked to provide assistance to developers who want to build projects. Businesspeople sometimes seek government incentives for their projects on the grounds that they would not otherwise be profitable. For instance, a developer might agree to build housing downtown if a special low-interest loan were provided. If public officials believed that downtown housing was a community priority, a local economic developer might consider whether it was advisable to provide the developer with a subsidy and, if so, how much of a subsidy. The profit projection, among other things, sheds light on the size of possible subsidies. If the analysis showed that the project would be profitable without public assistance, the case for a public subsidy would be weakened greatly. Even if the developer's data indicated that the project would not be profitable without public support, public officials may examine the model's assumptions carefully. The developer may have underestimated profitability to pressure the public officials into giving a large subsidy. In other cases, some developers might be overoptimistic, asking for a smaller subsidy than might really be necessary. Thus, public officials might be led to contribute to a project that was likely to fail, leaving the downtown with another empty building. Even publicly built projects such as parking garages, convention centers, and sports facilities should be subjected to a cash flow analysis to determine whether the project will infuse money into the public treasury or be a resource drain. Also, a public official may choose not to back a project that will not be successful based on the case flow analysis because a failed project, even if it is a private project, may hurt community development.

Land-Use Patterns

The activity with a residual sufficient to pay the highest price for a site will determine the land use. This section shows how competition among various activities results in systematic land-use patterns. First, the "monocentric city mode" is described. Patterns of land use are based on the assumptions that the central business district (CBD) is the point of maximum access and transpiration costs increase moving from the CBD in all directions. Later, some simplifying assumptions are relaxed and more complicated patterns of land use are described. However, two key principles are always evident: (1) activities seek access to urban goods and (2) the activity willing and able to pay the highest rent or price for a site determines its use.

THE MONOCENTRIC CITY MODEL

The moncentric city model is predicated on the assumption that land in the center of the metropolis is the most valuable because it provides firms located there with maximum access to urban goods such as customers and supplies. Thus, the CBD is the site where the firms would be willing to pay the maximum price. The amount the firms would be willing and able to pay for different sites is known as a rent-bid curve.

Each activity would have a different rent-bid curve, depending on the value of various types of access. Activities that have a strong need for access will tend to outbid other activities for prime CBD land. Also, activities that cannot easily substitute other inputs (say, travel time) for access afforded by central locations will tend to dominate CBD locations. Since most businesses desire access to similar urban goods, the rent bid curves will generally tend to be highest at the CBD and decline from that point. Figure 9.2 illustrates a pair of rent bid curves suggested by the concentric circle model and shows the land-use pattern that would result if the highest bidder determined the land use.

In urban areas, the most valuable properties are dominated by finance, legal, and administrative functions. The need for a central location is due primarily to the importance of face-to-face contact among executives. Individuals in these occupations may require frequent, short-notice meetings. Since the time of lawyers, financiers, or executives is valuable, their transportation costs are high. Individuals are expensive to transport, particularly highly paid executives. The prestige of downtown locations also influences the rent-bid curve, although such locations are becoming less prestigious in some places. Economic development officials often seek to improve the CBD as part of an effort to encourage administrative and financial activities to locate in their area.

Retail activities also value proximity to CBD locations (albeit less than in the past) because of the centrality of the CBD to customers. Industrial activities historically have been attracted to near-CBD locations due to access to ports, railheads, and roads. However, these ties have diminished since World War II. Today, new industrial facilities are oriented toward highway access points, contributing to suburbanization of manufacturing. Furthermore, zoning regulations have tended to exclude many industrial activities from near-CBD sites.

The value placed on CBD land for residential use is not as high as for financial and administrative uses in the United States for most people. This observation may change. Consequently, many types of households have located at varying distances from the CBD.

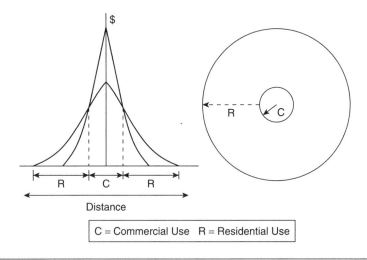

Figure 9.2   The Concentric Circle Model

NOTE: Competition among various activities may result in a concentric circle pattern of land use under certain theoretical assumptions.

THE DENSITY GRADIENT

CBD land is not only the most valuable, but it is also the most intensively used. This is no coincidence. Valuable resources tend to be used intensively. This explains why CBD land usually has dense daytime population and tall buildings.

Larger cities have higher CBD densities than do smaller places. Although urban growth at the fringe lowers the slope of the density gradient, if population is held constant, four factors normally affect the density gradient:

1. Newer cities developed around the automobile tend to use central locations less intensively than older, "trolley-car" cities.

2. Higher-income groups are more likely to decentralize. Thus, cities with high-income populations will have less concentrated densities.

3. Low-quality central city housing leads to urban decentralization and a lower density gradient.

4. Low manufacturing employment contributes to lower CBD densities.

American central cities have lower population densities than their European counterparts for many of the reasons cited above.

ROADS AND AXIAL DEVELOPMENT

The recognition of highway systems requires modification of the concentric circle approach to reflect lower transportation costs along the main arteries. A site near a main road may be farther from the CBD than are other sites, yet have better access. Various economic activities will be willing to pay more for a site near a road. Figure 9.3a is a land-use pattern that might exist if the assumption of equal transport costs in all directions were dropped from the concentric circle approach. Rivers and other natural disruptions could be incorporated to show how other variations in transportation costs affect land use.

The doughnut city may be an emerging land-use form. As beltways around cities provide good access to the entire metropolitan area and as the areas just a few blocks from the CBD are increasingly associated with urban bads, new development is concentrating near the beltways, whereas areas near the CBD are overlooked. Some fear that large parts of the central city may become the hole, with little economic activity, and the beltway development will become the doughnut.

The introduction of roads into the model also helps explain strip commercial development—commercial strips located on either side of major roads. Strip development reflects the desire of many businesses for access to a stream of customers rather that a stationary customer base.

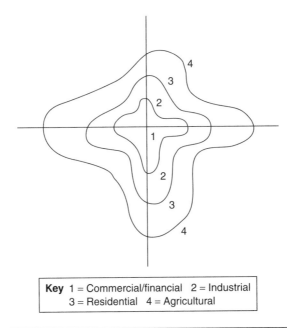

Key 1 = Commercial/financial   2 = Industrial
3 = Residential   4 = Agricultural

Figure 9.3   Roads and Axial Development

NOTE: The construction of a road system on the urban landscape will alter the access points and contribute to axial development.

AGGLOMERATION AND THE MULTIPLE-NUCLEAR CITY

The multiple-nuclear city is perhaps the most sophisticated model of the modern metropolis because it recognizes that land-use clumps appear because of agglomerations of economies within a single organization and among establishments. Intraurban agglomeration is an important aspect of the CBD's attractions, and the same set of forces can cause subcenters to develop beyond the CBD. A medical complex of several square blocks is an example of a specialized cluster. It would be ludicrous for a hospital complex to occupy a concentric circle around the CBD, as would be suggested by a literal interpretation of the concentric zone model. Agglomeration economics will also encourage clustering of groups of firms. Perhaps, firms needing access to a railhead (and firms needing access to firms that locate near a railhead) will form a cluster, and across town another cluster of manufacturing firms may form. Figure 9.4 illustrates the multiple-nuclear city.

Outlying retail centers such as regional shopping centers are important elements of the multiple-nuclear city. As cities grow, access to the CBD becomes more difficult for families living near the periphery. Retail centers develop to serve the increasingly large suburban markets. Additional activity such as

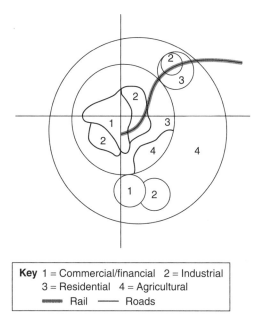

Key 1 = Commercial/financial   2 = Industrial
     3 = Residential   4 = Agricultural
     ▬▬ Rail   —— Roads

Figure 9.4   Agglomeration and the Multiple-Nuclear Models

NOTE: Agglomeration economies will contribute toward alternative centers of concentration and the multiple-nuclear model of urban form.

offices, entertainment, and residences may unfold around regional shopping malls, particularly if the transportation system is oriented toward the subcenter. As the metropolitan area expands, previously isolated communities may be brought into the metropolitan network. The enveloped communities will experience land-use changes, and they develop into subcenters with the metropolitan system.

SPECULATION

Sites are often maintained in low-density uses such as parking lots or agriculture while intensive development occurs nearby. The owners may be speculating that the land will be suitable for a different use in the future, and therefore, land values will increase faster than the return in current use.

Speculation involves differences of opinion about the future. Causes of differing opinions involve factors such as anticipated public improvements, the path of development, and the general state of the economy. The imperfect nature of the real estate market also contributes to speculative holdings. Consequently, land-use development is not smooth or incremental as implied by the model of axial growth. "Leapfrog" development will be observed.

ZONES OF TRANSITION

Inertia characterizes land-use changes. Urban landscapes change slowly, in part due to the long physical life of buildings. Coevolutionary development also contributes to land-use inertia. An initial land use may attract other activities and infrastructures that reinforce the original use. Businesses may be reluctant to relocate because they are supported by nearby residents, customer habits, traffic flows, and so forth. When people or businesses move, they tend to move short distances, thus preserving some neighborhood linkages.

In contrast to stabilizing forces, economic factors that influence land use also change. Consequently, zones of transition emerge and mixed land uses are observed. During a transition, land uses may seem incompatible. For instance, a commercial area may encroach on a residential neighborhood or vice versa.

THE SPREADING OF THE METROPOLIS

Metropolitan areas throughout the world are expanding. There has been an increase in suburban populations accompanying the spreading out of the metropolis. In some areas such as Latin America or Africa, the urban fringe is the residence for poor populations. In North America, suburban residents tend to be richer. Factors contributing to metropolitan spread include urban growth, declining transportation costs, new production techniques, new values, and income growth.

Growth

Growth increases center densities, but higher densities gradient also extend outward. Many parts of the metropolis are experiencing fewer dependencies with the center of the metropolis. Independent and generally autonomous activity centers are developing. The outward expansion of the metropolis has led to the development of edge cities (Joel Garreau, 1991). Unlike traditional bedroom suburbs, edge cities have an economic base of their own. Often these places develop around key highway intersections. Characteristics of edge cities include having comprehensive retail and office activities, having more jobs than homes, and having developed in the past 40 years.

Transportation Costs

Transportation cost declines have reduced the cost of access to the CBD for firms and households located in outlying areas. The preferences of firms and households that were initially indifferent between a nearer-CBD/higher-rent site and a more distant/lower-rent location have tilted toward more distant locations. Thus, lower transportation costs will contribute to metropolitan spread. Commuter-oriented highways and beltways have provided important transportation cost advantages to suburban areas. If the cost of gasoline continues to rise, metropolitan spread may slow or cease.

Production Techniques

Technologies that reduce the need for CBD access or increase the need for land have contributed to urban spread. It is often cheaper to produce a single-story facility with acres of nearby parking rather than build in a congested urban area on a site that may require off-site parking or may be environmentally questionable.

Computers allow more individuals to work at home rather than in an office. There is still a need for face-to-face communication and a social need for contact with individuals at work. Nevertheless, there is little doubt that telecommunication and computer technologies have decreased the importance of CBD access for both individuals and "back office" activities such as record keeping and processing.

Values, Image, and Amenities

Changing images and values represented by locations affect land-use change. In the United States, suburban locations are generally more prestigious and are associated with values of safety, families, and convenience. Downtown locations also convey positive images of sophistication. Both businesses and households may be attracted to the values and images connoted by places. In efforts to revive the downtowns, some cities have attempted to separate the CBD from nearby areas with lower images. Locations near the urban core tend to be more valued in places throughout the world than in the United States.

The images conjured by a rural lifestyle continue to attract many families to the urban fringes in the United States. Urban fringe areas that have an abundance of farmland or even small agricultural preserves tend to attract development (Roe, Irwin, & Marrow-Jones, 2004).

Incomes

As incomes increase, families tend to spend an increasing proportion of their income on housing. They may also want to alter the kind of shelter from multifamily housing, which is land-intensive, to detached, single-family housing, which uses more land per household. The best buys on single-family housing with large lots are distant from the CBD. In fact, such properties are rare in central cities. Thus, increasing incomes are associated with the spreading out of the city.

EVALUATING METROPOLITAN SPREAD (URBAN SPRAWL)

Many observers question the desirability of expansion at the urban periphery or urban sprawl. Critics have argued that sprawl contributes to pollution and excessive energy consumption due to greater reliance on the automobile associated with the suburban lifestyle. Other consequences associated with urban sprawl include (1) loss of agricultural land and wildlife habitats, (2) wasteful abandonment of inner city properties, (3) an ugly built environment with "ticky-tacky" housing, (4) political fragmentation and economic segregation (Rusk, 1993), (5) excessive public spending on roads and infrastructures, and (6) obesity due to our dependence on automobiles (Plantinga & Bennell, 2005).

Economists attribute part of the sprawl problem to externalities. A new resident on the urban fringe contributes to the costs shared by all residents. Longer commutes, increasing pollution, and congestion are costs shared by all. Metropolitan expansion also increases public infrastructure costs for roads, sewers, public buildings, and so forth. Yet potential movers to the urban fringes only consider private costs, not the costs imposed on others. Hence, the cost of moving to the suburbs is greater for society than for the individual. This situation is summarized in Figure 9.5. If the suburban home owner were required to pay the full additional (social) cost of a new dwelling, only 100 new units would be built. However, since home owners are not required to pay the full cost, 150 units will be built. When fringe dwellers are able to shift some of their costs to others, the quantity provided by the market will exceed the optimal level.

Land Use and Economic Development Tools

Local development officials recognize that efficient land-use patterns contribute to an area's economic strength. They rely on certain government powers to affect land use. A variety of distinct rights are associated with a particular property. Lawyers use the analogy that the multitude of rights are like a bundle of sticks, each stick representing a right. The government has taken the sticks called police power, taxation, eminent domain, and escheat. The first three sticks are important economic development tools:

1. *Police power* is the authority of the government to regulate use to enhance or preserve health, safety, and the general welfare. Zoning and building codes are the most important police powers.

2. *Taxation* affects the return that property generates and local revenues. Property taxes can affect land use since they lower the return on a real estate investment. Some states allow agricultural land to be taxed at a lower rate than is improved property. This differential discourages development and encourages urban sprawl.

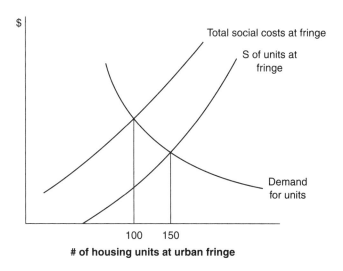

Figure 9.5   Housing and Sprawl at the Urban Fringe

NOTE: Overdevelopment occurs at the urban fringe because residents and developers of new real estate do not bear the full cost of development. Important externalities include public infrastructure and congestion.

3. *Eminent domain* is the right of the government to purchase property if its use is needed for a public purpose such as a road or a park. What constitutes "public purpose" has been a source of land-use debate about the appropriate role of government. This issue is discussed in more detail below.

4. *Escheat* is the government's right to all land for which there is no private owner. For instance, if someone dies without heirs, his or her property will be claimed by the government.

ZONING AND ITS CRITICS

Zoning is probably the most significant determinant of land use among the government sticks. Conventional zoning groups land uses into compatible categories. Compatible land uses are zoned near each other, and incompatible uses are separated. Thus, zoning prevents a slaughterhouse from locating in an established residential area. Zoning practice is not without critics.

There are at least five specific ways in which zoning may hinder economic development:

1. Changing land use becomes difficult. Zoning often prevents redevelopment of an area when, for example, a change from residential to commercial land use is needed. Mills (1989) showed that zoning encourages landowners to attempt to

have their property zoned in socially inefficient ways and suppress potential net social gains because it is often difficult to rezone a property.

2. Zoning may inflate land costs. Zoning restricts the amount of land available for certain industrial, commercial, and multifamily uses. This limits the supply of land for such purposes and artificially raises the land price for some uses.

3. There are aesthetic and social shortcomings of zoning. Architectural critics sometimes claim that zoning (and building codes) detracts from an area's quality of life.

4. Public planners make mistakes. Critics of zoning argue that public officials may be more likely to misallocate land than are developers, who may be more attuned to market signals. Furthermore, the government planners' mistakes may be quite harmful because they are large-scale mistakes.

5. Exclusionary and fiscal zoning occur. Many communities attempted to zone out the poor by prohibiting all but very expensive housing. Other communities allow only such construction as will generate more tax revenues than it will cost to service the property. Hence, apartments with three or more bedrooms are zoned out of many communities because such apartments will generate less in revenues than does a single-family house, but the large number of bedrooms implies that the tenants will have school age children. Such practices may enhance the economies of some areas, but they may create problems for central cities, which often bear a heavier cost of providing services for low- and moderate-income families.

FLEXIBILITY AND LAND-USE REGULATIONS

Numerous innovations in land-use regulations have made implementation more flexible and attuned to market signals.

An important theoretical contribution was made toward the implementation of land-use regulations when economists showed that under conditions of perfect information and freely transferable property rights, the free market could be a mechanism for efficient land use (Coase, 1963; Siegan, 1970). Contracts coupled with privately negotiated restrictions on future use could avoid incompatible uses. Consequently, land-use regulations have been administered more flexibly and have been attuned to market signals.

"Directed development" manages land use by scheduling building of public infrastructure. Infrastructure complements rather than replaces zoning. If a community wishes to discourage new development beyond a certain area, it may establish a policy whereby no roads, sewer lines, or other infrastructure will be built for a period of time. The type of planned infrastructure will influence the type of development. A lack of schools will discourage residential development, whereas a "theater district" could be encouraged by an appealing streetscape.

"Transferable development rights" are a flexible way to limit density. Traditionally, land-use planners have limited density by regulating the size of buildings. For instance, there might be a limit on the number of apartments in a building or on the number of stories. Developers could apply for variances on a case-by-case basis. Using transferable development rights, community officials may simply rule that within a particular area the number of units or floors may be no more than 100. The rights to build units will be distributed among landowners according to an equitable formula. Perhaps each acre could be assigned the rights to 10 units. If a landowner wants to build a project with more units than assigned, the extra development rights could be purchased from the owner of other area properties. Thus, the overall density of an area may be controlled. Yet rigid zoning is avoided.

"Planned unit development" allows developers to propose a comprehensive plan for an area that may mix land uses. For instance, a development plan might incorporate a mix of single-family housing, apartments, a retail center, and office space in a single development.

THE EMINENT DOMAIN CONTROVERSY

When land must be assembled for public purposes, the owner of a parcel may be expected to hold out for top dollar. To prevent this behavior, governments have been granted the right to acquire property by paying a fair market value.

Even if the purpose of the land acquisition is not for a direct public use, a problem may arise. For instance, a developer might have a plan for a large residential, commercial, and recreation development. The developer might need to acquire property from 20 owners to assemble the land. In this situation, it is reasonable for an owner to try to hold out for an above-market sales price. In fact, all owners may rationally pursue the same strategy. Accordingly, the developer may be unable to acquire the site.

To overcome this collective action problem, local governments have used the power of eminent domain to acquire property at the market value. They then resell it to a developer on condition that the land is used for the anticipated project. The use of eminent domain has been justified on the grounds that economic development is a public purpose.

Whether "public purpose" should be expanded to include private enterprises that contribute to economic development is in debate. However, without this tool, urban areas with fragmented property ownership patterns face a redevelopment obstacle.

RIGHTS TO LAND AND ECONOMIC DEVELOPMENT

Hernando De Soto (1989) showed that poorly defined rights to land can be a significant impediment to economic development. He believed that a lack of formal (i.e., government registered) rights to land in many developing nations makes it difficult for informal, traditional, or customary landowners to use their land as collateral for capital. Since farmers cannot borrow by using land as col-lateral, they cannot purchase machinery to improve their productivity or pur-sue other entrepreneurial ventures. Furthermore, government bureaucracies often make it difficult for persons living in shanty towns or in tribe situations to gain a title even if their families have had use of the land for generations.

De Soto's work has been widely influential. It is widely credited with sup-porting land reform in Peru. The government actively reduced barriers to granting land titles, and as a result, titles were given to more than 1.2 million families. His ideas have been credited with bringing political stability to Peru against an insurgent revolution.

Many economists believe that a well-defined system of property rights is critical to economic growth, development, and efficiency. When property rights are poorly spelled out, individuals may lack incentives to maintain or improve property because they are afraid of putting resources into a project when they may not capture the benefits.

The problem of poorly defined property rights constitutes an instance of a problem of the commons. Everyone has an incentive to overuse the resource, encouraging depletion, and few have incentives to conserve.

Summary

This chapter examined land use. An efficient distribution of land use contributes to local economic development prospects. The return to land is based on productivity. In the case of urban land, productivity is a function of access to goods in the environment. Land value equals the return to land (rent) divided by the discount rate. Rent is the residual to land after the other factors of production have been compensated. Land is fixed in supply, not created by the efforts of man, so some economists have maintained that the return to landowners is unearned.

The highest and best use of land is the most profitable use subject to legal restrictions. Access is an important determinant of the highest and best use. Market processes reinforce the tendency of land to be placed in its highest and best use.

A land-use study is frequently conducted to determine the appropriate use of a site. Developer goals are set; market, environmental impacts, and profit studies are undertaken; finally a decision is made. The critical step in a land-use study is a cash flow analysis to determine the present value of the future returns from a project. If the discounted present value of future returns is greater than the project's costs, the project is likely to be undertaken. Public officials and pri-vate developers often use the cash flow analysis in their negotiations.

The combination of individual development decisions results in land-use patterns. The simplest model of a metropolis is the concentric circle model. More complicated models can be developed by introducing roads, agglomeration economies, and speculation. However, all land-use models of urban development are based on the idea that firms bid against each other for land and the highest bidder (subject to legal restrictions) determines land use. In the theoretical models, rents will be greatest at the point of maximum access, the center of the metropolis, and will decline at points of less desirable access. However, the multiple-nuclear model allows for subcenters of activity and density.

Land-use patterns are changing in response to urban growth and changes in transportation costs, production technology, values, incomes, and other factors. Currently, the outward spread of the metropolis is a major land-use trend.

Political as well as economic factors influence land use. Zoning is the primary tool used to regulate land use, but not the only tool. Zoning is intended to reduce land-use spillovers. However, zoning has been criticized for being both ineffective and inefficient. The current trend is to allow developers more flexibility by providing greater scope for market-oriented decisions. In some developing countries, poorly defined property rights hinder efficient land-use decisions.

10

Housing and
Neighborhood Development

This chapter focuses on housing, the land use that most directly affects the welfare of individuals and families. Economic development officials are concerned about housing because it is a basic building block of neighborhoods, directly affects community welfare, generates local tax revenues, and affects the quality of life in the entire community.

Fundamentals of Housing Economics

Supply and demand analysis is useful in understanding forces that affect the housing market. Figure 10.1a illustrates a traditional supply and demand model for housing. The equilibrium price and quantity of housing are determined by the intersection of the supply and demand curves.

"Ceteris paribus," or "other things being equal," assumptions are necessary to allow the assumption that the equilibrium price and quantity remain stationary. Supply and demand curves represent the behavior of producers and consumers. However, their behavior is stable with respect to price and quantity only when all relevant variables other than price and quantity are held constant. The most common factors that must be assumed constant in supply and demand analysis of housing are shown in Table 10.1.

The ceteris paribus assumptions are seldom met in reality, but that does not diminish the usefulness of supply and demand analysis. Paradoxically, it is the violation of the assumptions that makes the model useful. When any of the factors that are assumed to be constant change, the relevant supply or demand curves will shift. Thus, it is these changes in the ceteris paribus assumptions that give predictive power to economic models. For instance, if an increase in

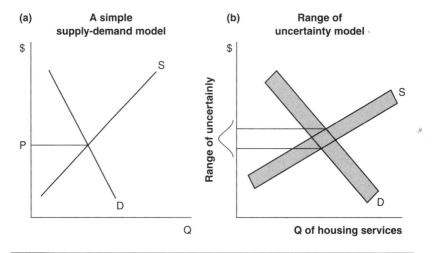

Figure 10.1   Two Models of the Housing Market

NOTE: The traditional supply and demand presentation implies that a single, observable price will emerge. In reality, "fuzzy" supply and demand curves might be used to illustrate the range of uncertainty.

Table 10.1   Important Ceteris Paribus Assumptions

General	Specific Real Estate Example
	Demand
1. Price of other goods	Price of home fuel
2. Consumers' tastes and preferences	Recent importance of family rooms
3. Size of the market	Number of families in a city due to factory relocation
4. Incomes of consumers	Incomes in a city or employment
5. Expectations	Inflation changes beliefs about future housing prices
	Supply
1. Price of inputs	Price of lumber, tools, etc.
2. Number of producers	Number of building contractors
3. Conditions of technology	Advances in factory fabrication of homes or plastic plumbing (where legal)

income were anticipated while other important factors remained relatively stable, housing prices would be anticipated to increase.

The horizontal axis traditionally measures the quantity of a homogeneous product per period of time. Yet houses are very dissimilar. To finesse the problem of what is being measured on the quantity axis, economists have assumed that housing can be defined in terms of "units of housing services." A mansion might contain five units of housing services while a small apartment might contain only half a unit of housing services. The level of housing services contained in a dwelling unit can vary with design, location, and other features. The neighborhood environment and local public services that residents may receive can also be considered part of housing services.

Price is also a slightly more complicated concept when applied to housing because some housing is purchased and some is rented. However, conversion between rent and sales price is straightforward. The value of a house is based on the discounted present value of the net rents. In a well-functioning market, value will equal sales price. Therefore, it is conceptually easy to move between rent and sales price. If rents rise, sales prices also rise (assuming factors such as maintenance cost and expected life of the property do not change). If housing prices rise, then monthly payments increase.

HEDONIC PRICING

Hedonic pricing models segment the housing-services bundle into detailed components and use statistical techniques such as regression to determine the marginal value of each component. The value of the entire housing bundle can then be determined by aggregating the value of various components.

The essence of hedonic pricing models can be summarized in Equation 10.1, which states that price is a function of housing characteristics:

$$P = f(C_i), \tag{10.1}$$

where P is the price and C_i is a vector of i characteristic (i.e., size, access, number of baths, etc.).

Equation 10.1 is a general functional form. When the function is specified, the coefficients associated with each variable express the value of that characteristic, holding all other characteristics constant.

For instance, if values were determined only by the square footage of the apartment and the number of bedrooms, the hedonic equation might be

$$PR = a + b_1(\text{sq. ft.}) + b_2(\text{bedrooms}), \tag{10.2}$$

where PR is the property rent per month, a is the intercept term, b_1 is the number of square feet of space, and b_2 is the number of bedrooms.

Using regression techniques, the values of a_1, b_1, and b_2 could be determined. Suppose the regression technique resulted in the following equation:

$$RR = 75 + 0.40(\text{sq. ft.}) + 2.0(\text{bedrooms}). \qquad (10.3)$$

Then, the rent for a three-bedroom, 1,000–sq. ft apartment would be expected to be $481 = [75 + ($0.40)(1000) + ($2)(3)]$. The model provides information on the components. For instance, an extra bedroom adds $2 per month to the rent, holding the apartment size and all other factors constant. Actual price models are much more complex than the simple, linear, two-independent-variable model illustrated by Equation 10.2.

The market-comparison approach has also been used to estimate value. Although the market-comparison approach lacks the statistical rigor of the hedonic price model, it is based on the same concept—housing is a bundle of related goods and services. There are four steps in the market-comparison approach. (1) Examine the subject property for which price is to be estimated. (2) Collect data for similar properties for which sales prices are known. (3) Adjust the sales prices of the comparables to reflect the price they would have sold for if they had the characteristics of the subject property. If a comparable property is better than the subject property in some respect, then the sale price of the comparable should be decreased. If a comparable property is worse than the subject on a particular feature, then the comparable's price is adjusted upward. Usually, judgment and experience are used in making adjustments. (4) Average values of the comparable properties to provide an estimate of value of the subject property. Table 10.2 summarizes this process.

UNCERTAINTY, MARKET
IMPERFECTIONS, AND COMPETITION

In perfectly competitive markets, such as the New York Stock Exchange or commodity exchanges, buyers or sellers are price takers. Real estate transactions are fundamentally different from competitive markets. One important difference between housing markets and competitive markets is that buyers and sellers can only guess the price for which a particular property will sell. Another important difference between real estate and competitive markets is that while there are generally hundreds of buyers and sellers in any real estate market at any given time, there may be only one or two sellers and only a few buyers for any particular property. Thus, each participant in a real estate market has some ability to affect price.

Because of the nature of real estate markets, price is seldom known before an actual sale has been made. The equilibrium price for a particular class of property in a given area may be better visualized as a range rather than as an

Table 10.2   The Market Comparison Approach to Value: Grid Analysis

Improvements	Comp A	Comp B	Comp C	Subject Property
Sale price	$156,000	$153,500	$148,000	Not known
Time of sale	Recent	1 year ago	18 months ago	Now
	0	+2,700	+3,500	
Location and neighborhood conditions	Better	Worse	Worse	Average
	−$5,000	+$5,000	+$3,000	
Architectural style	Worse	Better	Worse	Good
	+$500	−$1,000	+$250	
Total square feet	2,500 sq. ft	Same	Same	2,300 sq. ft
	−$7,000	0	0	
Kitchen size and design	Better	Same	Same	Average
	−$500	0	0	
Heating and air conditioning	Same	Same	Same	Electrical
Number of rooms	8	7	Equal	8
	0	+$3,000	0	
Number of baths	2	1½	2	2
		+$1,300	0	
Type of construction	Better	Better	Better	Poor
	−$1,200	−$700	−$1,500	
Physical condition	Same	Better	Worse	Average
	0	−$1,000	+$1,200	
Garage and other outbuildings	Same	Same	Same	1½ cars
Lot value difference	+500	Equal	Equal	Average
Indicated value	$56,000	$59,700	$54,450	Not known

Correlated value of subject property = ($156,500 + $159,200 + $154,450) /3 = $156,717 exact point. Figure 10.1b shows a modified supply and demand graph for a particular property as three-bedroom, one-and-one-half-bath ranch houses in the Saville subdivision. In most housing markets, the supply and demand curves are fuzzy, and a range of uncertainty exists.

Residential Location and Neighborhood Change

The choice of where to live is an individual decision shaped by larger social forces. Individual decisions have the cumulative effect of forming recognizable neighborhoods. This section describes the processes that result in the social and economic similarity of neighborhood residents. The models discussed in the sections will suggest levers that local development officials may employ to affect change.

THE FILTERING-DOWN THEORY

The filtering-down theory explains how lower socioeconomic groups come to occupy houses and neighborhoods previously occupied by higher-income families. As incomes among a high-income group rise, their demand for housing increases. Some individuals will be able to satisfy their increased demand for housing by buying newly constructed houses. The newly constructed houses are likely to group in new developments rather than locate in a scattered pattern among existing, older houses. New development is economical if the existing properties have value, and demolition and clearance costs are significant. Houses built in new neighborhoods also share infrastructure costs. The filtering-down theory does not necessarily require a growth pattern in which successive groups moved outward toward the urban fringes, but outward movement is typical.

The filtering process depends on what happens to the houses vacated by the families that purchased newly constructed houses. There are three likely possibilities:

1. *No filtering:* Families of similar economic backgrounds might purchase the vacated houses. In this case, there would be no change in the economic status of the neighborhood. The filtering process will not be effective in increasing the supply of housing to lower-income groups.

2. *Complete filtering:* Suppose that families of comparable incomes were not interested in moving into the vacated properties at the price the initial occupants paid. In this case, the price of housing in the neighborhood would fall and the house would be affordable to lower-income households. The house could be described as filtering down to lower-income families. This second case is the clearest example of how lower-income families benefit from the filtering process.

3. *Filtering and adaptation:* Houses will often undergo some adaptive change when they filter to a lower-income group. One important reason for the change in the housing stock is that lower-income groups may be unable to afford the same levels of maintenance as the previous higher-income group. Also, lower-income groups may wish to divide houses to accommodate more people than previously. In physical terms, the lower maintenance levels might be reflected in houses that were in need of paint, cracked windows, and so forth. Some adaptation will result in lower-quality housing services, although the quantity of housing services provided in a neighborhood may increase if properties are used more intensively. In this case, the housing units in the neighborhood filtered to a lower-income group, but the extent of the housing services increase would depend on the extent of the adaptive adjustment. If the decline in housing quality is slight, the adaptive filtering will probably lead to better housing for the lower-income group.

The three possibilities could describe what might happen to an individual house. If the focus of analysis is on the neighborhood, Possibilities 2 and 3 will change the socioeconomic composition. To the extent that adaptation occurs, the physical characteristics of the neighborhood will also change.

THE TRADE-OFF MODEL

The trade-off model explains the predominance of high-quality housing on the city perimeter in terms of the trade-off between access to central locations and household demand for space (Muth, 1969). The model is based on the assumption that as incomes rise, the rate at which households are willing to substitute access for cheaper land changes.

Space Versus Access

The model assumes that the land near the central business district (CBD) is a desired location because it provides the greatest access to work and other amenities. Desirability decreases with distance from the CBD. Picture a household with a significant income at location M in Figure 10.2. The location at M represents the optimal trade-off for the household between access to the central city, on the one hand, and lower land costs, on the other. Each household has two factors to consider in choosing its location. One consideration is the amount of space that it prefers. The larger the amount of space the household desires, the farther from the city center the household will tend to locate, all other things being equal. Second, costs of travel into the city must be considered. Travel costs include the out-of-pocket costs and opportunity costs of foregone activities while traveling. Empirical studies have shown that time costs of commuting are valued well below (about 25%) the commuters' hourly wage. These opposite pulls determine the slope of the individual access-price trade-off.

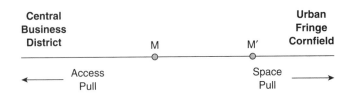

Figure 10.2   Space Versus Access as Income Rises

NOTE: Initially, the household is in equilibrium at point *M*. As income increases, the household will relocate to *M'* because the desire for more space plus the cheaper land near the fringe is stronger than the increased pull of the desire for better access.

As the income of the family located at *M* increases, the household will want more land. The desire for more land will tend to tilt the locational choice toward the periphery where land is cheaper. However, the increased income will also increase the opportunity costs of commuting. The increased opportunity cost of travel will tend to orient the optimal location toward the city's center where access is best. The stronger pull will dominate, but that cannot be determined theoretically.

Evidence in the United States indicates that the outward movement effect dominates. Therefore, neighborhoods of higher-income families are more likely to locate in the metropolitan area's outer ring. However, South American and European countries do not have as strong an outward movement. The difference suggests (not surprisingly) that the trade-off is affected by attitudes regarding the value of non–work time, laws, images of the city, preferred living accommodations, cultural dependence on automobile, and other sociopolitical factors.

Trade-offs in the Multiple-Nuclear City

There are multiple points within a metropolitan area that represent points of substantial access. The CBD is no longer the controlling access point in most major metropolitan areas, and jobs have shifted from the central city to suburban locations. Many large business agglomerations exist throughout most metropolitan areas. The model's assumption of minimum transportation costs at the CBD is not true for most families.

In light of the new realities of urban form, the trade-off theory requires modification to describe households as examining trade-offs among a variety of jobs and residential locations. In some situations, land costs may actually decline, moving toward the central city and away from a subcenter. However, the generalization that preferences for increased space are more easily attainable at the urban fringe remains valid, particularly if newly constructed housing is desired.

THE CULTURAL AGGLOMERATION MODEL

Cultural factors are also important in neighborhood formation. People often believe that they will find congenial friends or mates (or mates for their children) if they live near people like themselves. They also may feel uncomfortable among people from other ethnic groups. Thus, neighborhoods of individuals with similar social characteristics will form based on social desires and agglomeration economics.

The services that some ethnic groups desire may be provided economically only if economies of scale can be achieved. Therefore, groups may form neighborhoods around stores that reflect their buying patterns. Older individuals may congregate in neighborhoods that provide certain services, while families in the child-rearing stage may be overrepresented in a neighborhood with recreational facilities and good schools. Ethnic groups have formed neighborhoods around a church. The changing demographic composition of a neighborhood portends a change in the services available in the area. In addition to the forces that draw like groups together, there are discriminatory processes at work that tend to isolate poor and minority families. Burgess (1952) used the phrase "invasion-succession" to describe ethnic change.

Socially homogeneous neighborhoods have been criticized. Benefits of neighborhood diversity include (1) helping promote a stable social mix of community leaders, (2) providing alternative role models for individuals in the lower class, (3) encouraging artistic diversity, (4) encouraging cultural cross-fertilization, (5) increasing opportunities for the poor, (6) reducing social tension, (7) avoiding residential instability, (8) helping prepare residents for life in a diverse world, and (9) promoting neighborhood stability. The desirability of neighborhood diversity has been recognized and encouraged in some local development programs. However, the forces tending to segregate households along income and racial lines continue to be strong.

THE TIEBOUT MODEL

Tiebout (1956) developed a model that describes the relationship between local government programs, taxes, and housing prices. The model is often considered part of the public finance literature because it emphasizes the role of government services and taxes as a major element in neighborhood choice. The model is discussed here because it also has implications for neighborhood change. In fact, in a metropolitan context, a small suburb is similar to the neighborhood as a reference point. There are four necessary postulates.

1. A house purchased in a particular area embodies a bundle of services, including government services. For instance, the housing services in a particular neighborhood may or may not include garbage collection, adequate police service,

and quality public schools. These government-related services are in addition to the private housing services provided by the structure and nongovernmental amenities such as friendly neighbors and good shopping.

2. Individuals form preferences for an area based on the public services and other features of the external environment as well as the private services of the house.

3. Different levels of service provisions will often result in different tax burdens among municipalities. "Other things being equal"—that is, assuming equal service levels, the higher the tax burden, the smaller the housing demand in a jurisdiction will be. Negative features of the neighborhood, such as unsafe conditions, higher insurance premiums, and pollution, can be treated as negative features of the housing bundle.

4. Individuals differ in their preference and willingness to pay for private housing services and also for the goods associated with housing in a particular neighborhood. In other words, some individuals will be willing and able to pay different amounts for packages of neighborhood amenities and disamenities.

To understand the implications of the Tiebout model, assume that the legislative body in a small suburb voted to construct a major sports facility that includes tennis courts, swimming pools, and a gymnasium with an indoor track, weight rooms, and sauna. The facility would be available free to community residents only. Property taxes would increase by an average of $100 per household per year to finance the project. The tax boost includes maintenance as well as repayment of bonds issued to support construction. How will the change in the amenity-disamenity mix affect housing prices and the characteristics of individuals living in the neighborhood?

First, some residents will be deterred from living in the area because the higher taxes are more of a burden to them than the value they place on the sports facility. In other words, they would no longer be willing to pay as much as they previously would have paid for a house in that area. Demand among this group will decrease. Conversely, other individuals will be attracted to the municipality because they value the services of the sports complex more than they object to the extra costs. Thus, some individuals will move out of the community to avoid the high taxes, while others will move into the area because they want access to the facility.

The process of housing adjustment is best illustrated by the supply and demand model. Assume that there are two groups of individuals—"sports nuts" and "misers." The sports nuts are willing to pay for the extra facilities, while the misers are not. The responses can be analyzed by reference to Figure 10.3. Prior to the sports complex construction, the demand by the two groups may have been similar. Thus, the pre–sports complex demand curve D in Figures 10.3a and 10.3b is the same for both the sports nuts and the misers. After the increase in services and taxes, however, the demand for housing in the area increases among sports nuts and decreases among misers. The isolated effect of the sports nuts is to increase prices from $500 to $600 per month. The isolated effect of the misers is to decrease housing prices from $500 to $400. The combined effect depends on which group has the largest shift in demand. Figure 10.3c is drawn on the assumption that the sport nut effect outweighs the miser effect. Hence, housing prices rose to $520. Of course, the combined outcome could have resulted in lower property values; it depends on tastes and preferences.

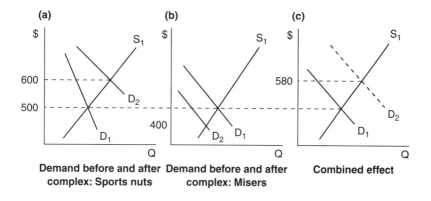

Figure 10.3   The Tiebout Model

NOTE: The public improvement made the community more desirable for some residents, but the higher taxes to finance the improvements made the community less desirable for others. The combined effect cannot be determined theoretically although in this example the net effect was to increase property values.

The adjustment process is also accompanied by spatial rearrangement of households. The misers will sell their property to both avoid higher taxes and capture the higher prices that the sports nuts are willing to pay. When they sell their properties, they will move to an area providing a better service/tax mix for their preferences. Sports nuts, on the other hand, will move into the suburb. In Tiebout's (1956) words, spatial arrangement amounts to "lumping together of all similar tastes for the purpose of making joint purchases" (p. 417). Individuals "voted with their feet" for the combination of amenities and disamenities they preferred.

The Tiebout hypothesis has been tested on several occasions. Oates (1969), for instance, found that, ceteris paribus, property values are higher in a community with more attractive public services. Oates was the first to show that property tax increases tend to be capitalized into the current value of property. School expenditures exert a particularly significant positive impact in the municipalities examined by Oates. Clotfelter (1975) has documented spatial rearrangement as a result of school desegregation using the Tiebout model as the basic theoretical framework. Economists have shown school quality to be a significant factor in shaping interurban locations, even holding racial composition constant. Differences in property insurance have also been shown to affect housing prices. With the rise of environmental concerns, avoidance of pollution also explains some price variations (Noonan, Krupka, & Baden, 2007).

An important implication of the Tiebout model is that individuals select areas that provide their preferred mix of services and taxes. Better services and lower taxes will increase housing demand within the area. Individuals will express their preferences by attempting to move into the district—a process termed *voting with their feet*. If a local area's property values increase more than the value of properties in similar areas, one reason may be that local officials provided a desired mix of taxes and services. Some observers have suggested that relative changes in housing prices are a measure of the performance of public officials. However, nongovernmental actions, such as establishment of an attractive shopping center nearby or a neighborhood escort service for the elderly, will also change the amenity-disamenity mix.

THE AGGREGATE ECONOMIC FALLOUT MODEL

Hill and Bier (1989) developed a model of neighborhood change that links changes in the economic base to neighborhood formation. Changes in the national economy may affect particular local sectors, and these impacts are, in turn, translated into changes in neighborhood characteristics. Their model suggests that neighborhoods have identifiable links to occupations and industries in the local economy. For instance, one neighborhood may have a disproportionate number of residents who are blue-collar workers in an automobile plant. Another neighborhood may be composed primarily of high-income professionals in the service sector, such as lawyers and bankers. A layoff in the automobile plant is likely to result in deterioration and lower property values in the neighborhood linked to the auto sector. Neighborhoods with occupational-industrial mixes that are not linked to the auto sector would be affected only indirectly. Hill and Bier use data from Cleveland to show that both the positive and the negative effects of industrial and occupational changes in the local economy spilled into neighborhoods where workers lived, affecting poverty levels and housing costs.

INITIATING AND PERPETUATING THE CHANGE PROCESS

Models of neighborhood formation and change complement one another. The filtering model best explains the adaptive adjustments that occur during neighborhood change. The trade-off model explains why wealthy families lead the suburbanization movement and create a process that allows filtering to occur. The concept of social agglomeration helps explain neighborhood changes in terms of ethnic migration patterns. The Tiebout model shows how neighborhood characteristics affect housing prices and how individuals vote with their feet for neighborhood characteristics and public services associated with a property. Neighborhood characteristics are also affected by macroeconomic forces. Although in some instances one model may have more explanatory power than another, in most cases each model provides an important perspective on neighborhood change.

The speed of change may be accelerated by real estate agents who use fear of change and steering of prospective buyers to encourage people to sell their homes. Deterioration may also be encouraged by lending practices. When lenders decide to reduce loan availability, housing prices may decline. Recently, "predatory" lenders have made loans to individuals who cannot afford to repay. This practice may contribute to abandonment. Lack of upkeep also contributed to neighborhood decline. Both economic and social factors influence the upkeep decision (Galster, 1987). High degrees of absentee ownership or simply not caring what the neighbors think also reduces upkeep.

In contrast to the cumulative decline perspective, there are countervailing forces that tend to stabilize neighborhoods. For instance, if property values decline significantly in a year, buyers' attention may increase if a reputation as a "bargain" neighborhood develops. Current residents may decide not to sell when they otherwise would have. Similarly, public policies may adjust to help prevent cumulative decline.

When a neighborhood starts to change, will the dynamics encourage further changes or will the neighborhood reestablish the original equilibrium? In most instances, a dramatic change in 1 year does not alter the long-run neighborhood future. For example, a spike in crime may cause more police activity in the neighborhood, decreasing the crime rate. The neighborhood returns to the original development path. The historic tipping points that characterized racial change appear to be anomalies (Galster, Cutsinger, & Lim, 2007).

The existence of a self-stabilizing mechanism in neighborhoods does not mean that neighborhoods will not experience improvement or deterioration. Rather, they indicate that powerful, long-term social and economic changes among a group of variables perpetuate neighborhood change. For instance, the movement of high-income families out of a neighborhood may create long-term deterioration. A spike in the crime rate may create conditions that bring the crime rate back to where it was, but long-run processes will not be altered. A possible policy implication for neighborhood development officials is that response to one or a few signs of deterioration may not be enough to reverse long-term decline. A broad-based effort that addresses multiple variables is necessary to reverse neighborhood decline.

Housing Policy Issues

Many housing policies operate indirectly or are very broad based rather than targeted toward low-income groups, for instance. Housing assistance is often provided through income tax laws. To the extent that mortgage interest and property taxes are deductible, an individual's taxable income will be reduced. Also, governments often attempt to keep interest rates low as a way of encouraging housing construction and purchase. This section considers more direct housing support efforts.

Local officials have considerable latitude in designing urban housing programs. Several policy issues need to be addressed in the development of local housing programs. The issues are described here as polar positions to make the distinctions as sharp as possible. However, policymakers often must select the appropriate middle ground.

RENT CONTROL VERSUS MARKET FORCES

The role of rent control in local housing policy is a perennial issue. Several cities have enacted rent controls. Tenant groups in cities where rents have increased rapidly have pressured their local legislators to enact controls. Rent controls take many forms. In some cities, rents are allowed to increase at a given amount per period. Often, the controls are lifted when one tenant moves and a new base is established. Even within a city, some units may be rent controlled while others are not, depending on the time, the location, and the conditions of construction.

In spite of the variety of rent controls, the issue is generally analyzed by the simple supply and demand curves shown in Figure 10.4. In this case, the market rent per unit of housing services is $1,000 per month. However, the rent is controlled at $700 per month. Consequently, more housing services are demanded at the controlled price than building owners are willing and able to supply.

The arguments for rent control are generally based on equity. Proponents of rent control argue that tenants may be exploited if building owners are allowed to raise rents according to what the market will bear. Furthermore, rent increases are frequently attributed to neighborhood or community-wide factors as opposed to actions of individual property owners. Therefore, tenants, as part of the community, might be as entitled to some of the benefits of increased community desirability as property owners. Since the buildings subject to control are already in existence and were built based on rent expectations at the time of construction, rent-control proponents view rent increases (above increases needed for tax and operating cost factors) as windfalls.

Opponents of rent control point out that if rents are prevented from increasing, property owners will reduce the housing stock. The housing supply

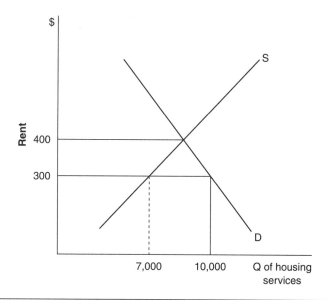

Figure 10.4   Rent Control

NOTE: The controlled rent of $700 per month will result in a shortage of 300 units of housing services.

will shrink until the supply is consistent with the lower-than-market rents. Mechanisms for decreasing the quantity of housing services include (1) reducing maintenance levels, (2) abandonment, (3) providing fewer amenities, and (4) lower rates of new housing construction.

Furthermore, the problem of rationing will remain. If rents are below the equilibrium, building managers will have to select among potential tenants. Criteria for choosing which tenants will occupy below-market-rent properties could include race or a willingness to pay kickbacks to the managers (an under-the-table means of raising rents).

Measures to skirt the intent of rent controls may also be attempted. Landlords may convert rental units to condominiums or tear down a building that is under rent control to construct a building that is either not subject to controls or subject to a less restrictive set of controls. Instances of property owners deliberately cutting heat or vandalizing their own buildings to encourage tenants to leave have been reported.

INCOME SUPPORT VERSUS HOUSING ASSISTANCE

One of the classic arguments in welfare economics is whether individuals would be better off receiving cash grants or assistance in kind of equal value. This question has been raised regarding whether cash should be given to poor families rather than giving them housing assistance. The conventional wisdom is that cash is preferable to in-kind assistance because, at the very least, the recipient would spend the full cash amount on the housing and be equally well-off with cash or the in-kind assistance. If only part of the cash were spent on housing and the rest spent on other things, the evidence of the choice is that the recipient would prefer less housing and more of other things that cash buys. Evidence indicates that if most families are given an extra amount of money to spend on housing, they will substitute some of their housing assistance for other things.

The rebuttal to the superiority of cash transfers argument is that while individuals may know what is best for them, they may not know what is best for society. Substandard housing has significant negative externalities. Housing assistance may not only house individuals better but also alleviate street crime, arson, visual pollution, and so forth. Thus, aid designed to alleviate housing conditions is intended to help ameliorate problems in the larger society as well as provide benefits directly to the recipients.

SUPPLY- VERSUS DEMAND-SIDE ASSISTANCE

A related debate concerns whether housing assistance should be provided by increasing the housing stock or by providing low-income families with the means to rent better housing through vouchers or other types of assistance.

One advantage of increasing the stock of low-income housing is that the construction or rehabilitation of low-income housing units will create additional jobs, albeit temporary jobs. Increases in housing supply will also reduce rents throughout the area, indirectly assisting others. Providing assistance directly to individuals so that they can buy better housing is demand-side assistance. Because demand-side assistance allows individuals to use the existing housing stock, it is generally cheaper than relying on new construction and allows recipients access to more choices.

GHETTO DISPERSAL VERSUS GHETTO IMPROVEMENT

The problem of housing segregation has led many policymakers to argue that policies should strive to disperse large ethnic populations. If assisted housing were more integrated, minority groups could be better integrated into society. Enforcement of fair housing laws has been the primary tool to encourage dispersal of minority populations. Provision of housing assistance in the form of new construction or subsidies for renting existing housing are also tools for housing integration.

An alternative policy approach has been termed *the gilded ghetto*. Some minorities may shun integration. Integration is sometimes seen as a threat to a group's culture. Furthermore, dispersal of minority populations throughout the metropolitan area would likely dilute a group's political strength. Assuming that voters are more likely to vote for someone of the same background, some minorities' strength would have a difficult time being elected or otherwise generating support for their issues if political strength were diluted across a large area.

DWELLING UNIT VERSUS NEIGHBORHOOD DEVELOPMENT

Closely related to the previous issue is the question of whether the focus of policies should be to improve the house or to improve the neighborhoods in which the low-income families live. The condition of housing units among the poor communities has improved dramatically in many places, yet there has been little improvement in the public perception of the "problem" of slums. The home itself may be but a small part of the environment. Social programs to eliminate crime, provide recreation, and clean up neighborhoods may be equally important to the quality of shelter.

Linkage Between Local Housing and Global Financial Markets

Three markets influence housing conditions and affordability. The first market involves the sale of the property itself. Second is the primary mortgage market. This market provides property buyers with loans needed to finance homes and other real estate purchases. If loans were unavailable, available only at high-interest rates, or subject to other strict terms, the market for property sales would experience price declines. Third is the secondary market. Primary market lenders (sometimes called originators) frequently bundle mortgages into multimillion dollar packages and resell them to international financial intermediaries such as life insurance companies, pension funds, and other institutions. The transactions in the secondary market provide liquidity to primary mortgage lenders, which in turn supports the housing market. At the same time, values established in the real property market influence the value of securities and stock held by global financial institutions since the real assets are the security for the financial assets. Thus, neighborhood housing is tied to international financial markets. Figure 10.5 illustrates the participants in each of the three markets and the benefits to the parties.

Retail and Commercial Neighborhoods

Commercial development is also part of neighborhood development. Observers say that "retail follows rooftops," suggesting that retail establishments

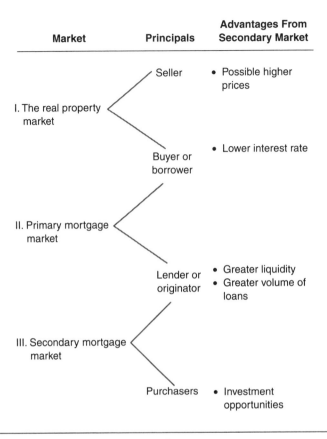

Figure 10.5   The Three Real Estate Markets

NOTE: The three real estate markets interact. Consequently, the secondary market may generate benefits and risks in the real property market.

emerge to serve expanding markets. But there is also a reverse causality. A weak or declining cluster of neighborhood retail stores will make areas less attractive to potential residents and contribute to further neighborhood decline.

Declining retail activity can spill over into neighborhood decline in several ways. First, retail activities are amenities that people value when selecting a home. The type of commercial activity contributes to the character and image of nearby housing. Commercial strips and malls are often "gateways" to residential areas, so a deteriorated retail area will contribute to a negative perception. In addition, the cost of travel for shopping purposes, while not as high as travel for jobs, can be significant and will increase as transportation costs increase. The decline of retail shopping in CBDs has detracted from the appeal of downtowns as residential areas. Furthermore, the closure of neighborhood businesses results in neighborhood job loss. Even small commercial strips can be an important employment center in some small neighborhoods.

Medical researchers have found that the lack of medical facilities (including pharmacies) is detrimental to the health of residents in the underserved areas. *Food deserts* is a term used to describe areas lacking nearby supermarkets that sell competitively priced fruit and vegetables (Powell, Slater, Mirtcheva, Bao, & Chaloupka, 2007). Often, neighborhoods lacking groceries have an abundance of fast-food outlets. The combination of inadequate supermarkets and a plethora of fast food contributes to an unhealthy lifestyle.

Retail revitalization has been shown to lead neighborhood regeneration (Lowe, 2005). Local economic development (LED) officials have intervened to strengthen retail neighborhoods expecting to encourage development. Commercial revitalization programs target particular retail areas in a coordinated way. Such programs often work through a neighborhood merchant association. Grants, loans, and infrastructure improvement are tools used to provide a "face-lift." Some owners of commercial properties have worked with government officials to form special tax districts whereby higher tax payments are linked to direct benefits to the district.

Retail businesses may eschew some poor neighborhoods because of the methods they use to identify markets. Many chain retailers and franchise businesses rely on nationally calibrated customer profiles in selecting sites. Retailers may apply their national profiles in selecting sites, causing them to overlook areas with atypical demographic profiles. These profiles may cause them to overlook potential inner-city markets with a more diverse demographic composition. For example, income is often underreported for low-income people (International Council of Shopping Centers and Business for Social Responsibility, 2001–2002). Many low-income areas have very high spending per acre due to high population density so that they may be good business locations even though they have low per capita spending. Also, many poor families depend on income earned in off-the-books employment. This unreported income will not be accounted in location decisions.

The Social Economy of Neighborhoods

Neighborhood residents, particularly those living in deteriorating or "left-behind" parts of the regional economy have created their own neighborhood-oriented development organizations. These organizations attempt to build neighborhoods from within. Among other tools, neighborhood development groups rely on nonprofit organizations and political activism.

COMMUNITY DEVELOPMENT CORPORATIONS

Community development corporations (CDCs) represent an important part of the social economy of neighborhoods. While there is no one, formal definition of a CDC, they are nonprofit enterprises that seek to improve neighborhood or small communities based on a three-pronged approach:

1. Increasing income and wealth or area residents

2. Improving the physical environment, especially the housing stock, public spaces, and the environment

3. Strengthening social capital, such as building networks, norms, and relationships

CDCs are characterized by a design to empower neighborhood residents and seek to be "grassroots" oriented.

Typical CDCs are initially capitalized by governments, foundations, and private investors. These institutions are sources of continuing funding as well. In addition to grants, CDCs are dependent on earnings from the projects they operate. CDCs have had positive impacts. They can "start a chain reaction of investment that leads to dramatic improvements to neighborhoods" (Galster, Levy, Sawyer, Temkin, & Walker, 2005). Increasing property values are used as an indication of neighborhood improvement, and many CDC activities are focused directly on housing improvements. Success in job training, job creation, and commercial development has also been demonstrated by some CDC (Williamson, Imbroscio, & Alperovitz, 2002).

A representative CDC project might be the revitalization of the housing stock in a particular small neighborhood. Drawing on their initial capital, perhaps supplemented by bank loans, government grants, or private investors, the CDC would purchase some dilapidated or abandoned housing. The houses would be restored, ideally using workers for the neighborhood who receive training in the building trades as well as compensation from the work. When the houses are sold or rented the revenues can be used for another project. When CDCs lose money on the projects, the capital stock dwindles. When projects are "profitable," additional community projects can be financed.

Critics of CDCs contend that the drive to maintain or increase the capital base has detracted from another important goal—community empowerment. Even though CDCs are nonprofit organizations, the extent to which they can operate unprofitably (by getting grants) is very limited. Individuals and organizations that help capitalize CDC—financial organizations, foundations, and corporations—are sometimes disproportionately represented on boards. Some critics contend that leaders of CDCs become part of the "establishment," making deals that benefit development interests at the expense of community empowerment goals, while grassroots representatives are sometimes excluded.

The concept of positive neighborhood changes can be so ambiguous that sometimes direct financial gain is favored over abstract goals like "participation." Increases in property values are one way to measure neighborhood improvement. If improvements in one neighborhood are not offset by value declines elsewhere, then they reflect positive impacts.

Conflicts among various groups in a neighborhood are reflected by considering renters and owners. A renter may have initially selected an area because it provided the right combination of amenities, access, and rent. After a successful revitalization program, property values and rents will increase. Thus, the renter will no longer have the optimum housing choice and may have to relocate. The process by which in extreme circumstances low-income populations are replaced by higher-income groups is dubbed "gentrification." Even property owners may be forced to leave an improving neighborhood as prices increase. However, property owners can sell their homes and capture the impact of property value increases unlike renters.

COOPERATIVES

Cooperatives are another form of place-based ownership. Cooperatives represent groups of people who voluntarily come together to pursue economic and/or social goals. Consumer-owned cooperatives provide goods and services to their members. A cooperative may charge a "membership fee" or require an in-kind contribution such as a few hours of work per month. In exchange, members of the consumer cooperative receive the benefits of the organization's bargaining power and operating efficiencies in the form of lower prices or distributions of "dividends." Consumer cooperatives are scattered in retail grocery, housing provisions, and health care. Cooperatives have addressed the problem of food deserts in some urban neighborhoods. Like CDCs, consumer cooperatives generally seek to build a sense of community and grassroots participation in the areas they serve.

COMMUNITY GARDENS

A discussion of innovative neighborhood socioeconomic institutions would be incomplete without a reference to community gardens. Community gardens are normally organized by nonprofit groups or governments. They divide small plots of urban land among a group of individuals. For instance, a 5-acre plot may be broken up into 1/16–acre gardens, and individuals from surrounding areas cultivate their individual plots. The community garden association may provide land only, or they may provide seeds, tools, a watering service, or other needs. Urban neighborhoods that have experienced population declines often have pockets of land that could become eyesores if not for urban gardens.

While many individuals see gardening as a nice hobby, most community garden advocates believe that the value of what can be produced, even on a very small tract of land, will substantially increase a family's real income. Furthermore, community garden associations help solidify neighborhood identity and impart values of sustainability.

Summary

Livable neighborhoods contribute to a community's quality of life and, hence, can be an important LED tool. Housing conditions are a big part of creating a livable local environment. The housing market can be analyzed using traditional supply and demand concepts. However, care must be taken to understand what the supply and price represent. It is useful to describe the quantity axis as "units of housing services" rather than a physical quantity. Price may be expressed as sales price of a stock of housing or as rent for a periodic flow of housing services. By discounting the present value of rents, one can convert between rents and sale prices.

Real estate markets are imperfect, characterized by few buyers and sellers and imperfect information. Consequently, bargaining is an important part of real estate transactions, and specialists are needed to assist buyers and sellers. There is also a range of uncertainty regarding price.

The hedonic pricing model splits the housing service bundle into detailed components and uses statistical techniques such as regression to value each of the components. Characteristics that affect price include features of the property itself as well as characteristics of the surrounding area. The market comparison approach is a "quick and dirty" application of the hedonic pricing method.

LED is often practiced at the neighborhood level. Five complementary models of neighborhood formation were described. According to the filtering model, as incomes rise, upper-income groups tend to purchase new housing on the urban periphery. The vacated houses become available to lower-income groups. The trade-off model emphasizes the space versus access trade-off. As incomes increase, the pull of cheaper space near the urban fringe increases more than the pull toward the CBD due to the desire for better access. Social forces contribute to the cultural agglomeration model. The Tiebout model describes the process in which individuals "vote with their feet" to live in the neighborhood that provides the best combination of housing unit, neighborhood amenities, public services, and housing prices. Improvements in neighborhood amenities, public services, and taxes become capitalized into property values. The aggregate economic fall-out model links neighborhood change to larger economic changes.

Low-income housing is an issue faced by economic developers. Related issues include (1) rent control versus market forces, (2) income support versus housing assistance, (3) supply versus demand assistance, (4) ghetto dispersal versus gilding, and (5) dwelling unit versus neighborhood development.

Through the sales and resales of mortgages, local real estate markets are linked to global financial markets. The need to strengthen commercial establishments is closely associated with neighborhood development. A strong retail sector can anchor a neighborhood and make it more attractive to residents. A neighborhood characterized by a weak retail sector can be a sign of neighborhood decline and detrimental to LED. Also, building the social economy—institutions with an economic function that have a social orientation—contributes to neighborhood development.

11

Poverty and Lagging Regions

Poverty reduction is an economic development goal with important spatial dimensions. Globally, poor countries tend to cluster in the Southern Hemisphere. Countries that are rather rich have less affluent regions. Urban areas have poverty neighborhoods. These lagging areas are the focus of special local economic development policies.

The first section discusses the types of poverty and its concentration among certain groups. Next, the causes of poverty are considered, followed by a discussion of the relationship between poor areas and the larger economy. The final section analyzes key policy issues.

The Nature of Poverty

Poverty can be associated with personal characteristics of the poor such as laziness or ill health. It also can be traced to characteristics of the local environment. Often individual characteristics and location are difficult to disentangle because poor people tend to live in low-opportunity areas. The ability to address spatial concentrations of poverty is hindered by disagreements about what poverty is and who is affected.

CONCEPTUAL APPROACHES

Three major conceptual definitions of poverty are often discussed: (1) absolute deprivation, (2) culturally or socially determined deprivation, and (3) relative economic position.[1]

Absolute Deprivation

Absolute poverty is a concept in which a minimum real living standard is established and anyone falling below that level is considered poor. When the focus of analysis is on absolute poverty, the poverty line should not change except to account for price changes. Individuals favoring the absolute concept believe it is the most clear-cut definition of poverty.

The official definition of poverty used in the United States is known as the Orshansky index named after the developer, Mollie Orshansky of the Social Security Administration. It is an absolute standard calculated as follows:

1. The U.S. Department of Agriculture determined the cost of an "economy food plan." It was the cost of foods that offered some variety and provided a balanced diet at a minimum cost for families suffering temporary financial hardship. It was a no-frills food budget. The cost of the economy food plan was calculated for various family sizes.

2. Since the average poor family spent about one third of their income on food, the cost of the economy food plan was multiplied by 3 to give the poverty income cutoff. Adjustments are made for family size and for farm families that grow some of their own food. In 1963, this figure was slightly more than $3,000 for a family of two adults and two children.

3. Each year, the poverty cutoff is revised to account for changes in the cost of living. In the United States the poverty line for a traditional family of four was $20,444 in 2006.

The official poverty line is considered an absolute poverty measure because, once set, it is adjusted only for inflation so it reflects constant purchasing power but it is not devoid of cultural influence. Establishing the poverty line at three times the minimum food budget reflected cultural standards and political considerations at the time. The portion of family income spent on food falls as income increases. Therefore, if the poverty line had been established in a period when families spent a higher portion of their income on food and then adjusted only for inflation, the poverty line would be lower than it is today. Conversely, if the same conceptual approach were used today, the threshold would be higher.

The World Bank also uses an absolute measure of poverty, known as the "$1 a day" standard. Thus, anyone earning less than $1 a day falls below the poverty line. The standard was developed in 1990 and has been adjusted to account for changes in the value of the dollar (measured as purchasing power). The fact that the bundle of goods consumers buy significantly varies among countries makes international comparisons problematic.

Sociocultural Poverty

An alternative approach is to base the poverty level on social norms at a given time and place. Individuals favoring cultural definitions of poverty point out that socially acceptable living standards change, so poverty definitions should reflect contemporary standards. Unfortunately, definitions that change with time and place make comparisons less useful. Thus, it is not a good standard for measuring progress. Also, a consensus about where the sociocultural poverty line is drawn will be problematic. In this regard, a culturally flexible standard of poverty sufficient to allow an individual to participate in "normal social life" has been proposed (Harrington, 1984). Inability to afford birthday parties for children, an occasional recreational event, cable TV, some new clothes, and education might be indicators of poverty in the United States.

The Gallup polling organization has operationalized a cultural definition of poverty. They regularly ask, "What is the minimum amount of money a family of four needs to get along in our community?" In 2006 the average response was "Over $50,000"—well above the Orshansky indicator.

The social/cultural definition of poverty is also reflected in the concept of the living wage. Many observers argue that a wage should be sufficient to keep a normal family above the poverty line with only one member working full time.

Relative Poverty

Some economists are concerned about relative poverty—the condition of the poorest portion of the population. Economists who focus on relative poverty are in fact concerned about the distribution of income. Increases in the proportion of total national income accruing to individuals in the bottom 20% would indicate reductions in poverty under this standard. An advantage of a relative definition of poverty is that it reflects the fact that individuals tend to feel poor when they are poor in comparison with others. "Happiness studies" indicate that a person's relative place in the income hierarchy affects the subjective feeling of happiness.

Critics of purely relative definitions of poverty contend that it confuses the concept of poverty with inequality and that it is logically impossible to eliminate a portion of the income distribution. There will always be a lowest 20%. However, a relative poverty definition has been used to target grants to poor areas or population groups. Thus, relative income definitions can be useful in policy implementation.

Each of the three concepts of poverty provides a different perspective, but they are not necessarily inconsistent with each other. Initially, all three definitions could coincide. However, over time, they will probably diverge. For example, suppose that in the early 1970s, $5,000 represented the threshold income for absolute, culturally determined, and relative poverty. Over time, however, average incomes increase as would the income of those in the lowest one fifth of the distribution. How the social threshold will change cannot be determined theoretically, but evidence indicates that perceptions about what it takes to participate in society will increase as average income's increase. The absolute poverty line, however, which may have been culturally influenced when it was set, will remain fixed. Therefore, a gap between the absolute definition and other poverty thresholds will increase.

Other Poverty Metrics

The study of poverty is complicated by various definitions of income. For instance, should income before or after taxes be the standard? How should the imputed value of assets such as houses and cars be treated? What about income from social programs or medical expenses? If an individual becomes ill and receives, say, $170,000 in medical care, most of us would not consider that person rich! Table 11.1 shows the distribution of income in the United States under four alternative definitions.

Poverty definitions are based on income. Wealth also influences the popular concept of poverty. Income is a flow of money, whereas wealth represents a stock of spending power that may be used in the future. In some cases, low-income individuals may be wealthy, but generally low-income families have low wealth. The lack of wealth makes living on a low income much more difficult because poor families have nothing to fall back on in the event of an emergency. For instance, someone with no wealth may be unable to fix their car if it breaks. Lacking transportation, he or she may lose a job. A person with

Table 11.1   Share of Aggregate Household Income by Quintile: 2005

Quintile	Money Income[a]	Market Income[b]	Post-Social-Insurance Income[c]	Disposable Income[d]
Lowest	3.42	1.50	3.24	4.42
Second	8.79	7.26	8.59	9.86
Third	14.42	14.00	14.33	15.33
Fourth	23.03	23.41	22.80	23.11
Highest	50.34	53.83	51.03	47.28

a. All cash income before taxes; excludes capital gains and lump sum payments.

b. Deducts government cash transfers from money income; includes imputed rental income and subtracts some imputed work expenses.

c. Adds non-means-tested government programs such as social security to market income.

d. Post-social-insurance income less taxes plus nontax transfers.

equal income but with enough wealth to pay for car repairs may keep the job and maybe rise to be president of the company.

DEMOGRAPHICS OF POVERTY

It is important to distinguish between the *incidence* of poverty and the portion of a poverty population with certain characteristics. For instance, the incidence of poverty is very high among unemployed workers. However, only about 20% of the poor are unemployed. A group that is a very small portion of the total population will normally represent only a small portion of the poverty population, yet a high parentage of persons in that group may be poor. This section focuses primarily on groups with high incidences of poverty.

Who Are the Poor?

Table 11.2 is a basis for understanding which groups tend to be poor in the United States. One characteristic that stands out is that the incidence of poverty is particularly high for female-headed households. The high poverty rate among females also contributes to the high childhood poverty rates. Observers have used the phrase "feminization of poverty" to describe the fact that nearly 30% of all female-headed households are below the poverty line and nearly three fourths of all are adult women or children.

In contrast to female-headed households, married couples have very low poverty rates. Family breakups are strongly associated with an increasing incidence of poverty. However, the relationship between family dissolution and poverty may be a chicken–and–egg problem. Lack of money is a source of marital tension, and economic difficulties often contribute to divorce or desertion.

Minorities, particularly blacks and Hispanics, are another demographic group with a high incidence of poverty. Because ethnic groups tend to live in racially segregated neighborhoods, the association between ethnicity and poverty is particularly visible in urban places where poor ethnic neighborhoods are an important factor in big city politics and tend to be the location of significant concentrations of other urban pathologies such as crime, school dropouts, vandalism, and so forth.

A disproportionate number of the poor population has health-related problems that limit their ability to participate in the labor market. Some health problems are visible, such as being confined to a wheelchair, but other problems are more subtle. Mental problems such as mentioned twice alcoholism and depression will inhibit work but may go undetected and untreated. Health and poverty may form a vicious cycle. A poor person may be unable to afford medical attention, which, in turn, may aggravate existing problems.

Table 11.2   U.S. Poverty Rates: 2005

Total	Percent Poor
White, not Hispanic	8.3
Black	24.7
Asian	10.9
Hispanic	21.8
People in families with no husband	31.1
Married couple families	5.3
Male	11.1
Female	14.1
Central-city resident	17.5
Non–central city	9.1
Nonmetropolitan	14.2
Children below 6	20.0
Children below 18	17.6
Age 65 and older	10.1
Families with at least one worker	7.3
Families with no worker	27.7

SOURCE: U.S. Census Bureau, "Historical Data," retrieved from www.census.gov/hhes/www/
poverty/histppov/histpovtb.html

The working poor have been described as a "large at-risk population . . . composed of unskilled, low-paid workers who are one recession, one illness, one accident away from being poor" (Harrington, 1984). While families with at least one worker have a below-average poverty rate, more than half of all poor families have at least one member who works some of the time during the year. Such families are poor because of unemployment, underemployment, employment at low wages, or illnesses that prevent full-time work. The escape rate for the working poor is high because they are able to take advantage of job market opportunities. However, escaping poverty does not preclude a lapse back into poverty.

The working poor present a challenge to rich countries because the working poor are generally viewed as doing what is expected—working hard and playing by the rules. If the economic system fails them, the problem may be with the economic system, not the persons themselves.

Income Mobility

Identification of the poor is complicated by income mobility, particularly among families near the poverty threshold. Poverty rates represent the average portion of individuals who are poor during the year. A poverty rate of 10% does not mean that the same 10% of the population are poor for their entire lives or even for the entire year. In fact, for many families, poverty status is temporary. Income mobility is particularly great among the poor who are willing and able to work because employment is associated with an increase in income.

If poverty represented a temporary condition that changes as people progress through different life stages, it would be of less concern than if poverty were permanent. Evidence indicates that many individuals do move among categories in different stages of life. But poor persons tend to move from poor to near-poor and back to poor in a cycle that prevents wealth accumulation. Changes in family status such as marriage or employment status are key determinants of income mobility. Changes in the national and local economy are also important in moving families out of poverty.

In contrast to individuals with income mobility, other persons may be poor their entire lives. Individuals who are permanently very poor are often referred to as the underclass. People in this category tend to be isolated from mainstream culture. Recent observation suggests that the rate of income mobility may be slowing.

Spatial Concentrations of Urban Poverty

Low-income families benefit significantly from aggregate economic growth. However, some areas are bypassed as the larger economy prospers. This section examines the nature of the relationships between poor areas and the larger economies of which they are a part.

REGIONAL LINKAGES: THE SPREAD AND BACKWASH EFFECTS

Myrdal (1957) pioneered the analysis of the relationship between rich and poor areas. Although his work was concerned with large regions rather than neighborhoods, it provides a foundation for understanding relationships between urban neighborhoods and metropolitan areas. Myrdal's concept was that the benefits poor regions receive from proximity to prosperous regions depend on two competing forces transmitted through the market. *Spread effects* reflect linkages that cause development in prosperous areas to spread into lagging areas. *Backwash effects* reflect factors that cause lagging regions to fall further behind. Spread effects imply a positive association between the poor area's growth and that of the prosperous area. The backwash effect suggests that the prosperous regions take resources from the lagging region. Thus, the faster the prosperous regions grow, the slower the lagging regions grow.

The spread effect operates through arbitrage. For instance, marginal productivity (and hence the rate of return) of capital may fall in the advanced region with abundant capital. As a result, investors will seek opportunities in capital poor areas. Hill and Wolman (1997) describe another, probably stronger, spread effect that operates through labor markets. As employment increases in the prosperous regions, employers seek to hire more workers without increasing wages. Hence, they may attempt to attract workers from labor surplus areas either by encouraging the workers to move to the prosperous areas or by moving businesses to the labor surplus area.

The backwash effect reflects the tendency of resources to flow to prosperous areas. For instance, investor's expectations may be more optimistic about new enterprises in growing areas. Workers may migrate to fast-growing areas, creating brain drains. Thus, sometimes the lagging regions may be harmed by proximity to a prosperous area.

EMPIRICAL STUDIES OF SPATIAL LINKAGES

Studies have employed regression analysis to examine the relationship between lagging regions and other areas. Figure 11.1 illustrates the nature of three possible relationships. In Figure 11.1a, no consistent relationship appears between changes in the welfare indicators such as income or employment in the benchmark economy and similar changes in the poverty region. This empirical relationship is consistent with the theory that what happens in the prosperous region does not alter conditions in the lagging region. There may be no linkages between the two economies, or the lack of a consistent relationship might reflect offsetting spread and backwash effects. In contrast, a strong, positive relationship between changes in welfare indicators in the two areas is shown in Figure 11.1b. Figure 11.1b is consistent with a strong spread effect—prosperity in the affluent area spreads to poor areas. Conversely, Figure 11.1c would be consistent with a strong backwash effect. Prosperity in the advanced area is associated with welfare decline in the lagging area.

Good empirical studies have generally included more than two variables as shown in Figure 11.1 in an effort to "hold other things constant." Nevertheless,

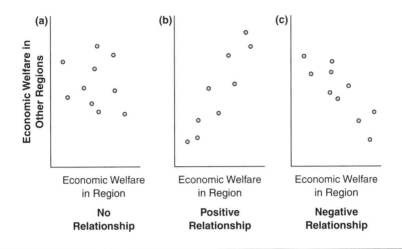

Figure 11.1   Possible Relationships Between Growing and Lagging Regions

NOTE: The correlations between changes in prosperity indicators in one regions and another may indicate whether growth transmission mechanisms are weak or strong. Most areas are positively linked with the surrounding region (b). However, some persistently poor areas may lack such ties and, therefore, not prosper as the rest of the area develops (a).

this approach has been employed to examine whether the welfares of various regions are tied together.

Generally, improvements in national welfare are associated with improvements among the poor, as indicated by Figure 11.1b. Positive correlations between improvements in metropolitan welfare indicators and improvements in central city welfare (Hill, Wolman, & Ford, 1995; Ledebur and Barnes, 1993; Voith, 1992) have been described. These associations are consistent with the idea that the lagging areas have important linkages with the prosperous areas in the suburbs. The findings have led some observers to conclude that cities and suburbs should cooperate with each other to ensure mutual development. However, extremely poor neighborhoods in urban areas do not appear to be linked economically with their metropolitan region (Blair & Carroll, 2007). Figure 11.1a best describes this relationship.

Correlation between one area's welfare and that of another does not prove causation. Both outcomes might be influenced by the same underlying events. For instance, a good national governmental policy could have an independent effect on both regions. Furthermore, statistical evidence does not indicate the direction of the causation. Theory suggests that prosperity in one area might contribute to prosperity in another region, but the effects could be mutual or run in the opposite direction.

SPATIAL LINKAGES AND
THEORIES OF SPATIAL POVERTY

The statistical evidence indicates that growth is often successfully transmitted to lagging areas but not always. Some areas remain poor in spite of significant growth in other area economies. This section describes traditional theories of poverty and the implications these theories have for the ability to create linkages to the mainstream economy.

Human Capital and Behavior

Human capital and behavioral theories of poverty recognize that lack of individual abilities and nontraditional behaviors create barriers to economic participation (Becker, 1975). Because there have been many studies among a variety of groups, locations, and time periods, the theories that cite lack of education or nonmainstream behaviors as contributing to poverty in neighborhoods are very powerful.

Education correlates with job success. However, education as measured by the number of years of schooling does not explain all the variation in earnings. Education is only a rough proxy for the ability to do a job. Individuals with the same number of years of education may have vastly different abilities. A high school diploma from a typical urban school is quite different from a similar diploma from a college preparatory, high-income suburban school diploma. In addition to education, "life skills," work experience, and other characteristics have been used as proxies for human capital (Wolaver & White, 2006).

Culture of poverty theories assert that educational deficits are only part of a larger complex of behavioral traits that perpetuate inner-city poverty. Linkages to mainstream behaviors such as dress, language, punctuality, and posture can greatly influence market acceptance. Behavioral deficits may be more difficult to change than education or skill levels because they are deeply ingrained. Moss and Tilly (2001), in a study of employment practices, conclude that "soft skills" may be a greater impediment to employment than concrete skills required for a job.

Observers claim that the poverty culture reflects reasonable adaptations to harsh economic realities and that faulting individuals for traits constitutes "blaming the victim." Nevertheless, these behaviors are impediments to attaining good jobs and help explain inner-city isolation (Ryan, 1976). Educational and hard skill deficits probably have cultural behaviors as roots, so the explanations are intertwined. Unfortunately, no one has disentangled the interaction between the two aspects that may prevent individuals living in low-income areas from getting jobs.

Inadequate work skills and nonmajority behaviors create deficits among residents of low-income areas that are significant and not easily remedied.

Employers may refuse to hire some inner-city workers even when no other workers apply or even at very low wages. As long as this barrier prevents populations living in inner-city neighborhoods from participating in the mainstream economy, inner-city neighborhoods will not benefit from mainstream economic growth. The relationship shown in Figure 11.1a will be descriptive.

Racial Discrimination

The most visible characteristic of poor, inner-city neighborhoods is that they are overwhelmingly African American. Race is so intertwined with other socioeconomic variables, including education, behavioral traits, and residential location, that it is difficult to disentangle the consequences of racial discrimination from other variables.

Direct racial discrimination is a barrier that can be overcome only by societal change rather than behavior changes on the part of the minority individual. Removal of other barriers to economic integration will be of limited value if racial barriers remain. Statistical and "matched pair" evidence exists showing racial discrimination persists. Theories of racial discrimination explain both segregated neighborhoods and poor education. However, the perspective fails to explain why some middle-class African American neighborhoods have strong ties to the dominant economy while others do not. To explain the persistence of poverty in inner-city neighborhoods but not in other predominantly black neighborhoods, direct prejudice theories need to be combined with other theories of spatial poverty.

The stronger the racial bias, the less likely it is that the "taste for discrimination" can be overcome and the less likely it is that those inner-city areas with largely black populations will benefit fully in regional expansions. Thus, if the barrier is strong, a weak or nil relationship between regional expansions and prosperity in black areas can be anticipated.

Spatial Mismatch

Another set of ideas about the causes of inner-city poverty is the existence of a mismatch between jobs and residential location (Kain, 1968). The spatial mismatch theory suggests that jobs are located in areas inaccessible to residents of inner-city neighborhoods. For instance, housing segregation often results in blacks living in poor inner-city areas that are inaccessible to jobs being created in the fast-growing suburbs. Therefore, African Americans have few opportunities to participate in the metropolitan economy. The spatial mismatch hypothesis has been frequently tested and found valid.

An important question in the spatial mismatch literature is "How much of the difference in earning is attributable to where blacks live and how much is attributable to being black?" Studies have tried to control for race and other determinants of employment to isolate the effects of location. They suggest that race may be a more important factor than space but inner-city locations are also an impediment to earnings.

Inner-city residence probably hinders integration into the metropolitan economy in several ways: (a) distance from a job and lack of access to public transportation increase the cost of applying for a job; (b) high travel costs reduce the benefits of having a job; (c) information about jobs is more difficult to obtain for workers in inner-city areas; (d) students in low-income areas often have lower educational attainment, and therefore, residential location probably correlates with human capital and behavioral deficits; and (e) employers discriminate against inner-city residents on the basis of their address or zip code.

The mismatch perspectives suggest that potential linkages between inner-city areas and the rest of the metropolis exist. However, residential isolation coupled with the lack of transportation, spatially biased information flows, and inadequate public service provision (particularly education) prevent individuals in poor neighborhoods from taking full advantage of metropolitan opportunities. The more difficult the barriers are to overcome, the more likely it is that there will be no or a very weak association between economic changes in metropolitan areas and similar changes in inner cities.

Selective Migration

Suppose regional expansion results in out-migration of individuals with good jobs and with the greatest capabilities of getting jobs in prosperous sectors. Inner cities are often "points of departure" for families moving up the economic ladder. Upwardly mobile residents benefit from this process, but other neighborhood residents who cannot leave may be harmed (Teitz & Chapple, 1998, p. 51).

Neighborhood residents with jobs or other linkages to metropolitan networks are likely to have more social capital than economically isolated residents (Putnam, 1993). As better-connected residents leave poor neighborhoods, linkages with the mainstream economy are also lost. The exit of individuals with connections to the metropolitan information network is likely to result in diminished employment and other information for those left behind. Out-migration may result in social isolation, weakened role models, and departure from dominant behavioral norms, exacerbating nonmainstream behaviors (Wilson, 1985). Neighborhoods can also lose links to important political institutions as out-migration reduces social cohesion.

Over a long time period, selective migration may result in increasing isolation of the neighborhood from the metropolitan economy. Selective migration is a "backwash" effect; accordingly, we might anticipate a negative association between metropolitan expansion and neighborhood income in the short run (see Figure 11.1c) and an exacerbation of economic isolation in the long run.

Inadequate Internal Development

Rather than highlighting barriers that prevent residents of poor neighborhoods from building connections to the mainstream economy, endogenous growth theorists emphasize the inability of poor neighborhoods to generate local businesses. In this case, poverty is attributed to too few neighborhood jobs and other opportunities.

Inadequate internal development may also be traced to a lack of linkages with the metropolitan economy. Metropolitan institutions may fail to reach into poor neighborhoods. Barriers to business formation include fear, lack of transportation, and cultural differences that hinder entrepreneurs and financial institutions from investing. Weak linkages with educational institutions, business development organizations, marketing agencies, and other support organizations may also hinder internal development.

To the extent that poor neighborhoods do not experience sufficient business formations and investments during growth periods, they will not fully benefit from metropolitan expansion. Furthermore, a lack of business development implies that even if poor residents attain jobs outside the area during periods of regional prosperity, the neighborhood will not experience the full spending or multiplier effects. Thus, any positive benefit to poor neighborhoods from regional growth is likely to be weaker than might otherwise be the case.

Accommodations to Capitalism

The radical or Marxist perspective views ghetto areas as spatial accommodations to the processes of capital accumulation (Harvey, 1976). The capitalist system determines a division of labor that, in turn, supports a geographic pattern of economic activity. The poor serve an important function in capitalism: They are the reserve army of the unemployed. Ghettos are the places where they live.

Although most perspectives regard poor neighborhoods as economically dysfunctional, the Marxist view assigns such places an important function. The residents keep wages from increasing. The availability of inner-city labor will prevent region-wide wages from rising significantly when labor markets tighten. In this view, poor areas may be strongly integrated with the mainstream economy and the capitalistic system, but those links do not contribute to inner-city prosperity. If linkages function as the theory suggests, regionwide expansion will increase jobs for inner-city residents. Unfortunately, employment slowdowns in a region will disproportionately disadvantage residents of poor neighborhoods: last hired, first fired. Marxist theories suggest significant linkages that will transmit growth to poorer places resulting in the kind of relationship depicted in Figure 11.1b.

Policy Issues

The numerous plausible and supportable theories explaining the existence of poor areas in the midst of prosperous regions suggest that spatial poverty is likely to be caused by a variety of factors. This section examines policy approaches to both individual poverty and lagging regions.

STRENGTHENING LINKAGES

Efforts to tie lagging regions to prosperous ones are evolving. Many local economic developers are addressing employment problems through direct linkage programs or provisional government incentives. Public officials negotiate agreements with private employers to hire local residents, often in return for development subsidies, zoning considerations, or other government incentives. Enterprise zones are areas where businesses have been encouraged to locate. Usually, direct linkage agreements do not require that particular persons be hired but only that area residents be considered or interviewed. In general, assessments of direct linkage programs have demonstrated good placement records, but they have not been applied on a large scale.

Rather than focusing on direct linkage policies, several observers have suggested building bridges between neighborhoods and economic organizations in the region. Porter (1997) feels that a sustainable inner-city economy can only prosper if it is based on "private, for-profit initiatives, and investments based on economic self-interest and genuine competitive advantage instead of artificial inducements, government mandates, or charity" (p. 24). He also argues that inner-city areas have major competitive advantages, including (a) a location near the heart of the region, (b) access to major regional clusters, (c) significant neighborhood demand that is being satisfied elsewhere, and (d) outstanding human resources. Impediments to exploiting these advantages can be overcome by better communication and information flows between inner-city representatives and business and political leaders.

Nowak (1997), a community development practitioner, feels that some local advocators have been too concerned with problems of housing and constituent service as economic development strategies. Consequently, poor areas have become detached from metropolitan "centers of job generation." Neighborhood business development should be "viewed as part of a chain leading to external [regional, not neighborhood] employment and business opportunities" (p. 7).

Incorporation of underground activities into the regional economy may also help integrate neighborhoods. To the extent that underground businesses must remain "underground," they are denied access to mainstream economic resources (Blair & Endres, 1994). Accordingly, economic development officials may want to attempt to bring businesses and talented entrepreneurs into the mainstream economy so that ties with the metropolitan areas can be developed.

In the future, scholarly efforts directed toward understanding the evolution of market linkages will be useful. The assumption is often made that if benefits can be gained by establishing relationships between economic institutions, linkages will almost automatically evolve to capture potential gains. A more comprehensive perspective, however, should acknowledge the importance of a social foundation to support the development of economic ties. Such a perspective should contribute to understanding how both market and nonmarket institutions can be better integrated into neighborhoods.

IMPROVING PRODUCTIVITY

Conventional microeconomic theory leads to the conclusion that worker pay will be equal to the value of the marginal product in a well functioning competitive labor market. The value of the marginal product measures the amount of increased revenue to the firm from employing an additional worker. It is the value of the extra worker's contribution to a firm's revenues, holding other inputs constant. The concept may be expressed as

$$VMP_i = MP_i \times MR,$$

where VMP is the value of the marginal product of the ith worker, MP_i is the additional output produced by the ith worker (marginal product), and MR is the marginal revenue attributable to a unit of extra output.

Accordingly, if the ith worker caused output to increase by five units and each unit of additional output sold for $2, the VMP_i would be $10. A firm would lose money (and therefore not hire) if it paid a worker more than the VMP. That circumstance would mean that the cost of hiring the worker was higher than the resulting revenue. But firms would be willing to employ additional workers as long as the value of the marginal product exceeded the wage. This theoretical relationship is the linchpin that links low productivity to low earnings and poverty. If productivity increases, the VMP will increase.

Figure 11.2 illustrates a conventional view of how labor markets operate. The right-hand graph (b) depicts the aggregate supply and demand in the entire labor market, while the left-hand graph (a) depicts the situation for a single firm. The solid lines indicate conditions prior to any productivity improvements.

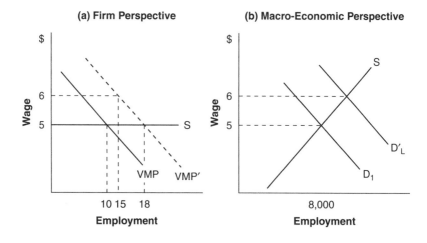

Figure 11.2   Productivity Increases: Single-Firm and Macroeconomic Perspectives

NOTE: If the productivity of a class of labor increases, the wage will increase depending on the elasticity of the aggregate labor supply (b). A single representative firm will consequently increase its demand for labor from VMP to VMP' and increase employment from 10 to 15.

The firm's VMP curve, in Figure 11.2a, represents the extra revenue that the firm could earn if it hired an additional worker, holding other inputs constant. The VMP is the firm's labor-demand curve. As the number of employees increases, the value of the marginal product will fall, for three possible reasons: (1) the law of diminishing marginal productivity states that after some point extra workers will contribute less to output than previously hired workers (remember, capital and land are held constant); (2) some producers may have to lower the product price in order to sell increase output; and (3) firms will hire the most productive workers first.

If the wage for the relevant class of workers is set by the market at $5 (see aggregate perspective in Figure 11.2b), the firm depicted in Figure 11.2a would hire no more than 10 workers because the 11th employee would increase revenue by less than the wage.

If the firm's productivity increase caused the VMP curve to shift upward to the right and the wage remained unchanged, the number of workers hired would increase from 10 to 18. This description could apply if the individual firm introduced a new method of production that causes the VMP of only its employees to increase. Note that the wage rate remained at $5, although more employees were hired. If the firm were a competitive employer in the labor market, its innovation would not significantly affect the overall demand, so it could hire as many workers as it wants at $5.

However, if the productivity of a whole class of workers increased, it would be improper to assume that the wage rate faced by the firm would remain unchanged. For instance, suppose all workers became better educated and more productive. The productivity increase of a whole class of workers would cause the aggregate demand for that type of labor to increase, as shown by the shift from D_L to D'_L in Figure 11.2b. Consequently, the wage rate would increase unless the aggregate labor supply was perfectly elastic. At the new, higher wage of $6, the firm would hire only 15 rather than 18 employees.

There are several ways in which individuals who improve their productivity will improve their labor market situation.

Productivity Directly Recognized

An employer or supervisor within the firm will recognize and reward an individual's productivity improvement. In this case, greater productivity will result in greater pay without changing jobs or job categories. When compensation is on a commission or piecework basis, this case often applies.

Productivity Facilitates Job Category Change

Workers within a particular class have similar skills and pay. If an individual's skills or productivity increases, he or she will move into another job class, such as from typist to secretary. The employee's wage in the new labor class will be higher than the wage being earned previously, reflecting the higher productivity.

Productivity Improves Place in Queue

Improved productivity will not affect an individual's particular class of labor or wage rate, but the more productive workers will be more likely to be hired early, and they will be among the last to be laid off. Hence, improved productivity may result in neither an increase in pay within a job class nor a change in job class. Nevertheless, productivity improvements may help an individual avoid the last-hired, first-fired syndrome.

Productivity Irrelevant

Some labor-market theorists believe that an individual's place in society is so constructed as to make pay impervious to productivity. Custom and tradition determine who is hired and what he or she is paid. A worker's productivity depends not so much on her or his personal skills but on the job she or he holds. According to this perspective, the job niche an individual fills determines the pay. Increases in productivity alone may not allow individuals to change their niche. For instance, jobs may have customary promotion and advancement ladders, and entry to a job ladder may require an appropriate social background. Even if individuals improve their productivity, increases in pay may be unlikely unless they are on an upward job ladder. Frequently, a college degree is required to get a job, although job duties may not require a college degree. The secondary labor market, where the poor and near-poor are confined, has few job ladders. Hence, productivity improvements do not lead to better pay within the job class. Furthermore, it is difficult to change job classes because of behavioral and other noneconomic requirements for jobs in the primary labor market.

ADDRESSING WAGE RIGIDITIES

Impediments to the movement of wages can contribute to unemployment and poverty. Frequently, high-paying occupations maintain above-equilibrium wages through union rules, institutional customs, or political muscle. To the extent that the poor are locked out of these jobs, poverty escape routes are limited.

Minimum-Wage Laws

Minimum-wage laws are sometimes cited as examples of labor-market imperfections that hurt employment prospects of the poor. However, whether minimum-wage laws hurt or help the poor is a matter of debate. To understand the issue, assume that only poor or near-poor workers have minimum-wage jobs. If the minimum wage were fixed by law at $6.00 per hour, then workers with productivity levels below that wage would be unemployed. Thus, lowering or abolishing minimum-wage laws would result in increased employment levels for such people.

However, many economists believe that a minimum wage increase may reduce poverty even as it decreases employment. An increase in the minimum wage has two important consequences: One would tend to hurt the poor and the other consequence would help the poor. First, individuals earning at or near the minimum-wage level could experience a decrease in income if they lose their job. Not all minimum-wage workers would lose their jobs, but some would. Second, those who maintain their jobs would experience an increase in income. The total impact of an increase in the minimum wage would depend on which of the two countervailing tendencies is greatest—the decline in employment or the increase in wages. The outcome, in turn, depends on how responsive employers' demand for labor is to a fall in the wage rate.

The impact of increasing the minimum wage can be analyzed with reference to Figure 11.3. Assume that only poverty-level families are affected by changes in the minimum wage. The total income of families at the market wage of $5.00 will be $5.00 times E. If a minimum wage of $6.00 is established, *total*

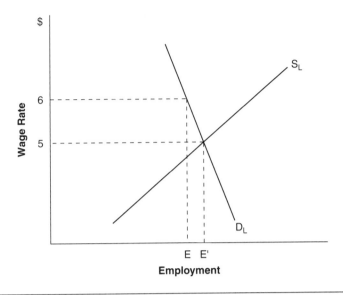

Figure 11.3   The Effect of Minimum Wage

NOTE: The effect of a decline in the minimum wage on the total wage bill depends on the responsiveness of the demand for labor to a drop in the wage.

wages may increase if employment declines are relatively small. Technically, if the demand for labor is inelastic, increases in the minimum wage will increase the total earning among that group.

Efficiency Wages and Other Wage Floors

Efficiency wages are wages that are deliberately kept above the equilibrium wage to provide employees with a reason not to shirk duties. Imagine a worker at the true equilibrium wage for a particular type of labor. What incentive would workers have to be on time, use company resources wisely, treat customers well, or otherwise go the extra mile? If they were fired, they could easily get a similar job since they were earning equilibrium wage. If, however, they were paid above the equilibrium wage, they would be concerned enough about keeping their job to apply extra effort—the above-equilibrium wage provides an incentive. One could even argue that jobs that give employees the most discretion will provide the greatest premiums above equilibrium to prevent misuse of that discretion.

The Harris-Todaro Model

Wages are supposed to encourage workers to migrate to areas where they are most needed or most productive. Rigidities can sometimes prevent wages from serving such a function and have perverse consequences for the national economy. Specifically, local development officials have been concerned that workers in agricultural regions, where their productivity is low, migrate to cities, where they become unemployed.

Compare metropolitan Area A with a $10 wage and an unemployment rate of 30% with rural Area B with a $5 wage and no unemployment. The expected wage is the wage times the probability of employment. Furthermore, let the probability of unemployment equal the unemployment rate. Therefore, the expected wage in A is $7 compared with $5 in B. It is perfectly rational to move from Region B to Region A. Migrants are willing to trade off the risk of unemployment against the potential for higher wages. The new migrant might find high wage employment but at the expense of another worker.

While the migration is rational from the worker's viewpoint, it is unproductive from the national perspective. The net result is movement from low productivity work to no work. This development pattern is particularly troublesome for many developing countries such as India, where migrants leave the rural areas for congested cities.

EMPLOYMENT GUARANTEE SCHEMES IN INDIA

India's economic development plans are strongly oriented toward assisting the poor, particularly in rural areas. Targeting the poor has been particularly difficult in rural areas because assistance to agricultural production may assist relatively wealthy landowners, and the poor benefit only through secondary or trickle-down mechanisms. In contrast, the Employment Guarantee Scheme in the Indian state of Maharashtra directly targets the rural poor. Similar programs exist in other Indian states. These programs are interesting because they reflect a popular belief that the government should serve as the "employer of last resort."

The heart of the program is a guarantee of employment to rural job seekers who are willing to do manual work on piece rate compensation. The manual work and low pay provide an incentive for program participants to seek jobs elsewhere. The piece rate compensation links pay to productivity and discourages shirking.

The program seeks to fund labor-intensive projects that create productive assets. Accordingly, irrigation systems, soil conservation efforts, wells, roads, and similar public works projects tend to be funded under the program. Participation in the program expanded during slack agricultural seasons, creating a countercyclical safety net. The overall design and oversight are at the state level, but there is significant local project planning and implementation. While the employment guarantee programs are generally considered effective, funding limitations prevent the programs from actually providing work for all who desire it, weakening the "guarantee."

Benefits of the Employment Guarantee Scheme are both direct and indirect. The most obvious source of assistance is the compensation paid to those employed in the Guaranteed Employment Scheme. Second, the poor benefit indirectly when the assets created improve agricultural productivity. Greater productivity may raise wages to agricultural workers. Also, the public infrastructure has directly improved the quality of life as, for example, when a well provided drinking water. Finally, as productivity is improved, individuals at all income levels will benefit because the entire economy will be more productive.

INCOME SUPPORT

Most antipoverty policies have emphasized improving the ability of individuals to earn income. However, some individuals may have no viable wage earner in the household: Therefore, transfers are their only source of income.

It is difficult to defend a sharp distinction between income-support programs and other governmental programs. All governmental programs support somebody's income. Numerous programs support middle- and upper-class families, including Social Security and Medicare, which help the elderly of all income levels. Unemployment compensation and agricultural subsidies assist the wealthy as well as the poor.

While antipoverty programs are intended to help poor persons, they also have strong constituencies among some producers. Medical programs support demand for medical services; food stamps (a program administered through the Department of Agriculture) support farmers and food prices; and housing programs (run primarily by the Department of Housing and Urban Development) benefit the construction industry. Middle-income families also benefit from income support programs. They provide a safety net and may relieve the burden of taking care of other family members, particularly parents. Political support from the nonpoor helps maintain assistance programs in tough budget battles. Income support programs are also important to the economy of many regions, especially low-income neighborhoods and retirement areas.

In-Kind Versus Cash Transfers

Economists have asked whether it is best to assist the poor by giving assistance in kind or money transfers of equal value. The traditional answer has been that cash transfers are preferable to in-kind support, assuming that (1) the recipients are knowledgeable about what brings them utility and (2) the purpose of the transfer is to increase the utility of the recipients. The argument in favor of cash transfers is as follows. Suppose a poor person received $100 worth of food. Assuming the cost of the food to society were $100, the government or grantor would be indifferent to the form of the cash or in-kind support. If transfer recipients received cash rather than $100 worth of commodities, they would either (1) spend all the cash on food or (2) spend it on other things, probably including some food. With the cash, recipients would be no worse than under the in-kind transfer program if they spent all their government support on food. If they had chosen to spend the cash support to purchase any other combination of goods, the choice suggests that it would make them better off than they would have been with $100 worth of food because that's what they selected.

Defenders of in-kind transfer programs suggest that some poor persons may not know how to manage their money and in-kind transfers may prevent spending on frivolities or harmful goods, particularly drugs, alcohol, and gambling. Second, governments may use poverty programs to achieve other goals. For instance, voters may feel better knowing that the poor have certain levels of food, housing, and medical care. They may not be concerned about the level of cable television.

Guaranteed Annual-Income Plans

Many observers have proposed guaranteed income plans as an antipoverty strategy. Initially, flat guaranteed-annual-income plans were proposed. A threshold level of income was set according to family size. If a family earned less than that amount, the federal government would transfer the difference to the family. The problem with this flat guaranteed income is that anyone who could earn near the threshold level would have little or no incentive to work. The government would maintain family income at the threshold even if no one worked. Essentially, the "tax" on any income earned by families receiving assistance would be 100%.

The negative income tax (NIT) has been proposed as an alternative to the guaranteed income. NIT could provide an income floor and still maintain work incentives. Under NIT proposals, individuals would be allowed to keep a portion of the extra income they earn. The marginal take-back rate, which was 100% under the flat system, can be reduced to some fraction of earned income.

The guaranteed annual income has been strongly supported by both liberals and conservatives. Milton Freidman popularized the idea of a guaranteed annual income as a substitute for in-kind and other social support programs. One advantage is that guaranteed income plans are simpler to administer than the variety of in-kind and other means-tested transfer programs. They would also give the poor more choices about how to spend, and they might cost less than the variety of hit and miss programs. A national NIT program might reduce the perverse location incentive and inequities in state-managed antipoverty programs.

The NIT has two major drawbacks. First, any proposal that has a guaranteed income floor near the poverty level and a reasonable take-back rate, say less than 0.40, results in excessive transfers to families that are not poor. For instance, in our example, a floor of $15,000 and a take-back rate of 0.50 would mean that families earning up to $30,000 would still receive some transfer. Second, it is difficult to envision the substituting income only for psychological, educational, and medical services provided by the government. Poverty is more than an income problem.

Summary

Elimination of poverty is a particularly important LED goal. Three major conceptual definitions of poverty are absolute deprivation, socially or culturally determined definitions, and relative poverty. A disproportionate portion of the poor are minorities, uneducated, and woman-headed households.

General overall economic growth helps persons living in low-income areas. The process of arbitrage operating through labor markets creates a "spread effect." Sometimes the poor areas may become even poorer due to the proximity of a prosperous area, due to a backwash effect. While the spread effect is typical, the outcome depends on the linkages between the poor region and the prosperous sector.

Theories of poverty suggest that the ability of residents in poor areas to take advantage of growth in prosperous areas may depend on the strength of barriers such as cultural and behavioral traits, racial and ethnic discrimination, access to the prosperous area, the extent to which beneficiaries leave the poor areas, internal economic integration, and the extent to which the unemployed serve as "the last hired, first fired." While each of these theories has a different implication regarding what policies should be pursued, they are not mutually exclusive. Each has some truth.

Attempts to address problems of poor areas have led to a variety of policy prescriptions. Some policies emphasize the need to build stronger linkages between poor and prosperous areas. Efforts to improve productivity through education, training, behavioral changes, and so forth are involved in the traditional approach. Some policies recognize the presence of wage rigidities. Both minimum wages and "efficiency wages" may be part of the wage rigidity problem. For individuals who have difficulty in getting employment, some countries have employment guarantee plans whereby the government becomes the "employer of last resort." Direct income supports, such as a guaranteed annual income or in-kind transfers, are ways to provide a minimum living standard. Both government employment and income support, programs raise concerns about creating disincentives that might prevent recipients form seeking market employment.

Note

1. While this section describes poverty largely in the U.S. context, the analysis is, however, generalizable to other countries.

12

Local Governance, Finance, and Regional Integration

The role of government in economic development goes beyond subsidies and tax abatements that directly affect business decisions. An equal or more important role is performing a variety of traditional tasks well, creating an overall atmosphere that encourages economic development. Accordingly, local economic development (LED) officials are involved in a wide variety of local governance issues. This chapter describes how important public finance issues relate to economic development.

Spatial Perspectives on Government Functions

Local governments that either over- or underprovide government services can detract from economic development prospects. Musgrave (1959), in a classic analysis of government functions, concluded that government has three basic functions: maintaining a stable economy, providing an adequate distribution of income, and ensuring the appropriate production of goods.

Historically, the stabilization function involved national fiscal and monetary policy. More recently, LED has become an increasingly important part of stabilization policy for both nations and localities. National economies benefit from fast-developing localities, and those localities often provide nations with critical linkages to the global economy. Because local stabilization is the major theme of this book, this section focuses on distribution and allocation activities that contribute to economic development.

DISTRIBUTION AND THE RACE TO THE BOTTOM

Local governments may alter the distribution of income either deliberately or through unintentional redistribution programs. Many analysts contend that geographic differences in local distribution programs influence residential choice. Communities that tilt too far in favor of programs that assist the poor at the expense of wealthier population cohorts face the destabilizing prospect of attracting more poor and discouraging wealthier residents. In an intergovernmental setting, state and local governments may seek to attract businesses and wealthy residents at the expense of low-income groups. A race to the bottom can develop in which benefits to low-income groups are reduced to make the area more attractive to more affluent groups.

Distribution activities are conceptually distinct from the government decisions regarding what types of goods to produce (allocation). But in practice, it is difficult to separate the functions. For instance, there are many services that are financed by tax dollars so that the cost of the service usually falls disproportionately on the wealthy, since they tend to pay more taxes. However, benefits may accrue disproportionately to low-income groups.

LED officials often feel that they walk a "tightrope" when confronting equity issues. On the one hand, they recognize that an appropriate income distribution is a legitimate goal. Greater equity can even encourage growth in some circumstances. On the other hand, many steps that assist low-income groups can discourage business investment, result in out-migration of wealthy residents, and discourage growth. Because of this dilemma, many observers believe that income distribution programs should be a national effort.

LOCAL ALLOCATION

Local governments play a major role in the allocation of goods. Sometimes, unregulated markets fail to allocate resources appropriately. In these cases, governmental involvement is often appropriate. This section considers cases of public goods, goods with significant externalities, merit goods, imperfect information, and monopolies.

Public Goods

Public goods can be consumed by one person without significantly diminishing the consumption of that same good by anyone else (i.e., the marginal cost of an extra consumer is zero) and where exclusion of potential consumers is not feasible. If a good has either of the characteristics of a pure public good, the private market will not provide the good. No one will have an incentive to voluntarily pay. But if no one paid, how would production be financed without tax subsidies? The solution is to force people to pay through taxes.

National defense is a classic example of a pure public good at the national level. If national defense were financed privately, rational individuals (in the economic sense of utility maximizing) would refuse to pay because their contribution would be too small to affect output or their benefits. And there is no practical way to exclude nonpayers (creating the free-rider problem). Hence, citizens must be forced to pay for public goods.

There are also goods that have characteristics of "publicness" only within the confines of a geographic area, such as police or fire protection. Within a jurisdiction, everyone may receive similar benefits regardless of whether or not they pay, and it may be impractical to exclude nonpayers. In addition to contributing to overall economic stability, LED activities have important public goods characteristics. If a new enterprise is attracted to an area, the benefit may be widely shared among related firms and workers. It is also usually impractical to exclude people who have not contributed to economic development efforts from receiving benefits. The public goods characteristics apply to broad activities such as planning or training programs as well as specific projects such as improving part of the transportation grid.

Externalities

Goods with externalities (spillovers) are another instance where local governments should alter outcomes of the private sector to ensure that a proper quantity of goods is produced. Externalities may be either positive or negative. Positive externalities provide benefits to third parties, whereas negative externalities impose costs on third parties. Laissez-faire markets will tend to underproduce goods that have positive externalities and overproduce commodities with negative externalities. Furthermore, externalities may be produced by either production or consumption processes.

Local governments face two kinds of externalities. First, they must deal with externalities that occur strictly within their jurisdictions. For instance, a crowded shopping area may impose negative externalities on nearby residents. Second, local and regional governments must address intrajurisdictional externalities. For instance, Jurisdiction A could allow a large shopping mall to be constructed on A's side of the boundary separating A and B. Jurisdiction A's actions could create externalities in the form of congestion, noise, and air pollution for residents of Jurisdiction B.

LED efforts generate important interjurisdictional externalities. If Community A subsidized the expansion of a new plant, many of the employees may live in neighboring Jurisdiction B. The residents in B may receive positive spillover benefits due to City A's economic development program.

Monopolies and Natural Monopolies

Monopolists keep prices higher and output lower than under competition. Accordingly, consumers are disadvantaged and government intervention may be appropriate. Most discussions of monopolies envision a market within a nation. In practice, it is difficult to define a monopoly, particularly in a local context. Consider a grocery. A community might have only one full-service grocery. But if there are similar stores in nearby towns, the grocery's monopoly power may be negligible. In contrast, a corner gasoline station may be only one of hundreds in a city. Yet the store may have some monopoly power over customers traveling in a certain direction because it is the only convenient stop on some routes during certain times of day.

Local officials seldom, if ever, attempt to directly alter a firm's monopoly position. However, general attempts to attract new businesses and particularly import substitution strategies can have the effect of creating competition for existing businesses and improving community welfare.

Natural monopolies are important to local economies. Natural monopoly industries are characterized by technologies that require very large economics of scale. Consequently, many communities have market sizes sufficient to support only one business efficiently. Natural monopolies tend to be in the utility, transportation, and communications industries. These sectors influence a wide range of community activities, including the ability to attract new businesses so that local officials are concerned with their performance.

Information

Market failures also occur when individuals lack the information needed to make good decisions. Federal government efforts to ensure food and drug quality help consumers who individually lack the resources to monitor quality themselves. Most of the local government's activities have only a modest role to play in enhancing information. But information is critical to economic development. Providing information either in response to direct questions or as part of service on a committee is an important part of the job.

Merit Goods

There are goods or services considered so meritorious that the market will not provide them in the optimal quantities. Higher education, cultural events, or health care may be examples of merit goods, although the exact definition is vague. Merit goods play an important role in creating a community image and building a reputation for a high quality of life, so the provision of merit goods often enhances economic development.

PUBLIC TRANSPORTATION: AN EXAMPLE

Public transportation—such as trains and buses—has several characteristics that make free-market provision problematic. First, it is a natural monopoly.

Costs per traveler are minimized when operated at full capacity, yet the size of local markets is seldom sufficient to exploit scale economies. Second, significant externalities are associated with public transportation because when commuters use buses, road congestion is reduced. Also, transportation has good qualities since getting around is critical to urban life. Furthermore, public transportation is relied on disproportionately by individuals who cannot afford private automobiles, so there is a distributional element to public involvement.

Declining Costs

The natural monopoly problem associated with public transportation revolves around the very low marginal cost of an additional unit of service. Optimum-pricing theory implies that no one should be excluded from a service if the value is more than the marginal cost. In the case of a bus trip, for example, an extra rider would not significantly increase costs to the bus company (or society) because the bus would travel whether there were n or $n + 1$ passengers. Yet fare changes will reduce ridership, resulting in a loss of social benefits without a compensating reduction in social costs. The fixed cost of public transportation systems is large, but the marginal cost is small. The marginal cost is below the average cost, as shown in Figure 12.1.

What price and service level should result from the situation depicted in Figure 12.1? Once the price is set, the service level will be determined by the demand, so any equilibrium ridership level will represent a point on the demand curve. Let us consider the advantages and disadvantages of price-quantity combinations A, B, and C.

At Point A, profits for the transportation provider are maximized, and 500 people would travel. The marginal-revenue curve (not shown), would intersect marginal cost at passenger level 500. The problem with the 50-cent price is that the marginal rider (500th passenger) values an additional trip at 50 cents, but the cost of providing the marginal trip is only 2 cents. Hence, social welfare could be increased by increasing ridership. Increased ridership could be attained by lowering the price. However, lowering the price could also lower profits for the transportation provider.

At the price-quantity combination indicated by Point B, total revenue would equal total cost (both equal 0.15×700). The transportation provider would break even, but profits would be zero. In comparison with Point A, the net social benefits are greater at Point B, reflecting the extra ridership at relatively low social costs. However, a further increase in ridership would increase social benefits since marginal social benefit is greater than marginal social cost (MSB > MSC) at 700.

Finally, consider Point C, where net social benefits will be maximized. Let the price be set at 2 cents, the marginal cost. Ridership would increase to 900.

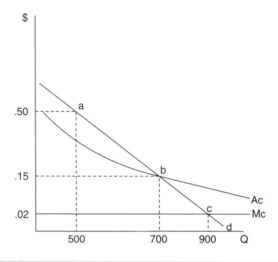

Figure 12.1   Pricing Under Conditions of Decreasing Cost

NOTE: The optimal price/quantity combination is indicated by Point C. This is not the profit-maximizing combination.

This level of ridership is socially optimal because the demand curve (marginal social benefits) equals marginal social costs. The problem with solution C is that revenues will not cover costs. Therefore, some kind of subsidy may be necessary to cover costs. To avoid subsidizing the service, complicated access permits and price discrimination plans have been employed.

Positive Externalities

Public transportation systems also provide positive externalities. When 10 people ride the bus during rush hour, automobile congestion on major roads may be reduced, providing benefits to drivers. Another positive externality is the reduced pollution that may accompany the use of buses rather than cars.

The positive externalities may be illustrated by imagining the MSB curve in Figure 12.1 increasing beyond the private demand curve (the marginal private benefit curve). Accordingly, optimum ridership will exceed 900 if positive externalities are recognized.

Size and Scope of Local Governments

This section contrasts two perspectives on optimum governmental size. The traditional approach to optimal size has been to examine the economically efficient (lowest cost) size of production to determine the appropriate size of government. Alternatively, decision-making costs have been viewed as the most important consideration in determining governmental size.

ECONOMIES AND DISECONOMIES OF SCALE

Some economists have believed that the appropriate size for a local government should be the population size that allows the government to provide services at the lowest average cost.

There are three serious problems with this approach. First, costs are influenced by the type of people being served. For instance, provision of police services will increase in areas with a high propensity toward crime. Second, the relationship between average cost and population may be different for each of the many local governmental functions. Consequently, the lowest-cost population size depends on the number and type of services provided by local governments. Third, the minimum-cost approach fails to recognize that communities may purchase selected governmental services from other cities. Therefore, the size of the producing unit does not have to be the same size as the consuming unit. A small city may enter into an agreement with another jurisdiction to pay a part of the cost of the fire department in return for fire protection. Since local governments do not have to produce all the services they provide, low average production costs need not be a factor in determining optimum government size. The ability of communities to purchase services from other governments offers potential for significant efficiencies. However, the potential efficiencies have not always been exploited.

DECISION-MAKING COSTS

Another approach to local government size is to consider preference match and decision-making ability of citizens as government size changes. Do decisions reflect citizen preferences, and are the costs of reaching a decision low?

Preference Mismatch

If the set of goods and services provided by the government does not match the preferences of residents, then a preference mismatch exists. The most efficient size for satisfying individual preferences would be a government serving only one person. In this case, an individual's preferences can be accommodated exactly. However, a one-purpose government is contradicted by the nature of government activities. Since citizens receive similar services, someone who does not prefer what the government provides bears a cost. The larger the political jurisdiction and the more diverse the citizen preferences, the more likely it is that some citizens will be dissatisfied with the mix of government services. The preference of the median voter is a likely outcome of a two-party democratic process (half the voters wanting more and half wanting less). If citizens have a narrow spread of opinion, preferences will align, and the extent of dissatisfaction will be small. Such communities are well positioned to work in a cooperative manner for community goals, including economic development. Areas where preferences are diverse and far apart are likely to experience high levels of preference mismatch.

Citizen Effort and Government Scope

Decision-making costs are also influenced by citizen effort to gather information. The decision-making effort depends on the number of issues voters are expected to decide. On the one hand, proliferation of special purpose jurisdictions usually makes decision-making harder because voters must know about a greater number of potential officeholders. On the other hand, if there were only one general-purpose government, specific issues might not get the attention they deserve. In large, general-purpose governments, high-profile or "hot-button" issues, such as abortion or crime, often dominate voter attention, while issues such as the need to separate garbage receive no attention.

Thus, in attempting to minimize decision-making costs, the scope of government should balance the ability of voters to express their opinions on specific issues with the information costs that would exist if a separate representative or unit of government existed for narrow sets of public issues.

Improving Government Efficiency

A well-functioning public sector contributes to LED not only through explicit development programs but also by providing traditional functions efficiently.

USING PRICES AND FEES

The city has been described as "a distorted price system." The "failure to price . . . in the public sector of the metropolis is at the root of many, if not most of our urban problems" (Thompson, 1968). User fees are prices charged by governments that can provide "market mimics." Appropriate user fees can assist public decision making in several ways.

Signals

User fees can be employed to inform decision makers about citizen preferences. Consider the demand for a public golf course or other recreational facility.

Often citizens can use such facilities for free or at a greatly subsidized cost. Consequently, the facilities tend to be very popular. Because of the lack of reliance on price, the high usage may be seen as evidence of high demand. Citizens may complain about "overcrowding" at the facilities, creating pressure on local officials to build additional facilities to relieve the crowding. Citizens who use particular services sometimes organize to keep the services they use high quality, ample, and free. Politicians are of course under pressure to respond. But does this result in an efficient use of resources?

Figure 12.2 illustrates the efficiency and welfare loss due to poor pricing policy. As is true with most production, there is a cost associated with each additional unit produced or each additional customer served. In this case, the MC curve represents the cost of serving an additional citizen. Following the traditional view, the value of the benefits received by consumers or citizens declines as they use more units. The MB curve shows how many units consumers would buy at various prices.

Assume that the price is zero, as is typical for many publicly provided goods and services. The residents will want 100 units if they are provided free. Consequently, they will place a value of $0 on the last (100th) unit consumed. (When the price is $0, goods will tend to be consumed to the point where they provide no *additional* satisfaction.) Consequently, the local government will be paying to produce some things that have zero value to citizens. User fees

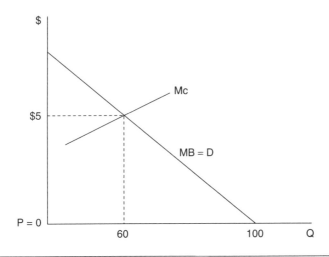

Figure 12.2   Welfare Loss From a "Free" Good

NOTE: A zero price results in overuse and inefficiency as the last unit consumed gives consumers no additional satisfaction.

can help policymakers understand the true value residents place on publicly provided goods.

Rationing

Prices also contribute to efficient rationing. Setting a zero price often does not negate the need to ration. With reference to Figure 12.2, if government produced, say, 60 units and no price existed, there would still be a need to determine who gets the 60 units when 100 are wanted. So providing something for free does not eliminate the need to ration. Often, resources spent on rationing a free government good are both excessive and unrecognized. For example, people may spend time and gasoline cruising for a parking space or they may wait in line to see a museum exhibit at particular times of the day.

Greater efficiency can also be obtained by varying user fees according to the time of day, month, or season. Such price variations are known as peak load pricing. Peak time users create congestion and contribute to the need for new capacity. By charging more to use facilities at peak times, citizens may spread their use more evenly. New scanning technologies have expanded the scope of user fees. Centuries before the widespread adoption of scanning, a theoretical economist suggested incorporating identification codes in cars. As they passed points, the place and time could be used to assess usage of public roads and to send them a monthly bill.

Expanding Choice

User fees can also be employed by the government to enlarge the range of services provided. Government goods tend to be the same for all who receive them. Yet many citizens may desire a little more or less or better or worse services. As the range of services increases, it will be easier to satisfy preferences without "voting with your feet" and reduce the "tyranny of the majority." Garbage collection can serve as an example. In most communities, all households receive the same level of service. People bring their garbage to the curb on a specified day for collection. Suppose, some rich and/or lazy persons would prefer to have the garbage person pick up the cans from the backyard. Such persons might prefer an option to pay more and thus not be required to lug the garbage to the curb themselves.

Affecting Behavior

User fees can also be employed to change behaviors. For instance, a new urban rail system might charge a low fee to encourage riders when the system is new. Conversely, vigorous fines could be used to enforce building regulations or avoid abandoned cars, just as traffic fines might be used to encourage safer driving. If local governments could use fines more and jails, probations, or court-ordered "treatment" less, behaviors could be changed at a significantly lower cost. Some California jails are allowing prisoners to pay extra for private cells, with special amenities—an interesting combination of using fines to change behavior while enlarging the range of choice.

LOCAL TAXATION AND ECONOMIC DEVELOPMENT

Taxes are required payment that may be unrelated to use. A fair and efficient tax system at the state and local level can be an important economic development tool. Businesses consistently rank taxes as an important location and expansion factor. This section first discusses general criteria for evaluating taxes. The principal criteria for a good local tax are efficiency, equity, and revenue elasticity.

Tax Efficiency

An efficient tax is one that does not adversely alter outcomes of private economic activity. An income tax, for instance, can be considered inefficient because a high income tax may encourage some individuals to work less. A head tax, on the other hand, will not distort the work/leisure choice because the taxpayer cannot escape the tax by working less. Most taxes create some distortions. Some taxes may deliberately distort prices to correct for other imperfections in the economy. Hence, taxes on goods with negative externalities may be efficient even if they alter existing incentives.

There is a saying that "an old tax is a good tax." Once the market has adjusted to a tax, it may be more disruptive to remove an existing tax and replace it with a theoretically more efficient tax than leave the distorting tax alone. The old tax/good tax principle implies that stability is an important efficiency characteristic.

Tax shifting must be considered when examining either efficiency or equity. Determining tax equity is difficult because the party that actually pays the tax to the government may be able to pass the tax forward to consumers or backward to producers. If a tax can be passed to someone other than the direct payer, the tax is said to have been shifted. The party that actually has a reduction in income because of the tax bears the "tax incidence."

Figure 12.3 illustrates the shifting process. Suppose S_1 and D represent the original supply and demand curves prior to the imposition of a tax. Then a tax is imposed on taxi trips equal to $1 per trip. Assume that cab drivers are responsible for collecting the tax. The initial effect of the tax will be to reduce the supply of taxi trips at each price the consumer pays. This is shown by the backward shift of the supply curve to S_2. The new equilibrium price will be $2.75. In this case, 75 cents of the tax has been shifted forward to the consumer because he or she pays 75 cents more than before the tax, and 25 cents is shifted backward to the driver. Often, the fare might be expressed as "$1.75, plus $1 tax." When expressed this way, it appears the consumer is bearing the full incidence, but in reality, the price of the taxed service drops somewhat, forcing the producer to bear part of the burden.

The relative elasticities of supply and demand determine the extent of shifting. If firms face consumers with inelastic product demand (i.e., prices can be increased without consumers significantly decreasing their purchases), producers will be able to shift a high portion of the tax forward to consumers; but if consumer demand is elastic, producers will have difficulty passing taxes forward. Similarly, if the product being taxed has an inelastic supply, as would be the case if the resources used in production had few alternative uses, the tax would tend to be shifted backward to producers. Producers with greater options would tend to avoid the tax, and it would be shifted to consumers.

Shifting has important implications for LED officials. Suppose, a small jurisdiction imposes a sales tax on a particular type of store, which consumers could easily avoid if they shop at competitive stores outside the taxing jurisdiction. Consumers could be said to have elastic demands for products sold

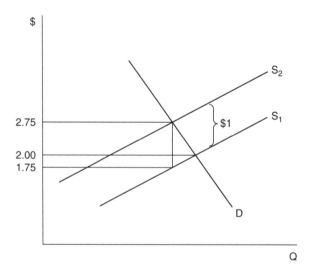

Figure 12.3   Tax Shifting

NOTE: Out of a $1 tax, 75 cents will be shifted forward. In this example, 25 cents will be shifted backward. The extent of shifting depends on the elasticities of supply and demand.

within one specific jurisdiction in a metropolitan area. Therefore, it will be difficult for business owners to shift the tax to consumers. Thus, the incidence will fall on the store owner. If the store was not making excess profits before the tax, it could easily be driven out of business. Similarly, local taxes on businesses that sell their products in competitive metropolitan, national, or international markets may be harmful to the firm and the community. A local tax on a business with an elastic demand will be shifted to consumers. Likewise, a statewide or national sales tax is more likely to be shifted forward to consumers. Since consumers have fewer nontaxed options, their demand will be less elastic.

Supply elasticity is also an important determinant of tax shifting. Factors of production with elastic supplies can move to untaxed areas, thereby escaping the tax, whereas immobile factors of production cannot avoid the tax. Building on the previous example of a sales tax, if shop owners were mobile and able to relocate to an untaxed district, they could escape the tax.

The property tax is considered to be born primarily by property owners in the very short run because the supply of property is inelastic. Thus, the tax will not affect supply or demand, and therefore, rents will not increase. However, beyond the very short run, the housing supply could decrease due to a tax as investors cut back on upkeep and new construction slows. Thus, the longer the time period, the greater the likelihood that increases in property taxes will be passed forward to renters.

Tax Equity

Equity refers to fairness, not equality. The main criteria for judging the fairness of a tax are the (1) ability-to-pay and (2) benefits-received principles. The ability-to-pay principle asserts that taxes should be levied based on a person's ability to pay. Since income is a major indicator of ability to pay, the principle is usually interpreted as implying that high-income families should pay more taxes.

The benefits-received principle links tax payments to benefits received from governments. The benefits-received principle is most useful in situations where benefits of the government program accrue directly to the recipient and where the value the recipient places on the good is easily determined. A motor fuel tax is based on the benefits-received principle since it is assumed that the use of gasoline represents use of roads. Direct user charges for public services, such as garbage collection, are an increasingly popular form of user fees.

Revenue Elasticity

Another important characteristic of taxes is their revenue elasticity, their elasticity with respect to growth in the economy. One measure of local tax revenue elasticity (RE) is

$$RE = \frac{\text{Percentage of change in tax revenues}}{\text{Percentage of change in local income}} \qquad (12.1)$$

Most communities want a tax base that increases at least proportionally to national income. However, they also desire a revenue source that is stable during economic downturns, because local expenditures are difficult to reduce during downturns. Often, these two goals conflict.

ACCOUNTABILITY

Public choice is a branch of economics that studies decision-making processes in the public sector from the perspective that everyone acts in their self-interest, regardless of whether they are public officials, private sector entrepreneurs, or the employees of a business. Therefore, government reward systems must be designed so that when government officials act in their self-interest, they will also do what is in the public interest.

Elected Officials

Rather than trying to achieve the public good, elected officials may use their office to maximize their own self-interest subject (usually) to legal constraints. Frequently, politicians will enhance their chances of being reelected by doing what is in the public interest. However, there may be instances when self-interest and public interest conflict.

Political officials are often judged by their ability to attract high-profile economic development projects. Consequently, insecure or ambitious politicians may feel the pressure to provide subsidies to businesses in excess of the amount that is necessary to achieve the legitimate economic development objective. Pressures may be strong, particularly near election times or if there is a major political need for a success story.

Narrow special interest groups also may exercise disproportional power in the economic development process. Most citizens are uninformed and/or don't care about the outcome of most public decisions. The costs (effort) of obtaining information on issues that barely affect them are too high to make it worthwhile. However, the few who are directly affected will be the ones who make their voices heard. On the one hand, the votes and campaign contributions among these few may hinge on the outcome of that single issue. On the other hand, citizens not directly affected may have only a vague idea about the costs and related issues. Their votes will not hinge on the outcome of the single issue. To get reelected, it may behoove politicians to decide issues in favor of special-interest groups rather than the community as a whole.

Bureaucrats

Nonelected public employees may also lack incentives to do what is in the public interest. Bureaucrats may seek more pay, better perquisites of office, or hassle-free work environments rather than serving the citizens better according to the public choice view. Also, public employees often operate under looser constraints than employees in profit-seeking firms because (1) public outputs are often difficult to measure (i.e., effective teaching); (2) responsibility for performance is often vague ("buck passing" is likely); and (3) there is no "bottom line," such as profits, to measure success. It is therefore hard to make some bureaucrats accountable. In addition to a tendency toward inefficiency, public employees may have incentives to expand services beyond the level desired by most citizens. Essentially, bureaucrats become another special-interest group. Public workers also constitute an important voting block that would probably support higher pay and better working conditions for local government workers.

Strengthening the Invisible Hand in Government

Simple, or some would say naive, economic theory suggests that the private sector will generally be more efficient that the government because incentives motivate people better. This assumption has not been proven. Nevertheless, to create an "invisible hand in government," reformers have proposed the introduction of market-like mechanisms. However, the task of restructuring government so that public officials do what is in the public interest is a continuing challenge. The nature of government lends itself to opportunities for government employees to put their interests above the public good. Because the public interest is seldom precisely defined and because the public outputs are elusive, accountability is hard to achieve. The conflict-of-interest problem is particularly acute in the practice of LED because local governments often assist in the creation of large sums of private wealth.

Currently, some reform groups are attempting to make government more responsive by introducing market-like mechanisms to traditional functions. Two pillars of reform are expanding choice and making public employees accountable. By giving citizens choices, public agencies that do not provide adequate services will lose "customers" and may eventually be terminated. Public officials may receive signals about the kinds of services consumers want as they vote with their vouchers. Employee accountability may be addressed by reward systems that encourage certain behaviors and discourage others.

Developing an invisible hand in government is constrained by the nature of government activity. Nonmarket factors are important in all government decisions. Governments do things that markets will not do. Many public decisions involve issues that transcend economic calculus, such as which amenities provide a high quality of life, what values schools should instill, which activities should be exempt from taxes, and how much effort should be directed toward the homeless. Furthermore, while theory suggests that the private sector will generally be more efficient, this assumption has not been established. After all, big companies are bureaucratic and have numerous incentive conflicts.

INTERGOVERNMENTAL COMPETITION

The benefits from competition in the private markets are widely discussed—better services, lower prices, and innovation. Economists are currently asking whether intergovernmental competition will provide similar benefits. The Tiebout model (see Chapter 10) suggests that governments have checks that restrain waste similar to checks in competitive businesses. It showed that under certain conditions, individuals would move to communities that provided their preferred mix of governmental services and taxes. Conditions necessary for citizens to vote with their feet are more closely approximated in the context of residential choice within a metropolitan area than in the context of interstate or international location choices because relocation costs are low.

Competition in the private market leads to greater efficiency as firms compete for customers. The Tiebout model implies that local governments may be forced to compete with each other for residents. Similarly, some businesses may vote with their feet. Shrinking residential populations may not be as direct a threat to a public employee's job security or advancement as shrinking profits to a private worker, but they may provide a check on government waste. Governmental competition may also contribute toward efficiency through a "demonstration" effect. When citizens see neighboring governmental units performing well, political pressure may increase for their government to replicate the good performance.

Theories of government behavior have led to the "Leviathan theory." In a nutshell, it suggests that lack of competition will reduce constraints, causing more government programs and less efficiency. Therefore, governments will be largest where competitive discipline is least.

Empirical studies have examined the extent to which competition among government units affects performance. Competition is normally measured by the number of local governments in a particular area. Many small government units represent a more competitive structure than a few large units. The research is not definitive, but as intergovernmental competition increases, the total size of government decreases, productivity increases, and quality improves (Taylor, 2000).

While the effects of government competition appear to be positive, there may be exceptions. Some economists argue that in the area of economic development, competition leads to the local government squandering resources chasing after mobile firms. Each local government tries to give potential new businesses more than other areas. In addition, local government competition may result in a race to the bottom as benefits to the poor are cut and environmental protections are reduced in an effort to appeal to business and well-off population groups.

INTERGOVERNMENTAL GRANTS AND COORDINATION

Intergovernmental grants can improve efficiency by improving coordination. Two reasons are generally given for intergovernmental grants. First, there is a need to encourage positive spillovers and discourage negative spillover effects that governments impose on each other. Second, some intergovernmental grants are to rectify fiscal disparities among jurisdictions. Grants to rectify fiscal disparities have both equity and efficiency objectives, since they may help poor areas undertake activities that they otherwise might not. Grants almost always flow from larger units of government to smaller units (of course, taxes flow in the opposite direction).

Efficiency and Spillovers

Externalities between local governments are common. For instance, excellent parks in one jurisdiction may be used by residents of another jurisdiction. In this case, nonpayers (nonresidents) will receive a positive externality. Economic theory suggests that when positive externalities exist, the good in question tends to be underprovided. When negative spillovers are present, the good tends to be overproduced. Some intergovernmental spillovers are the cost of having local government.

The suburban/central-city exploitation thesis is based on the idea of intergovernmental spillovers. The thesis is that suburban residents benefit from the services provided by the central city, but they do not pay their fair share of the cost. Because so many suburban residents work in the central city, they use many central-city services during the day. Suburban residents also use cultural and recreational facilities often found in the central city. But to the extent their property taxes are paid to suburban localities, they may not pay for city services. Accordingly, the charge has been made that suburban residents exploit residents of the central city. The empirical evidence for central-city exploitation is mixed (Green, Neenan, & Scott, 1976; Neenan, 1972; Ramsey, 1972). States often provide extra grant support to central cities in recognition of the spillovers.

Central-city/suburban spillovers are particularly cogent in the job creation process because many of the high-paying jobs held by suburban residents are located in the central business district. The efforts to maintain a viable downtown help suburban residents. These economic interdependencies have caused many metropolitan areas to create institutions that encourage interjurisdictional cooperation in the area of economic development. The presence of job creation externalities supports the idea that cities and suburbs should cooperate more in LED efforts.

The external benefits that flow from economic development are one of the reasons for the rapid growth in economic development grants from federal, state, and county governments to local jurisdictions. A single jurisdiction might encourage economic development to the point where program costs equal benefits to the jurisdictions, but the state (or neighboring local governments) might wish that the jurisdiction went beyond that point to achieve additional benefits. To encourage additional economic development spending, the state might provide grants to stimulate additional economic development.

Jurisdictions can also be encouraged to reduce negative externalities through the use of intergovernmental grants. For instance, grants for sewage improvements reduce the water pollution that affects downstream communities. Expressed differently, we could say that water purification carries positive externalities and a grant to increase purification efforts will increase the level of this output.

Equity

A second reason for intergovernmental transfers is to ensure that unequal burdens are not placed on individuals living in jurisdictions with different taxing abilities. Often, poor districts with small tax bases must impose higher tax rates on residents, yet the district collects less total revenue than more affluent communities. This imbalance is a particular issue in the funding of education where higher units of government seek to provide equal educational opportunities.

Suppose Individuals A and B earn equal incomes, but A lives in a rich city and B lives in a poor city. Furthermore, assume that their tastes and preferences are the same and taxes are proportionate to income. Given the assumptions, it would be advantageous to be a resident of the wealthy community because the local tax burden would be smaller. This situation violates the tax principal that "equals should be treated equally." Thus, transfers to ensure that A and B receive equal fiscal residuum may be appropriate.

Furthermore, given the potential disadvantageous tax treatment of resident B, an incentive would exist for B resident to relocate to the richer community. There are two potential problems that arise from the fiscal incentive to live in a wealthy jurisdiction. First, the rich political jurisdictions will get richer, and the low-income residents in the poorer district will be more isolated. Excessive income segregation could result in increased racial or social problems. Second, the provision of public services is often characterized by congestion costs. Migration could increase costs in the richer jurisdiction, and increased congestion could reduce the quality of services.

REARRANGING FUNCTIONS

Several types of intergovernmental rearrangements have been suggested to relieve pressures on local governments and improve efficiency. Particularly in the field of economic development where government competition can be destructive, many areas are seeking ways to better coordinate efforts and work toward government cooperation. These include reassignment of functions, regional tax-based sharing, and annexation.

Reassignment of Responsibilities

Reassigning responsibilities is a solution that usually involves shifting the financial burden upward where the ability to pay is perceived to be greater. In some areas, local governments have created metropolitan-wide economic development agencies as part of this reform. There are two limiting problems, however. First, as fiscal responsibility shifts upward, there is a tendency for control to shift upward, too. Yet many programs are best controlled and administered at the local level, where opportunities and needs can be identified more clearly. Thus, the ability to shift programs upward is hindered by the propensity to lose local control. Second, higher units of government may not necessarily have greater fiscal ability. After all, a state's taxable base is ultimately equal to the individual areas that make up the state.

Tax Sharing

Under tax sharing, increases in metropolitan taxes are shared among local jurisdictions. For instance, suppose the economy and the property tax base are growing in the northern suburbs, while the central-city tax base declines. Under a tax-sharing system, the growing district might turn over a certain percentage of the increase in taxes to the central city as well as to other local jurisdictions.

Tax sharing has been supported for two reasons related to economic development. First, employment growth often depends on a variety of regional factors, including a vibrant downtown. Expenditures of the central city often make the entire region more attractive to industry, so the central city should benefit from growth that occurs elsewhere in the region. Second, tax sharing may reduce the "zero-sum game" aspect of economic development. Intra-metropolitan competition for a larger tax base will be reduced if they share tax revenues. Such competition among local governments has resulted in such generous tax abatements that even jurisdictions with increasing employment and tax bases have failed to increase their revenues.

Annexation

Many communities have attempted to solve fiscal problems through annexation of the surrounding areas. If a city annexes industrial, commercial, or prosperous residential areas, it may expand its tax base by more than the cost of providing services to the annexed area. (Low- and moderate-income residential areas normally cost governments more than the tax revenues received.) Likewise, annexation of undeveloped land can provide sites for the growth of future taxable property.

Rusk (1993) found that annexation is one of the principal determinants of central-city success. Unfortunately, there are several drawbacks to an annexation strategy. First, only a limited number of central cities can benefit from annexation because they are surrounded by previously incorporated suburban jurisdictions. It is usually difficult to annex another city. Second, while annexation may help increase per capita income in a jurisdiction, it may do little for the inner-city populations still trapped in a vicious cycle of economic decline. For the metropolitan region as a whole, one community's annexation gain is often another's loss: Jurisdictions benefit, but people may not—place rather than people prosperity. Third, many suburban areas resist annexation by major cities because of the poor image and other problems that central cities have.

PRIVATIZATION

Many individuals consider private-sector activities to be more efficient than public operations. The private sector has been shown to provide some services at a lower cost than governments. If the private sector is in fact more efficient than government, citizens may be better served if private businesses deliver services traditionally provided by governments. Even if efficiency were not a concern, financially pressed governments might want to shed some activities and let them be private.

Privatization can also be achieved when local governments contract with private firms to provide a service the government previously provided. For instance, a city that may hire a private cleaning service to clean public buildings rather than having public employees do the job. Private organizations have been hired to provide services such as school lunches, transportation, and safety services. A local government may grant or franchise the right to provide certain services to private firms. The private provider may charge the public for the services, although the price and conditions are regulated by the terms of the franchise agreements.

Voucher systems allow the government to pay for a stipulated service level, but the choice of provider is left to the individual. The voucher will support a minimum level of service. Under many plans, if recipients wish to spend in excess of the voucher amount, they may do so. The individual is responsible for arranging for the services, and the service will normally be produced by a private source. Food stamps and rent assistance are the most well-known types of voucher. Many observers have proposed using vouchers in education (see below). Although vouchers are not widely used by local governments, their popularity is increasing.

Interest in using volunteers is increasing as another way of shedding responsibility. A local government may "hand over" a traditional responsibility to volunteers. The use of volunteers in schools, social service agencies, and other organizations has been viewed as a way to avoid hiring new employees. In providing social services, volunteerism has been linked to churches.

MARKET-BASED REFORMS IN EDUCATION

Education is an increasingly important aspect of local development (King, 2005). Families consider the quality of education in selecting where to live and are willing to pay premiums for a house in a school attendance area with perceived good schools. The educational system is also a foundation of a productive workforce that contributes to higher incomes and job growth. Business location studies frequently include school quality as an important element on corporate "must have/want" lists. Not surprisingly, state and local governments devote considerable efforts to improving educational outcomes.

Schools also have institutional problems associated with government goods provision. First, the nature of the output of education is difficult to measure. Home influences affect learning outcomes more than what happens in the school. Educational theory cannot prescribe a single, best pedagogy, so directly observing which schools are the best is impractical. Because of the positive externalities, education is mandatory, so schools don't worry too much about losing "customers." Incentive problems in producing education also exist. Teachers sometimes confront conflicts between their own self-interests and the interests of students. For instance, a teacher may have to choose between staying late to meet with a parent or going home and mowing the lawn. Due to the importance of education and the inherent public provision problems, there have been numerous efforts to improve school performance. These efforts have not focused on what should be done differently in the classroom. Rather, they have emphasized changing the system. In other words, they have tried to create an invisible hand in government. Three of the most noted reforms are charter schools, education vouchers, and standardized testing. This section is intended to show how these recent reforms are intended to bring market mimics to education. However, it is not an analysis of the pros and cons of market-based reforms in education.

Charter Schools

Charter schools are institutions established outside the traditional educational bureaucracy. They may be stand-alone schools or part of a corporate chain. The schools are free to try new approaches and techniques that may be difficult to implement in established systems because of existing rules or customs. In some cases, they may hire teachers with different sets of qualifications, teach nontraditional subjects, have different standards of discipline, or operate on different calendars.

In many cases, charter schools have challenged the educational bureaucracy and reduced the power of teacher organizations. For instance, charter schools often have the flexibility to pay teachers below existing salary scales, hire teachers with qualifications that are not acceptable elsewhere, fire teachers without cause, or require teachers to perform extra duties. Charter schools often have more flexibility to use merit pay systems that address incentive problems.

Of course, there are state-imposed limits to the flexibility of charter schools, such as minimum attendance days. Nevertheless, charter schools are based on the idea that they should be generally freer to try new approaches. "Let a thousand flowers bloom" might be a slogan. If an innovation is successful, it will attract students and other schools will copy the innovation. As families are given greater choices, people can "vote with their feet."

Vouchers

Educational vouchers are often a means of paying tuition to attend charter schools or private schools. The idea was pioneered by Milton Friedman (1962), a strong advocate for less government and greater reliance on laissez-faire markets. The heart of his scheme was to give parents vouchers to pay for their children's education. The vouchers would be given to schools to pay for educational services. They could be supplemented if the selected school cost more than the vouchers' amount under some plans. Children with special needs could receive more valuable vouchers.

The vouchers program would create an effective demand (want plus purchasing power) for schools outside the traditional school system. According to his approach, parents will seek the best schools for their children because parents have the children's interests at heart. A school that could not appeal to parents would lack a market and go out of business. Only the schools that are successful in the market would survive.

Surviving in the free market is a sufficient test of quality, according to many charter backers. Surviving means earning revenues at least sufficient to cover all costs, including nonaccounting costs such as returns for owners and managers. Even nonprofit schools often seek to generate an "overage" above costs to spend for whatever purpose the directors wish. The drive for profits or overage among nonprofit institutions will also constrain services to students and result in market-disciplined choices. The value of each service will be compared with the additional revenues (including vouchers) that the service brings to the school. Only activities where revenues exceed costs will be provided.

Standardized Testing

For markets to work, individuals must not only be able to choose, but their decisions must also be informed. Even with charter schools and vouchers, an information problem exists in education. How can parents tell which schools are good? The information problem may be decreased if students took a standardized test and the outcomes of each school compared. Increasingly, schools are required to administer standardized tests as a condition of receiving government funding. The results of the tests can then be used by parents in selecting schools.

Test results are also being used as part of the merit pay process for teachers and administrators. Presumably, the teachers with students showing the highest test scores, or perhaps teachers with students showing the greatest improvement in standardized test scores (the value-added approach), deserve the highest pay. Thus, teachers are more accountable for student performance.

Many observers object to "high-stakes" testing on the grounds that some teachers will "teach to the test," so that high scores do not indicate more general knowledge. Critics have noted that individual teachers or schools have cheated to boost the scores of their students. A third concern is that standardized testing is not a valid measure of education because education is such a broad concept that includes values, behaviors, and creativity in addition to the ability to take tests.

The research about the success of market-based education reforms is mixed. Some analysts suggest that market incentives improve education, but others disagree. Many studies reflect a bias because the issues are politically charged and because both public and private educational systems have moneyed interests in the outcomes. One reason that market reforms are hard to evaluate is that they have been implemented in a variety of combinations and in different environments. Generalization is difficult because market reforms appear to be successful in some places but not in others. Also, there are inadequate measures of outcomes. Most evaluations focus on standardized test scores since they are the easiest to measure, confirming a perennial incentive problem—you get what is easy to measure.

Fiscal Impact and Benefit-Cost Studies

Fiscal impact and benefit-cost studies are useful tools for economic development planners. Fiscal impact studies can be used to assess the impact of development projects on the government treasury. Benefit-cost studies analyze not only fiscal impacts but other costs and benefits that may accrue to citizens.

FISCAL IMPACT STUDIES

Fiscal-impact analyses are useful for forecasting the effects of economic development and other projects on an area's fiscal health. LED officials should consider fiscal impacts in planning and supporting new ventures. They vary greatly in scope and detail. However, there are certain steps that are common to most fiscal impact studies. A formula developed by Muller and Dawson (1972) provides a basic framework.

$$NFI = W - (X + Y), \qquad (12.2)$$

where W is the present value of development-linked revenue, X is the present value of development-linked operating expenditures, Y is the present value of development-linked capital expenditures, and NFI is the net fiscal impact.

Although the net fiscal impact formula is very clear conceptually, in practice, it is usually difficult to estimate the various components.

Estimating Revenues

Local revenues include property tax revenues, sales tax revenues, income tax revenues, intergovernmental transfers, and user charges/fees. Separate calculations may be made for each type of revenue. The importance of specific types of revenue sources will vary from district to district.

Residential developments are likely to generate most revenue through the property tax. The approximate value of new residential properties will be known when a fiscal impact study is undertaken because developers normally know the price range of houses in their development. Therefore, increased property tax revenues are relatively easy to estimate by multiplying the effective tax rate by the increase in the tax base. Revenues from sales taxes and income taxes may be more difficult to determine because they depend on shopping and work patterns. However, based on shopping and employment patterns of existing residents as well as the income levels that could be assumed based on the value of the residences, reasonable estimates may be derived. Intergovernmental transfers depend primarily on population size and the number of school-age children, although other factors may enter some grant formulas. Since family size can be estimated from the type of residential development proposed, roughly accurate estimates of intergovernmental revenues may be obtained.

Property tax revenues from commercial developments are also fairly easy to estimate based on the value of the proposed development stated in the zoning request or building permit. Local payroll tax revenues may also increase to the extent employment increases. Sales taxes will increase to the extent sales increase. Sales can be estimated based on the type of business and the estimated square feet of development. An analyst must be careful to adjust revenue estimates if increased sales or employment come at the expense of other local businesses.

Estimating Operating Expenditures

A major difficulty in measuring operating expenses is that costs may remain fixed when usage increases by a small amount, so that marginal costs are near zero. Such might be the case for small increases in road use. Other governmental services may face sharply increasing marginal costs as demand increases, as might be the case if new roads were required to accommodate development-related traffic increases. In the absence of data on marginal cost, analysts often assume that the marginal cost of public services will equal average cost.

Operating expenses for residential developments may be analyzed by considering whether demand for governmental services (1) is concentrated among low-income households, (2) increases with income, (3) changes with the size of the units constructed, and (4) varies in other relevant variables. Such considerations may be compared with the type of project being proposed. Operating expenses of commercial enterprises may be estimated based on the average costs of similar businesses in the area.

Estimating Capital Expenditures

Capital expenditures caused by a new development include (1) facilities necessitated because of the proposed project and used only by the project, such as sewer lines or fire stations; (2) facilities that would have been constructed regardless of the new development but in which new residents will share; and (3) facilities that will have to be constructed because of the new development but that will be shared by other residents. Theoretically, only the marginal costs of a new development are relevant. However, marginal costs are seldom the basis for evaluating a development's capital costs because they are difficult to determine and may differ from citizens' concepts of fair-share burden. In practice, the new project is normally charged for the entire cost in the first instance. In the second case, the new development may not be charged for any of the costs, or an average cost may be assigned. In the third case, the development may be charged for a disproportionate share of the incremental costs.

BENEFIT-COST ANALYSIS

Benefit-cost analysis is a decision-making tool that can be used to improve governmental decision making by going beyond narrow fiscal impacts and examining a broader range of costs and benefits. It attempts to measure all social costs and social benefits of public projects. If the benefits outweigh the costs, then the presumption is that the community would be enhanced by the project. If, on the other hand, the costs exceed the benefits, then the aggregate value of the resources required to build a project is greater than the benefits placed on the output. The former case is intended to be the public-sector equivalent of a profitable business venture, and the latter case is the counterpart of an unprofitable business.

The formula central to benefit-cost analysis is:

$$B/C = \sum_{i=0}^{n} B_i \bigg/ \sum_{i=0}^{n} C_i, \qquad (12.3)$$

where

B/C = benefit-cost ratio,

$\sum_{i=0}^{n} B_i$ = the sum of the discounted value of social benefits (0 = present year), and

$\sum_{i=0}^{n} C_i$ = the sum of the discounted value of the social costs.

The concept of benefit-cost analysis is simple: Measure and compare the benefits and costs. Yet there are conceptual difficulties and implementation problems. Social costs and benefits will differ from private costs and benefits if there are spillover effects or externalities. The private costs of producing a commodity are costs to the producer. Social costs include both private costs as well as spillover effects. However, the comprehensive perspective creates an implementation problem, since the consequences—both good and bad—that stem from a project are too numerous and often too small to measure. It might be said that the theoretical reach of benefit-cost studies exceeds the implementation grasp.

Steps in Benefit-Cost Analysis

The discussion of potential difficulties of benefit-cost analysis suggests that benefit-cost studies should be structured and implemented to avoid potential abuses. The steps in a benefit-cost study may be briefly summarized as follows:

1. *Describe the nature of the project:* This step is necessary because the purposes of benefit-cost studies are not always the same and the purposes may affect methodology. Benefit-cost analysis can be either a decision-making tool or an evaluative tool. For example, one study may answer the question "Should the school be built?" and another, "Should the school have been built?" There may also be relevant constraints that will affect the outcome or nature of the study. For example, a budgetary constraint may prevent analysis of a bigger project that might appear better. The question of whose costs and benefits are being considered should also be addressed. What is the geographic scope? The results may differ if a neighborhood, a state, or a nation is the region for which the benefits (costs) are being considered.

2. *Delineate the set of choices:* Benefit-cost analysis is not feasible for comparing all governmental projects. In describing the choice set, the analyst should specify the alternative projects being considered. In the simplest case, where only one project is being considered, the issue may be whether the benefit-cost ratio is greater than a certain level. The choice will become more difficult if projects are mutually exclusive or otherwise interdependent.

3. *Describe the benefits and costs of the project:* This step and the next are possibly the most difficult in the analysis. The benefits and costs should include not only direct but also indirect impacts. The analyst might even choose to discuss "speculative effects," so that those factors that might or might not result would at least be mentioned. Sometimes, nonquantifiable benefits are as important as those that can easily be monetized. Also, one of the significant lessons learned from evaluations of federal urban programs is that unintended and unanticipated effects often turn out to be more significant than planned impacts.

4. *Estimate the monetary value of the costs and benefits:* Techniques and examples for estimating social benefits include the following:

- The benefits of a road can include time savings valued at the traveler's hourly wage in addition to direct savings on transport cost.
- Consumer surplus is often estimated as part of the benefits.
- The value of mass-transit facilities includes the benefits to automobile drivers, who will save time because mass-transit facilities reduce driving time.
- Public housing benefits have included the estimated value of crime prevention.
- The value of public parks and other recreational facilities has included the price paid for admittance to similar private facilities, plus the value of travel time saved because of the nearness of the facility.
- Surveys have been used to determine what individuals might be willing to pay.
- The increased property values of land near public improvements have been a measure of benefits of parks.
- Flood control projects have included the value of the increase in agricultural output.

Of course, there are still significant estimation problems with attempts to quantify elusive outcomes. All attempts to estimate value are subject to criticism. Some analysts prefer simply to list or set aside some qualitative benefits.

5. *Select a discount rate:* An important dimension of benefit-cost studies is the time when benefit and costs occur. The further in the future the costs and benefits take place, the less weight they will be given. This process is known as discounting.

The selection of the discount rate for government projects is a controversial aspect of benefit-cost analysis. Since most government development projects involve large, current expenditures and provide a flow of benefits over many years, a low discount rate increases the net present benefits and, hence, also increases the number of projects that can be justified. Among the possible discount rates that can be used are these:

- Private rate of return, because it represents the opportunity cost of capital used in the project
- A rate slightly lower than the private rate of return, to adjust for the risk of public projects
- The rate at which the government borrows
- A rate that reflects appropriate concern for future generations

There is yet to be a final resolution of the discount rate issue. While the conceptual problems inherent in this step may be great, a rate is usually selected based on rates in effect at the time of the study.

6. *Discount the costs and benefits:* The first five steps are preliminary to the actual calculation. Once the appropriate benefits, costs, and discount rates are established, this step is mechanical.

7. *Perform sensitivity analysis:* While not always necessary, repeating the fifth and sixth steps with different assumptions will provide an indication of how sensitive the results are to changes in the discount rate or in values placed on some intangible benefits. If the results are sensitive to small changes in, say, the value of time savings resulting from construction of a road, then doubt will be cast on the project.

8. *Describe conclusions and caveats:* Many benefit-cost studies leave the impression that if the benefit-cost ratio is greater than 1, it is obvious that the conclusion should be to construct the project. However, if a result is sensitive to the discount rate, or to one of the variables that the analyst could only roughly estimate, then the conclusion would be in doubt. There could be a discussion of how the inclusion of qualitative variables may have affected the analysis. Furthermore, because of budget constraints, the cutoff point for government projects may be a benefit-cost ratio greater than 2 rather than greater than 1. In addition, funding a project with the highest benefit-cost ratio may

not maximize the difference between the total benefits and total costs. Consequently, the reasoning behind any cutoff point should be discussed.

Conceptual and Implementation Issues

The theoretical justification for benefit-cost analysis is that when a project's benefits outweigh a project's costs, net social wealth will increase. With the increase in social wealth, the government could redistribute income so as to make at least one person better off without making anyone worse off (called a Pareto move). Society may decide not to redistribute income because they prefer the existing distribution; but as long as everyone can be potentially better off, the project should be undertaken. Thus, benefit-cost analysis is based on efficiency rather than equity criteria.

One method for dealing with the distributional issue is to assign different weights to various income groups. Thus, $1 of benefits or costs to a low-income family could be weighted by a factor of 1.2 or 1.7. Whatever the weight (even if all are weighted equally), the analyst is making a value judgment, not a scientific judgment. Some writers have suggested a "balance sheet" approach, whereby the benefits and costs that accrue to individuals in different income categories are separated.

Several criticisms of benefit-cost analysis have been discussed in the literature. One criticism is that all the costs and benefits cannot be counted. Since almost every action sets off numerous second-, third-, and greater-order consequences, tracking down and valuing all the ramifications are impossible. While this criticism is true, benefit-cost studies should attempt to count the costs of the major consequences. An analyst may have to assume that unforeseen or remote costs and benefits balance out.

A second criticism has been that local governments cannot afford to undertake all projects for which the benefit-cost ratios are greater than 1. Consequently, another standard must be developed to select among projects. Most analysts recognize this point. As a result, benefit-cost studies are more appropriate as a guide to an agency selecting among similar projects than as a guide to a legislature trying to allocate funds among very different projects such as health and road maintenance. A small agency may also lack the resources to undertake all projects with positive benefit-cost ratios; but it could have a decision-making rule requiring benefit-cost ratios of more than, say, 1–5, before a project could be undertaken.

The presence of intangible costs and benefits presents another problem. It is nearly impossible to place a monetary value on some activities. Frequently, critics suggest that since we can't place a value on a human life, benefit-cost studies are not appropriate to projects where such issues are involved. However, some benefits and costs that cannot be valued may be set aside, so the benefits or costs could be expressed as "$10,000,000 less extra health problems for 100 people." Thus, the decision makers are still left with the decision regarding how to handle the trade-off.

Finally, critics contend that benefit-cost studies remove decisions from the political decision makers and place them in the hands of technocrats. When benefit-cost techniques are employed, citizens lose the ability to engage in debates and affect outcomes. It is true that benefit-cost studies can be used to "snow" people and make a political decision appear to be only a technical decision. However, this abuse can be avoided in well-implemented studies.

Summary

Most public programs influence economic development prospects either directly or indirectly, intentionally or unintentionally. Economic development officials are often involved in many phases of local government.

The federal government has a dominant influence in stabilization activities through monetary and fiscal policy. Local governments lack the capacity to control overall levels of economic activity, but LED efforts are a form of stabilization policy. Distribution functions are also difficult to implement at the local level because of problems associated with the race to the bottom. However, modest redistribution efforts occur at the local level. Allocation activities constitute the bulk of state and local government activity. Allocation activities include the provision of public goods as well as adjusting market outcomes for externalities and merit goods.

Many observers examine economies of scale to determine the appropriate size of local governments. But some economists argue that local governments can purchase services from elsewhere, so there is no need to have a government large enough to achieve economies of scale. More recently, economists have claimed that decision-making costs should be the key factor in determining government size. Three important aspects of decision-making costs are preference mismatches, decision-making effort, and intergovernmental spillovers.

Efficiency of local governments may be improved by better use of prices and fees, efficient taxes, accountability including strengthening the "invisible hand in government," intergovernmental cooperation, an effective system of grants, the distribution of functions, and privatization.

Fiscal impact and cost-benefit studies are useful tools for fiscal management. Urban development specialists should understand the strengths and limitations of these tools.

13

Planning, Future Studies, and Development Policy

conomics, future studies, and urban planning provide important perspectives on the local economic development (LED) process. Local planners
need reasonable estimates regarding the likely course of future events to anticipate needs and develop policy responses. Economics is usually at the heart of
planning processes because planners are interested in economic outcomes:
Economic methods are used in the planning process, and economic factors
constrain what can be done. The influential planner George Sternlieb (1986)
described the orientation of planners to economic concerns when he said, "In
a word we have all suddenly become economists" (p. 154). In practice, it is
often difficult determine whether someone engaged in planning or policy
development has an academic background in economics, planning, futurism,
or some other field.

Futurists and planners have learned a great deal from economists. But economists can also learn from futurists and urban planners. This chapter reviews
some futurist and urban planning perspectives on LED. It should stimulate
thought, speculation, and wide-ranging thinking.

The Future and Local Development

The process of thinking about the future is frustrating because nobody knows
the future with certainty. Yet decision makers want to know the future. Most
decisions are predicated on assumptions about the future, so some type of
futures analysis is almost inescapable. Usually, decisions have an implicit
assumption—the future will be pretty much like today. That assumption is
often roughly accurate, but not always. Often we look back on events and
realize that they could or should have been anticipated. Futurists, like

economists, are careful not to imply that they can "predict" the future. Rather, they use phrases such as "if trends prevail," "scenarios," "forecasts," and "projections" when describing what the future might be like.

Futurist thinking is diverse and usually involves a wider range of possible changes than customary economic studies deal with. This section examines four areas that illustrate the futurist perspective.

CONCERN WITH VALUES AND ATTITUDES

Economics has been considered a science of values. Planners attempt to guide economic development to achieve certain values. Choice is the observable reflection of values, yet economists generally take individual values as given. Economists are concerned with how individuals behave *given* a set of values or preferences. Futurists are concerned with changing values. They ask what value changes are likely to occur and how those changes may affect the way we will live.

One theory of why values change is that inconsistent values create personal, institutional, and political agitation. Eventually, one of the values will prevail, or a third value that rationalizes the conflicting values will emerge. Individual choices and institutions will change to reflect value shifts. An example of conflict of values is the existence of slavery in a country that professed that "all men are created equal." The conflict between these two values created a "house divided," and new principles and ways of doing things emerged.

Another view is that values are functional and they will change if they no longer serve the individual or society. For instance, the right of private property is functional because (among other things) it contributes toward economic efficiency. However, the values of private property have had to give way when they conflicted with other social goals. Governments are allowed to take property for the public good under some circumstances, and it is not considered stealing. Taxation requires individuals to give up their private property, yet some taxation is necessary for social stability. There may be a "metavalue," such as the greatest good or cultural survival that determines which values are functional and which are not.

Value changes continually influence LED and practice. Examples include the following:

1. Concern with green values has contributed to the rise of ecotourism. Costa Rica has built a thriving industry around this value change. Similarly, the anti-sprawl or "smart-growth" movement is shaping patterns in an effort to save urban land and avoid commuter-oriented energy use to protect the environment (Weiner & Brown, 2005).

2. The quality of life and the value of leisure activities are more important factors in economic development. Accordingly, businesses recognize that they need

more than high wages to attract some employees. Community planners use their region's amenities as bragging points and describe their amenities in promotional literature. At the same time, many businesses seek high-quality-of-life locations so that they can better attract employees.

3. Social justice is not a new value, but it is increasingly placed in a global context. There is more pressure on regions and businesses to avoid "sweatshop" conditions, provide a just wage, avoid child labor, and so forth. Economic globalization may reduce value diversity among localities, resulting in a spreading concern for basic living standards throughout the world.

4. Values placed on racial and ethnic segregation or integration have shaped urban life in a variety of ways. In many countries, changes in these values reduced social tensions and increased integration. In other countries, increased discord and extreme segregation are leading to "ethnic cleansing."

TECHNOLOGICAL CHANGE

Technological change refers to new ways of organizing activity. Technology does not have to be embodied in a physical product. For instance, the reorganization of a plant so that employees became more efficient could reflect a change in technology even if no new machines were used. Futurists are concerned with the impacts that technological changes can have. In fact, technological forecasting is an established subarea of future studies. Futurists are concerned not only with what new technologies may be developed but also by how they will affect society.

Technological change influences development in numerous ways. Changes in transportation technology influence the urban hierarchy, the shape of cities, and so forth. Construction technology has had similar impacts. Observers have noticed that technology contributed to the financial feasibility of the horizontal construction that has supported the development of greenfields and suburbanization. Examples of how technology affects local economies would themselves fill a book. In recent years, technological advances have been so widespread that they have made futures analysis even more problematic.

Economic developers and planners have become particularly concerned with attracting and supporting high-tech developments to such an extent that "advanced technology cluster" has become a buzz phrase in local development plans. *Advanced technology* is such an elastic phrase that most communities can point out local businesses that either make high-tech products or use advanced technology in their production processes. Consequently, a great many LED efforts can be justified as part of a high-tech development strategy. Furthermore, the development of almost any large business in an area can be considered evidence that a high-tech businesses development was working.

Baumol (1967), in a classic work on technology, divided the economy into two parts. One sector was susceptible to cost reductions due to technological progress, and the other sector was not. Sectors where technology reduced costs tended to be in object-oriented production such as manufacturing. He believed that service activities such as teaching or social work have fixed ratios of service providers to clients and so it is more difficult to apply technology. Accordingly, relative costs in the technologically progressive sector can be anticipated to decrease, and increased costs can be anticipated in service activities.

From this analysis, Baumol drew the conclusion that the costs of urban services—education, police services, trash pickup, and so forth—would become increasingly expensive. Government costs and taxes will grow disproportionately compared with production of things, a situation known as Baumol's disease. However, cost increases among services may not be a crippling problem because the increased productivity in the technology sector would compensate.

In retrospect, Baumol's analysis did not fully account for the ability of technology to extend to the services sector. Adaptations such as online classes or computers in police cars have lowered the cost of education and police services. Also, technology has improved the quality of some services such as medicine at the same time that costs have increased. Nevertheless, an understanding of why technology affects relative costs provides planners, futurists, and economists with insights regarding areas in which the public may require increased government spending and which industries can generate cost savings.

SYSTEMS ORIENTATION

Like economists, futurists have a systems orientation. They realize that because of interrelatedness within a subsystem, a change will have repercussions on many variables. "You cannot change just one thing," a systems thinker quipped. Futurists usually assume a more open or interdependent system, and they often take a global perspective. Economists usually limit their analysis to a few variables, such as the price and quantity of a good. Although no one can examine all of the changes that spring from an event, futurists try to track a wider variety of the repercussions because they are less limited by the boundaries of traditional academic disciplines.

Cumulative Causation and System Stability

Many complex systems are stable. When an event alters a stable economy, such as an urban economy, it normally returns to the original equilibrium. For instance, if a local business closes, wages may fall, making the area more attractive as a place to hire workers, thus restoring equilibrium. One reason why local economies tend to be stable systems is that numerous factors contribute to the current state of the economy. For instance, a full systems perspective might conclude that the size of a local economy is influenced by a variety of components ranging from direct economic activity to seemingly peripheral features. When components of systems reinforce each other, any single change is unlikely to alter significantly the underlying characteristics of the economy.

The stability of systems helps explain why some economic development policies fail. Consider an attempt to increase local incomes. Direct efforts to increase incomes, say an external grant, might achieve that goal in the short run. But unless the basic structure of the economy changes, incomes are likely to revert to previous levels when the grant ends. Very interdependent systems are likely to require substantial analysis to determine which factors (systems analysts might say parameters) can permanently influence outcomes.

In addition to stability, some systems can experience prolonged periods of cumulative causation. *Cumulative causation* refers to the process in which a change in one direction may reinforce other tendencies for change in the same direction. The change may operate toward a better or worse economy. Myrdal (1957) believed that disequilibrium paths were not uncommon in economic development:

> In the normal case, a change does not call forth countervailing changes, but, instead, supporting changes which move the system in the same direction as the first change but much further. Because of such circular causation, a social process tends to become cumulative and often to gather speed at an accelerating rate. (p. 13)

Consider the prospect of a downward cumulative causation. The process might be imitated by the closing of a local business. As a result, wages and purchasing power decrease. Additional businesses may fold. Sometimes it is difficult for policymakers to identify these points of cumulative decline, but when they believe that the economy is approaching such a juncture, extraordinary efforts to reverse the course may be appropriate.

Unanticipated Consequences

Complex systems often generate unintended consequences because policymakers are only concerned with part of a system and don't adequately trace the impacts on other parts of the system. Would public policy have been as supportive of the automobile had decision makers anticipated costs including 50,000 deaths annually, hundreds of thousands of injuries, billions of dollars of property damage, urban sprawl, oil dependency, and unwanted pregnancies? Of course, the benefits of the automobile may still outweigh the costs, but even desirable changes have some undesirable impacts.

Harman (1974) observed the existence of "problems of success." In the novelist Isaac Asimov's words, "There are no happy endings to history." Problems of success that affect LED include the following:

1. Prolonging life expectancy exacerbates problems of caring for the elderly.

2. Technological innovations dislocate workers.

3. Increased per capita incomes lead to increased isolation of the urban poor.

4. Efficient production systems result in dehumanization of some work.

5. Affluence results in increased energy use and pollution.

6. Satisfaction of basic needs results in revolutions of "rising expectations."

7. Economic growth results in inequality between rich and poor.

IMPORTANCE OF TIMING

Economists recognize the importance of time in forecasting. Anyone can correctly forecast an economic expansion or recession. Eventually, such an event will occur. But such forecasts do little good unless the forecast explains when the event will occur. Futurist writers often are not precise about the timing of events when they describe qualitative or speculative trends. (Futurists are more speculative then economists.)

The future has been categorized as follows: (1) immediate future—starting now and extending generally up to 1 year in the future, (2) near-term future—1 to 5 years from now in the future, (3) middle-range future—5 to 20 years from now, (4) long-range future—20 to 50 years from now, (5) the far future—more than 50 years from now. Economic forecasts tend to be in the "now." Planners for government and business tend to operate in the near-term and middle-range future. Futurists tend to think of the middle-range future and the long range-future. While this time horizon may seem excessive, the economic life of a major public building could be a century.

Futurists are very sensitive to how rapidly change occurs, and many futurists believe that the rate of change is accelerating. Some trends spread very rapidly. Factors that determine the spread of some changes include whether the changes are supported by enthusiastic proliferators, whether the trend "sticks" when another person is exposed to it, and the context of the situation (Gladwell, 2000).

The timing of events can also be controlled. If a society makes a particular project a high priority, it can often be accomplished quickly. For instance, it required only 4 years to develop the nuclear bomb once the decision had been made to give that goal a high priority. Eight years after President Kennedy announced the goal of reaching the moon, we were there. Of course, the scientific knowledge base for accomplishing these goals took centuries to develop. Yet at the time that the goals were announced, most people considered them unattainable in the near future.

Planning Perspectives on LED

The term *planner* frequently connotes an urban land-use planner. However, land-use planning is only one type of planning activity. Near-, middle-, and long-range planning have become important functions in both public and private sectors. Private firms such as real estate development companies engage in planning. Almost all major corporations engage in some types of strategic planning. Local governments have planning departments to help accomplish a variety of goals, including economic development. Social service agencies or transportation authorities might use a planner to develop goals and strategies for specific activities. The discussion below is primarily concerned with urban planning in the public sector; however, the principles are applicable to private planning as well.

THE PLANNING PROCESS

Most planners agree that the planning process is important because it serves as a vehicle for participants to think about the future. The process is often considered to be more important than the document or "plan" that results from the process. Often "plans" are put on the shelf, while the thinking that went into the plans has a significant influence. Figure 13.1 illustrates a generic planning process. The principal steps are (1) goal articulation (i.e., increase employment) and projections (i.e., employment growth will be inadequate if nothing changes), (2) intervention choice (i.e., a low-interest loan program), and (3) implementation (i.e., create an economic development bank). Goal articulation requires a vision of what the city should look like at some time in the future. Future goals should be based on a realistic understanding of what is possible rather than a wish list. Interventions are required to alter likely outcomes. Finally, the implementation process should feed back into the plan so it can be updated to reflect changing circumstances.

Goals and Projections

Many cities have master plans that establish future goals. Historically, urban master plans have been strong in describing physical development goals such as where the new shopping centers, sewage treatment facility, and other developments will be. They are increasingly including social goals.

Goals must be developed from a base of where the community is and where it will be if current trends continue and resources are available to affect change. Goals should be realistic. Consequently planners need to understand and analyze the community and its resources before or simultaneously with the development of goals. The development of realistic goals is sometimes accompanied by a visioning process where realism is set aside and a world is imagined where resources are more abundant than in reality.

The selection of the most appropriate goals is more difficult in public planning than in private planning. Private companies often have a clear goal—maximizing profits or stockholder wealth. Public agencies have a variety of

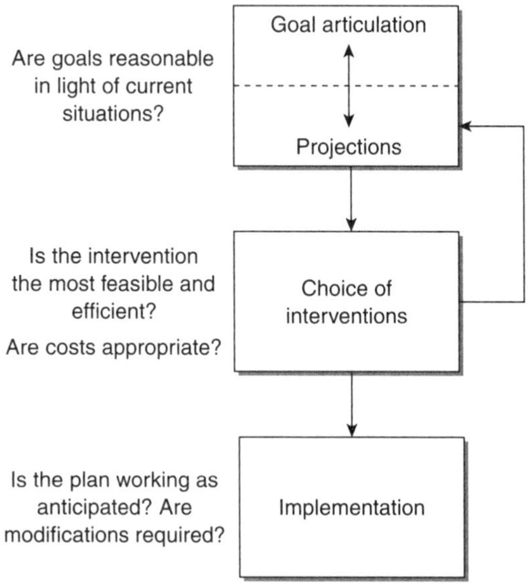

Figure 13.1   The Planning Process

NOTE: The planning process may include feedbacks so that goals may be revised or new interventions selected.

goals that reflect competing interests within the community. For instance, the goal of open space could conflict with the goal of industrial employment growth.

In addition to determining where the community is now, it is important to determine where the community will be if current events run their course. How well can analysts predict the future? Some things such as demographic composition can be predicted very well. Other elements of the urban future are easy to predict because local officials can control the outcome. For instance, the land-use pattern might be predictable if a particular land-use pattern were of a high political priority. However, most aspects of the urban future are neither easy to predict nor totally controllable.

Comparing goals with projected outcomes in the absence of deliberate interventions is useful to determine whether intervention is necessary. Frequently, goals must be changed if they are unrealistic or the result of strong trends that policies may not change significantly.

Selection of Interventions

What changes could be made to alter the course of events in order to achieve desired goals? There are many ways to achieve particular ends: Planners usually consider a variety of policies to achieve particular goals.

A first step in selecting policy interventions is to determine whether proposed interventions are feasible. Can the intervention be implemented given the community values, political patterns, budget constraints, and national trends? A proposal that cannot be implemented is seldom useful. It is also necessary to determine whether the intervention will actually bring about the desired goal. Like a less than adequate dosage of medication, some policies may be insufficient to accomplish the tasks, and too little may be worse than nothing. Many proposed interventions may be rejected at this stage.

Since many ends can be achieved through a variety of interventions, the planning process should select one of the various feasible interventions. Four criteria for selecting an appropriate intervention are as follows: (1) the most likely to produce the desired outcome, (2) the least costly, (3) the one with the lowest risk of negative outcomes, and (4) the most likely to contribute to other desirable outcomes. Selecting among feasible interventions can be complicated because some interventions may affect more than one planning goal. Therefore, an intervention that is less efficient in achieving one particular goal may be preferred because it helps achieve other goals. In the planning process, goals may have to be adjusted if the necessary interventions are not feasible.

Implementation

Many, many plans have failed because planners have not been concerned with implementation. The plan may be set on the shelf, or unanticipated snags may result in a scrapping of the plan. Most planners believe that a plan should be updated regularly. These rolling plans require a link to the implementation process so that the plan can be modified to reflect unanticipated events or implementation problems. A 10-year plan might require revisions every 2 years. The fact that a plan must be modified to reflected changes in the environment does not mean the initial plan was inadequate.

A suboptimal plan may be better than a technically "best" plan if the "suboptimal" plan has the support of the individuals involved in implementation. During implementation, buy-ins and the cooperation of many people are required. An excellent plan introduced in an uncooperative environment will probably be sabotaged. Furthermore, unanticipated events normally require changes in a plan, and these same changes provide opportunities for the individuals charged with implementing the plan to undermine it. The more broadly based the planning process, the more likely it is that individuals responsible for implementing the plan will support it. Of course, some plans must be introduced in situations where the implementers are hostile, as might be the case when one political faction reverses a previous plan of action. In this case, implementation may face sabotage concerns.

LIMITS OF PLANNING

LED planning has increased in importance. Today, large and medium-sized communities throughout the world have either economic development plans or a strategic plan in which economic development is a major part. Numerous consulting firms specialize in economic development planning, and federal and state governments provide financial assistance for such planning. There is a wide variety of economic development plans, reflecting differing regional resources, opportunities, and differing philosophies of the planners.

Planning, however, is limited in its ability to shape the environment because imagination and knowledge are limited. Furthermore, local financial resources are inadequate for many tasks. Another planning limitation is the need to coordinate plans with other communities, particularly higher levels of government. Sometimes these coordination requirements bind local planners to certain approaches or limit what can be considered. Another key limitation to planning in a capitalist environment is that other groups are usually needed for plan realization. The private sector is probably the largest force in LED, and most comprehensive plans will fail if they do not account for how private individuals in pursuit of their self-interest will react. At the same time *self-interest* is not synonymous with *selfish*, and many individuals will devote time and private resources out of a desire to see their community do well.

Planning and Future Studies Tools

The tools that economists bring to the study of urban futures are powerful. They include modeling, forecasting, and other econometric techniques, and, perhaps most important, the ability to apply economic theory. There are some tools that have been useful for understanding future events that are unfamiliar to many economists. This section describes tools that can be used in the planning and futures analysis—Delphi forecasting, games, scenario development, and environmental scanning.

DELPHI FORECASTING

Delphi forecasting is useful in developing answers about future events for which technical knowledge is required and where judgments are important ingredients. The Delphi technique is a way of combining expert opinion with group discussion and learning. To illustrate the use of the Delphi forecast, suppose you wish to know if and when a new regional airport will be built.

First a group of experts about the subject to be explored are convened. Delphi forecasting avoids "averaging ignorance," which might taint some random public opinion surveys, thus the reliance on experts. Next, a questionnaire is developed and distributed to the experts asking questions relating to when or whether a new airport will be feasible. The reasoning of participants and their degree of confidence might also be asked. After the responses have been tabulated, the results may be sent back to the panel of experts and the question asked again. In the second round, the experts will be able to reevaluate their original forecast in light of the opinion and information given by other experts. For instance, one expert might have said that a new regional airport would be built by 2015 because of traffic control problems. Another expert might have replied that new technologies in traffic control would relieve the congestion problem without the need for an additional facility. An economist might suggest that high construction costs and local budgetary limitations make the construction unfeasible in the near future. Faced with the new information, the individual who thought the airport would be needed very soon might revise the estimate to, say, 2020. The second-round projections would be informed by the results of the first round. Generally, the expert opinions will converge after successive rounds, as indicated by Figure 13.2.

The Delphi technique is versatile. The rounds can be conducted by mail, by phone, face-to face, by computer network, or through other means. The moderator can instruct the panel to accept certain assumptions as given so that various alternatives can be explored and a sensitivity analysis conducted. For instance, an assumption about regional population growth could be built into the question regarding the need for a new regional airport. Cross-impact analysis can be combined with futures analysis so that the impacts forecast in one

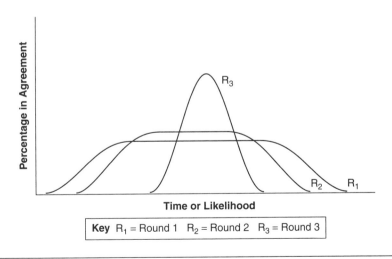

Figure 13.2   Convergence of Opinion in a Delphi Forecast

NOTE: During a successful Delphi, the opinions of experts will tend to converge.

Delphi conference can be used as assumptions in other Delphi studies to ensure that events projected in various studies are consistent.

There are two significant dangers in implementing and interpreting Delphi forecasts. First, situations where the results represent an averaging of ignorance should be avoided. The advantages of an expert panel will be negated if the questions are about things the respondents are unfamiliar with. However, the experts need not have similar backgrounds. In fact, it may be useful to include experts in a variety of fields in some forecasts. Second, a dominating personality can sometimes force individuals to conform to an opinion simply to avoid being contrary. The moderator should be particularly careful not to dominate the expert panel.

GAMES

Games are characterized by the assignment of a role to various participants. Individuals behave as they believe they would, given their role. The game should be structured so that the participants face constraints similar to the situation being simulated. An urban development game might include such roles as mayor, land developers, factory owners, and workers. A game master would create a situation and set parameters. As the game proceeds, the players might make demands on each other, form coalitions, or negotiate particular outcomes. The games are useful in helping players grasp the complex interactions that might be involved in real-life situations. The rules of the game might be changed to determine how the outcome would differ under different situations.

Games have been a major tool in military planning. War games often involve actual soldiers, but war games can also be played in a more abstract setting. Military games played by think tanks such as the RAND Corporation help demonstrate the problems with a strategy of "massive retaliation" and help demonstrate the need for flexible responses in addition to all-out war.

SCENARIOS

A scenario is a plausible story. It is a description of a series of events that the writer could imagine happening. Scenario writing appears simple, but complete and plausible scenarios are difficult to write. They require imagination and discipline. If the occurrence of a future event can be described as the logical outcome of a series of likely intermediate events, a higher probability should be given to the likelihood of that event. Often when a historian looks back on an event, the steps that led to it appear logical and predictable. With hindsight, it may appear that a scenario of the future could have been written easily. Conversely, if intermediate steps leading to a future event cannot be reasonably envisioned, the future event can be deemed unlikely.

Scenario development seems simple because we are so familiar with the technique. Many novels are scenarios. Using this approach it is not sufficient to say that an event will take place in the future. How it can be realized must be shown. A scenario is a way of describing how a future state can be achieved. Developing a plausible scenario that leads to a nonobvious conclusion about the future is a difficult but valuable accomplishment.

ENVIRONMENTAL SCANNING

Social scanning is a rather simple technique. It consists of monitoring newspapers and other current events and attempting to spot trends. Corporate boards and advisory committees are often composed of individuals from diverse fields to serve a scanning function among other things. Futures analysis may be formalized in the process by selecting a group of monitors from different fields. Thus, one team member might be asked to focus on value changes, while another might focus on technological or governmental trends. The scanning group may meet occasionally to discuss the trends (or hypothesis) they have identified and determine potential interactions. Trends that tend to reinforce one another are more likely to be realized. For instance, an environmental consciousness and the problem of pollution reinforce each other, suggesting that "environmental concerns" will be a long-term trend (Bodell, 2006).

Summary

The purpose of this chapter is to develop a future perspective on LED. Almost by definition, economic development is a forward-looking subject. Economic development planners must think strategically and plant seeds that may bear fruit only after many years.

Futurists have diverse points of view; yet there are common threads in their analyses. Futurists avoid suggesting that they can predict the future. They describe likely events if certain trends prevail or if certain changes occur. Concerns about value changes, technological developments, the interrelatedness of social and ecological systems, and the importance of timing are important in futures analysis. All these factors can be critical in economic development planning.

Planners need to be able to understand future possibilities and the ability to describe the means of achieving desirable futures. Planners in both public and private sectors frequently rely on economic paradigms. Most planners believe that the planning process is as important as a final document or plan. The planning process can be a vehicle for thinking about the future. A three-step planning process would include (1) the development of goals and projections, (2) selection interventions, and (3) implementation. The planning process is iterative, and monitoring is useful. Planning can affect the course of LED, but it is limited because most decisions are not under the direct control of planners.

Several useful tools are available for planning and futures analysis. First, Delphi forecasting can be used to help understand the future by drawing on expert opinion. Second, games can be used to simulate the possible course of events. A well-structured game includes realistic constraints on the behavior. Third, scenarios are descriptions of events that could evolve from the current flow of events. The more realistic the scenario, the more likely the future event is to occur. Finally, environmental and social scanning attempt to identify trends that will affect the locality through an organized monitoring of newspapers and other current services.

References

Alexander Grant. (1985). *General manufacturing climates of the forty-eight contiguous states of America.* Chicago: Author.

Allen, D. N., & Hayward, D. J. (1990). The role of new venture formation/entrepreneurship in regional development. *Economic Development Quarterly, 4*(1), 55–63.

Ashton, D. J., & Sternal, B. K. (1978). *Business services and New England's export base.* Boston: Federal Reserve Bank of Boston.

Bartik, T. (1990). The market failure approach to regional economic development policy. *Economic Development Quarterly, 4,* 361–370.

Bartik, T. J. (1984). Business location decisions in the United States: Estimates of the effects of unionization, taxes, and other characteristics of states. *Journal of Business and Economic Statistics, 3,* 14–22.

Bartik, T. J. (1991). *Who benefits from state and local economic development policies?* Kalamazoo, MI: W. E. Upjohn Institute.

Bartik, T. J. (1992). Effects of state and local taxes on economic development: A review of recent research. *Economic Development Quarterly, 6*(1), 102–110.

Batheldt, H., Malmber, A., & Maskell, P. (2004). Clusters and knowledge: Local buzz, global pipelines and the process of knowledge creation. *Progress in Human Geography, 28*(1), 31–56.

Baumol, W. J. (1986). Productivity growth, convergence, and welfare: What the long-run data show. *American Economic Review, 76*(5), 1072–1085.

Baumol, W. (1967). The macroeconomics of unbalanced growth: The anatomy of urban crisis. *American Economic Review, 57*(3), 415–426.

Beauregard, R. (1993). Constituting economic development: A theoretical perspective. In R. Bingham & R. Mier (Eds.), *Theories of local economic development: Perspectives from across the disciplines* (pp. 267–283). Newbury Park, CA: Sage.

Becker, G. (1975). *Human capital* (2nd ed.). New York: National Bureau of Economic Research and Columbia University Press.

Bell, M. E., & Bowman, J. H. (1987). The effects of various intergovernmental aid and local own-source revenues: The case of property taxes in Minnesota cities. *Public Finance Quarterly, 15*(3), 282–297.

Berry, B., & Parr, J. B. (with Epstein, A., Ghosh, A., & Smith, R.). (1988). *Market centers and retail locations.* Englewood Cliffs, NJ: Prentice Hall.

Beyers, W. B., & Alvine, M. J. (1985). Export services in post–industrial society. *Papers of the Regional Science Association, 57,* 33–45.

Blair, J., & Carroll, M. C. (2007). Inner-city neighborhoods and metropolitan development. *Economic Development Quarterly, 21*(3), 263–277.

Blair, J., & Endres, C. (1994). Hidden economic development assets. *Economic Development Quarterly, 8*(3), 286–291.

Blair, J. P., Fichtenbaum, R., & Swaney, J. (1984). The market for jobs. *Urban Affairs Quarterly, 20*(1), 64–77.

Blair, J. P., & Premus, R. (1987). Choosing a location for an industrial facility: What influences the corporate decision maker? *Perspective, 14.*

Blinder, A. S. (1987). *Hard heads, soft hearts: Tough–minded economics for a just society.* New York: Addison-Wesley.

Blomquist, G. C., Berger, M. C., & Hoehn, J. P. (1988, March). New estimates of the quality of life in urban areas. *American Economic Review,* 89–107.

Bloomberg, W., & Sandoval, R. M. (1982). Hispanic-American urban order: A border perspective. In G. Gappert & R. Knight (Ed.), *Cities in the 21st century* (pp. 112–132). Beverly Hills, CA: Sage.

Bodell, L. (2006). Best practices in social scanning. *The Futurist, 40*(5), 5–8.

Bolton, R. (1985). Regional econometric models. *Journal of Regional Science, 25*(4), 495–518.

Booth, D. E. (1986). Long waves and uneven regional growth. *Southern Economic Journal, 53*(2), 448–460.

Borjas, G. J. (1987). Immigrants, minorities, and labor market competition. *Industrial Labor Relations Review, 40*(3), 382–392.

Borts, G. H., & Stein, J. (1964). *Economic growth in a free market.* New York: Columbia University Press.

Bowen, H. P., Leamer, E. E., & Sveikauskas, L. (1987). Multicountry, multifactor tests of the factor abundance theory. *American Economic Review, December,* 791–809.

Bridge, G. (2007). A global gentrifier class? *Environment and Planning A, 39*(1), 32–46.

Bureau of Economic Analysis. (1993). *Regional multipliers.* Washington, DC: Department of Commerce.

Burgess, E. W. (1952). The growth of the city. In R. Parks, E. Burgess, & C. McKenzie (Eds.), *The city.* Chicago: University of Chicago Press.

Carlino, G. A. (1980). Contrasts in agglomeration: New York and Pittsburgh reconsidered. *Urban Studies, 17, 3.*

Carlton, D. (1983). The location and employment choices of new firms: An econometric model with discrete and continuous endogenous variables. *Review of Economics and Statistics, 65,* 440–449.

Castells, M. (1996). *The rise of network society.* Oxford, UK: Blackwell.

Charney, A. H. (1983). Intraurban manufacturing locational decisions and local tax differentials. *Journal of Urban Economics, 14,* 184–205.

Chinitz, R. (1961). Contrasts in agglomeration: New York and Pittsburgh. *American Economic Review, 51, 2.*

Christaller, W. (1966). *Central places of southern Germany.* Englewood Cliffs, NJ: Prentice Hall.

Christensen, J. L., & Drejer, I. (2005). The strategic importance of location: Location decisions and the effects of firm location on innovation and knowledge acquisition. *European Planning Studies, 13,* 807–814.

Clark, G. L. (1983). *Interregional migration, national policy and social justice.* Totowa, NJ: Rowman & Allanheld.

Clotfelter, C. (1975). The effect of school desegregation on housing prices. *Review of Economics and Statistics, 57*(4), 446–451.

Coase, R. (1963). The problem of social cost. *Journal of Law and Economics, 3*, 1–44.

Coates, J. F. (1982). New technologies and their urban impact. In G. Gappert & R. Knight (Eds.), *Cities in the 21st century* (chap. 10). Beverly Hills, CA: Sage.

Crowder, K., & South, S. (2005). Race, class, and changing patterns for migration between poor and nonpoor neighborhoods. *American Journal of Sociology, 110*(6), 1715–1736.

Cutler, H., England, S., & Weiler, S. (2003). Determining regional structure through cointegration. *Review of Regional Studies, 33*(2), 164–183.

Danziger, S., & Gottschalk, P. (1986, September). Work, poverty, and the working poor: A multifaceted problem. *Monthly Labor Review*, 7–25.

Department of Housing and Urban Development. (1988). *The President's national urban policy report 1988.* Washington, DC: Author.

De Soto, H. (1989). *The other path.* New York: Harper & Row.

Dickson, K. (Fall, 2005). Pounding the pavement. *Economic Journal*, pp. 27–31.

Dietzenbacher, E. (2005). More on multipliers. *Journal of Regional Science, 45*(2), 421–426.

Doeringer, P. B., & Terkla, D. G. (1992). Japanese direct investment and development policy. *Economic Development Quarterly, 6*(3), 255–271.

Eberts, R. W., & Grorberg, T. J. (1989). Can competition among local governments constrain government spending? *Economic Review, 24*(1), 2–9.

Erickson, R. A. (1987). Business climate studies: A critical evaluation. *Economic Development Quarterly, 1*(1), 62–72.

Fagan, M., & Longino, S. F., Jr. (1993). Migrating retirees: A source for economic development. *Economic Development Quarterly, 7*(1), 98–106.

Feser, E., Sweeney, S., & Renski, H. (2005). A descriptive analysis of discrete U.S. industrial complexes. *Journal of Regional Science, 45*(2), 395–419.

Feser, E. J., & Sweeney, S. H. (2002). Theory, methods, and a cross-metropolitan comparison of business clusters. In P. McCann (Ed.), *Industrial location economics* (pp. 222–259). Cheltenham, UK: Edward Elgar.

Florida, R. (2002). *The rise of the creative class.* New York: Basic Books.

Fortune. (1977). *Facility location decisions.* New York: Author.

Friedman, M. (1962). *Capitalism and freedom.* Chicago: University of Chicago Press.

Friedman, T. L. (2005). *The world is flat: A brief history of the twenty-first century.* New York: Farrar, Starus & Giroux.

Gabe, T. M., & Bell, K. P. (2004). Tradeoffs between local taxes and government spending as determinants of business location. *Journal of Regional Science, 44*(2), 21–41.

Galster, G. C. (1987). *Homeowners and neighborhood reinvestment.* Durham, NC: Duke University Press.

Galster, G. C., Cutsinger, J., & Lim, U. (2007). Are neighborhoods self-stabilizing? Exploring endogenous dynamics. *Urban Studies, 44*(1), 1–19.

Galster, G. C., Levy, D., Sawyer, N., Temkin, K., & Walker, C. (2005). The impact of community development corporations on urban neighborhoods. Washington, DC: Urban Institute.

Gappert, G. (1982). Future urban America: Post affluent or advanced industrial society? In G. Gappert & R. Knight (Eds.), *Cities in the 21st century* (chap. 1). Beverly Hills, CA: Sage.

Garreau, J. (1991). *Edge city: Life on the new frontier.* New York: Random House.

Garrison, W. L., & Levinson, D. M. (2006). *The transportation experience: Policy, planning, and development.* New York: Oxford University Press.

Gerking, S. D., & Weirick, W. N. (1983). Compensating differences and interregional wage differentials. *Review of Economics and Statistics, 65,* 483–487.

Giese, A., & Testa, W. A. (1988). Can industrial R&D survive the decline of production activity? *Economic Development Quarterly, 2*(4), 326–338.

Gillis, W. (1987). Can service-producing industries provide for regional economic growth. *Economic Development Quarterly, 1*(3), 249–255.

Gittell, R., & Vidal, A. (1998). *Community organizing: Building social capital as a development strategy.* Thousand Oaks, CA: Sage.

Gladwell, M. (2000). *The tipping point: How little things can make a big difference.* Boston: Little, Brown.

Green, H. L. (1959). Hinterland boundaries of New York City and Boston in southern New England. In H. M. Mayer & C. F. Kohn (Eds.), *Readings in Urban Geography.* Chicago: University of Chicago Press.

Green, K. V., Neenan, W. B., & Scott, C. D. (1976). Fiscal incidence in the Washington metropolitan area. *Land Economics, 52,* 13–31.

Greenwood, M. J. (1985). Human migration: Theory, models, and empirical studies. *Journal of Regional Science, 25*(4), 521–543.

Gwartney, J., & Lawson, R. (2006). *Economic freedom of the World 2006 annual report.* Vancouver, British Columbia, Canada: Fraser Institute. Retrieved June 2006 from www.freetheworld.com.

Hajiran, H. (2006). Toward a quality of life theory: Net domestic product of happiness. *Social Indicators Research, 75,* 31–43.

Hanson, R. L., & Berkman, M. B. (1991). Gauging the rainmakers: Towards a meteorology of state legislative climates. *Economic Development Quarterly, 5*(3), 213–228.

Harman, R. (1974). The coming transformation in our view of knowledge. *The Futurist, 8*(3), 15–24.

Harper, D. A. (2003). *Foundations of entrepreneurship and economic development.* New York: Routledge.

Harrington, M. (1984). *The new American poverty.* New York: Penguin Books.

Harris, J. R., & Todaro, M. P. (1970). Migration, unemployment and development: A two sector analysis. *American Economic Review, 60,* 126–142.

Harrison, B. (1974). Ghetto economic development. *Journal of Economic Literature, March,* 1–37.

Harvey, D. (1976). *Social justice and the city.* Baltimore: Johns Hopkins University Press.

Haug, P., & Ness, P. (1993). Industrial location decisions of biotechnology organizations. *Economic Development Quarterly, 7*(4), 390–402.

Heckman, J. S. (1982). Survey of locational decisions in the South. *Economic Review, 67,* 6–19.

Henderson, J. W., Kelly, T. M., & Taylor, B. A. (2000). The impact of agglomeration economies on estimated demand thresholds: An extension of Wensley and Stabler. *Journal of Regional Science, 40*(4), 719–733.

Henry, G. (1954). *Progress and poverty.* New York: Robert Schalkenbach Foundation. (Republished in 1992)

Hill, E. W., & Bier, T. (1989). Economic restructuring: Earnings, occupations, and housing values in Cleveland. *Economic Development Quarterly, 3*(2), 123–134.

Hill, E. W., & Wolman, H. L. (1997). City-suburban income disparities and metropolitan area employment: Can tightening labor markets reduce the gaps? *Urban Affairs Review, 32*(4), 558–582.

Hill, E. W., Wolman, H. L., & Ford, C. C., III. (1995). Can suburbs survive without their central cities? *Urban Affairs Review, 31*(2), 147–174.

Hirschman, A. O. (1972). *Strategies of economic development: Processes and problems.* New York: John Wiley & Sons.

Hoover, E. M. (1948). *The location of economic activity.* New York: McGraw-Hill.

Howarth, R. B., & Farber, S. (2002). Accounting for the value of ecosystem services. *Ecological Economics, 41,* 421–429.

Hoyt, H. (1939). *The structure and growth of residential neighborhoods in American cities.* Washington, DC: Government Printing Office.

Huff, D. L. (1964). A probabilistic analysis of shopping center trade areas. *Land Economics, 39,* 81–90.

Hunt, J. C., & Kau, J. B. (1985). Migration and wage growth: A human capital framework. *Southern Economic Journal, 51*(3), 647–710.

Ihlanfelt, K. R., & Sjoquist, D. L. (1991). The role of space in determining the occupations of black and white workers. *Regional Science and Urban Economics, 21*(2), 295–315.

International Council of Shopping Centers and Business for Social Responsibility. (2001–2002, Winter). Underserved markets—An untapped bonanza? [Electronic version]. *ICSC Research Quarterly, 8*(4). Retrieved from www.icsc.org/government/underserved_markets.pdf#xml=http://icscsearch.icsc.org/texis/search/pdfhi.txt?query=business+for+social+responsibility&pr=IcscLiveNew&prox=page&rorder=500&rprox=500&rdfreq=500&rwfreq=500&rlead=500&sufs=0&order=r&cq=&id=47b243a0e8

Jacobs, J. (1969). *The economy of cities.* New York: Random House.

James, J. B., Lee, C. F., & Sirmans, C. F. (1986). *Urban econometrics: Model development and empirical results.* Greenwich, CT: JAI Press.

Jargowsky, P. A. (2003). *Stunning progress; hidden problems: The dramatic decline of concentrated poverty in the 1990s.* Washington, DC: Brookings Institution.

Kain, J. F. (1968, Spring). Housing segregation, Negro employment, and metropolitan decentralization. *Quarterly Journal of Economics, 23,* 7–27.

Kasarda, J. D. (1990). City and jobs on a collision course: The urban underclass dilemma. *Economic Development Quarterly, 4*(4), 313–319.

Kay, A. (2005). Social capital, the social economy and community development. *Community Development Journal, 41*(2), 160–173.

Keil, S. R., & Hirschel, T. A. (1986). Identifying export potential in the export sector. *Growth and Change, 55,* 1–10.

Kenny, C. (2005). Does development make you happy? Subjective well-being and economic growth in developing countries. *Social Indicators Research, 73*(2), 199–219.

Kieschnick, M. (1981). *Taxes and growth: Business incentives and economic development.* Washington, DC: Council of State Planning Agencies.

King, K. A. (2005). Impacts of school choice on regional economic growth. *Review of Regional Studies, 35*(3), 356–368.

Klaassen, L. H., & Pawlowski, A. (1982). Long-term forecasting, meditations of two pitfall collectors. *Man, Environment, Space and Time, 2*(1).

Kozlowski, P. J. (1987, Summer). Regional indexes of leading indicators: An evaluation of forecasting performance. *Growth and Change,* 62–73.

Kratke, S. (2007). Metropolisation of the European economic territory as a consequence of urban agglomeration in the knowledge economy. *European Planning Studies, 15*(1), 1–27.

Ladd, H. F. (2002). *Market based reforms in urban education.* Washington, DC: Economic Policy Institute.

Ledebur, L., & Barnes, W. R. (1993). *All in it together?* Washington, DC: National League of Cities.

Lejano, R. P., & Wesse, A. T. (2006). Community development: Seeking common ground in discourse and in practice. *Urban Studies. 43*(9), 1469–1489.

Leniz, R. (1989). Business expansion and retention programs: A panoramic view. *Economic Development Review, 3*(1), 15–18.

Levy, J. M. (1985). *Urban and metropolitan economics.* New York: McGraw-Hill.

Lichtenberg, R. M. (1960). *One-tenth of a nation.* Cambridge, MA: Harvard University Press.

Losch, A. (1954). *The economics of location.* New Haven, CT: Yale University Press.

Lowe, M. (2005). Regional shopping centers in the inner city: A study of retail lead community development. *Urban Studies, 42*(3), 449–470.

Markusen, A. (2004). Targeting occupations in regional and community economic development. *Journal of the American Planning Association, 70*(3), 253–268.

Martin, R., & Sunley, P. (2003). Deconstructing clusters: Chaotic concept or policy panacea? *Journal of Economic Geography, 3,* 5–35.

Mayo, S. K. (1991). Theory and estimation in the economics of housing demand. *Journal of Urban Economics, 9,* 90–211.

McCann, E. (2004). Best places: Interurban competition, quality of life and popular media discourse. *Urban Studies, 41*(10), 1909–1929.

Mills, D. E. (1989). Is zoning a negative sum game? *Land Economics, 65*(1), 1–12.

Mills, E. S. (1993). The misuse of regional economic models. *CATO Journal, 13*(1), 29–40.

Mills, E. S., & Hamilton, B. W. (1984). *Urban economics* (3rd ed.) Glenview, IL: Scott Foresman.

Mills, E. S., & Lau, M. R. (1964). A model of market areas with free entry. *Journal of Political Economy, 72.*

Miriam, A. (2006). Identifying employment-creating sectors in South Africa: The role of service industries. *Development Southern Africa, 23*(5), 627–647.

Morgan, W. (1964). *The effects of state and local tax and financial incentives on industrial location.* Unpublished doctoral dissertation, University of Colorado.

Morse, G. (1996). Moving from R @ E's to jobs. In *The expansion and retention of existing businesses.* Ames: Iowa State University Press.

Moss, P., & Tilly, C. (2001). Stories employers tell: Race, skill, and hiring in America. New York: Russell Sage Foundation.

Moulder, E., & Hall, G. (1995). *Business retention initiatives in local government.* Washington, DC: International City Managers Association.

Muller, T., & Dawson, G. (1972). *The fiscal impact of residential and commercial development*. Washington, DC: Urban Institute.

Musgrave, R. A. (1959). *The theory of public finance*. New York: McGraw-Hill.

Muth, R. F. (1969). *Cities and housing*. Chicago: University of Chicago Press.

Myrdal, G. (1957). *Rich lands and poor*. New York: Harper & Row.

Neenan, W. B. (1972). *Political economy of urban areas*. Chicago: Markham.

Neenan, W. B. (1981). *Urban public economics* (chap. 3). Belmont, CA: Wadsworth.

Nel, P. (2003). Income inequality, economic growth, and political instability in sub-Saharan Africa. *Journal of Modern African Studies, 41*(4), 611–639.

Noonan, D., Krupka, D. J., & Baden, B. M. (2007). Neighborhood dynamics and price effects of superfund site clean-up. *Journal of Regional Science, 47*(4), 665–692.

Norgaard, R. (1984). Coevolutionary development potential. *Land Economics, 60,* 159–176.

Nowak, J. (1997). Neighborhood initiative and the regional economy. *Economic Development Quarterly, 11,* 3–10.

Noyelle, T. J., & Stanback, T. M., Jr. (1984). *The economic transformation of American cities*. Totowa, NJ: Littlefield, Adams; Rowman & Allanheld.

Oates, W. E. (1969). The effects of property taxes and local public spending on property values: An empirical study of tax capitalization and the Tiebout hypothesis. *Journal of Political Economy, 77,* 957–970.

Oates, W. E. (1981). On local finance and the Tiebout model. *American Economic Review, 71*(2), 93–98.

Obwona, M. B. (2001). Determinants of FDI and their impact on economic growth. *African Development Review, 13*(1), 46–81.

Olfert, M. R., & Stabler, J. C. (1994). Community level multipliers for rural development initiatives. *Growth and Change, 25,* 467–486.

Olsen, E. O. (1969). A competitive theory of the housing market. *American Economic Review, 59,* 612–621.

Partridge, M. D., & Rickman, D. S. (2003). Do we know economic development when we see it? *Review of Regional Studies, 33*(1), 17–39.

Pastor, M., Dreier, P., Grigsby, J. E., III, & Lopez-Garza, M. (2006). *Regions that work: How cities and suburbs can grow together*. Minneapolis: University of Minnesota Press.

Pellegrini, L. (2004). Corruptions effect on growth and its transmission channels. *Kyklos, 57*(3), 429–456.

Persky, J., Ranney, D., & Wiewel, W. (1993). Import substitution and local development. *Economic Development Quarterly, 7*(1), 18–29.

Plantinga, A. J., & Bennell, S. (2005). A spatial economic analysis of urban land use and obesity. *Journal of Regional Science, 45*(3), 473–492.

Porter, M. (1997). New strategies for inner-city economic development. *Economic Development Quarterly, 11*(1), 10–42.

Porter, M. E. (1990). *The competitive advantage of nations*. New York: Free Press.

Porter, M. E. (1998a). Clusters and the new economics of competition. *Harvard Business Review, November/December,* 77–90.

Porter, M. E. (1998b). *On competition*. Boston: Harvard Business School Press.

Powell, L. M., Slater, S., Mirtcheva, D., Bao, Y., & Chaloupka, F. (2007, March). Food store availability and neighborhood characteristics in the United States. *Preventive Medicine,* 189–195.

Pred, A. (1977). *City-systems in advanced economics* (chap. 1). New York: Wiley.

Pred, A. R. (1966). *The spatial dynamics of U.S. urban-industrial growth.* Cambridge: MIT Press.

Premus, R. (1982). *Locational high-technology firms and regional economic development* (U.S. Congress, Joint Economic Committee Report). Washington, DC: Joint Economic Committee.

President's Commission for a National Agenda for the Eighties. (1981). *Urban America in the eighties: Perspectives and prospects.* Washington, DC: Government Printing Office.

Putnam, R. (1993). *Making democracy work: Civic traditions in modern Italy.* Princeton, NJ: Princeton University Press.

Ramsey, D. D. (1972). Suburban-central city exploitation thesis: Comment. *National Tax Journal, 25,* 599–604.

Reilly, W. J. (1931). *The law of retail gravitation.* New York: Pillsbury.

Reinke, J. (1998). How to lend like mad and make a profit. *Journal of Development Studies, 34*(3), 44–58.

Ricardo, D. (1821). On the principles of political economy and taxation. 3rd ed. London: John Murry.

Ricci, F. (2007). Channels of transmission of environmental policy to economic growth. *Ecological Economics, 60*(4), 688–699.

Riefler, R. F. (2007). State patterns of occupational earnings: Implications for long-term growth. *Economic Development Quarterly, 21*(1), 34–48.

Roback, J. (1982). Wages, rents and the quality of life. *Journal of Political Economy, 90*(6), 1257–1278.

Roch, C. H., & Poister, T. H. (2006). Citizens, accountability, and service satisfaction. *Urban Affairs Review, 41*(3), 296–308.

Roe, B., Irwin, E. G., & Marrow-Jones, H. A. (2004). The effects of farmland, farm preservation, and other neighborhood amenities on housing values and residential growth. *Land Economics, 80*(1), 55–75.

Romans, T., & Subrahmanyam, G. (1979). State and local taxes, transfers, and regional economic growth. *Southern Economic Journal, 46,* 435–444.

Rostow, W. W. (1966). *The stages of economic growth.* Cambridge, UK: Cambridge University Press.

Rubin, D. S. (2005). Identifying small business opportunities using a shift-share analysis: An assessment and application. *Journal of Global Marketing, 19*(1), 95–109.

Rubin, H. J. (1988). Shoot anything that flies: Claim anything that falls. *Economic Development Quarterly, 2*(3), 236–251.

Rusk, D. (1993). *Cities without suburbs.* Baltimore: Johns Hopkins University Press.

Ryan, W. (1976). *Blaming the victim.* New York: Vintage Books.

Sassen, S. (1991). *The global city.* Princeton, NH: Princeton University Press.

Savitch, H., Collins, J. D., Sanders, D., & Markham, J. P. (1993). Ties that bind: Central cities, suburbs and the new metropolitan region. *Economic Development Quarterly, 7*(4), 341–357.

Schmenner, R. W. (1981, January). Locational decisions of large firms: Implications for public policy. *Commentary,* 3–7.

Schmenner, R. W. (1982). *Making business location decisions.* Englewood Cliffs, NJ: Prentice Hall.

Schunk, D., & Porca, S. (2005). State-local revenue diversification, stability, and growth: Time series evidence. *Review of Regional Studies, 35*(30), 246–265.

Scott, A. J. (2001). Globalization and the rise of city-regions. *European Planning Studies, 9*(7), 813–826.

Shafaeddin, S. M. (2005). Towards an alternative perspective on trade and industrial policies. *Development and Change, 36*(6), 1143–1162.

Siegan, B. (1970). Non-zoning in Houston. *Journal of Law and Economics, 13,* 71–113.

Skinner, G. W. (1964). Marketing and social structure in rural China—Part I. *Journal of Asian Studies, 24,* 3–33.

Skora, C. L. (1985). Ranking of state business climates. *Economic Development Quarterly, 2*(2), 138–152.

Smith, B. C. (2003). The impact of community development corporations on neighborhood housing markets. *Urban Affairs Review, 39*(2), 181–204.

Stabler, J. C., & Williams, P. R. (1973). The changing structure of the central place hierarchy. *Land Economics, 49,* 454–458.

Steponaitis, V. P. (1981). Settlement hierarchies and political complexity in nonmarket societies: The formative period of the valley of Mexico. *American Anthropologists, 83,* 320–365.

Sternberg, E. (1987). A practitioner's classification of economic development policy instruments with zone inspiration from political economy. *Economic Development Quarterly, 1*(2), 112–120.

Sternlieb, G. (1986). Grasping the future. In E. Rose (Ed.), *New roles for old cities* (chap. 14). Brookfield, VT: Gower.

Stevens, B. H. (1985). Location of economic activities: The JRS contribution to the research literature. *Journal of Regional Science, 25*(4), 663–685.

Storey, D. J., & Johnson, S. G. (1987). Regional variations in entrepreneurship in the U.K. *Scottish Journal of Political Economy, 34*(2), 161–173.

Stratton, L. (2002). Examining the wage differential for married and co-habiting men. *Economic Inquiry, 40,* 199–212.

Sweeney, M. (2004, Winter). The challenge of business incentives for state policy makers. *Spectrum,* 8–15.

Taylor, L. L. (2000). The evidence on government competition. *Economic and Financial Review, Second Quarter,* 2–10.

Taylor, M. (2005, August 2–5). *"Clusters": The mesmerizing mantra.* Paper presented to the International Geographical Union's Commission on the Dynamics of Economic Space, Toledo, OH.

Taylor, M., & Plummer, P. (2003). Drivers of local growth: Ideologies, ambiguities and policies. *Australian Journal of Regional Studies, 9*(3), 235–257.

Taylor, P. J. (2004). Regionality in the world city network. *International Social Science Journal, 56*(181), 361–372.

Taylor, P. J. (2005). Leading world cities: Empirical evaluation of urban nodes in multiple networks. *Urban Studies, 42*(9), 1593–1608.

Teitz, M., & Chapple, K. (1998). The causes of inner-city poverty: Eight hypotheses in search of reality. *Cityscape: A Journal of Policy Development and Research, 3*(3), 33–70.

Thisse, J.-F. (1987). Location theory, regional science and economics. *Journal of Regional Science, 27*(4), 519–528.

Thompson, W., & Thompson, P. (1985). From industries to occupations: Rethinking local economic development. *Economic Development Commentary, 13*(4), 12–18.

Thompson, W. R. (1968). *A preface to urban economics.* Baltimore: Johns Hopkins University Press.

Thompson, W. R., & Thompson, P. R. (1987). Alternative paths to the revival of industrial cities. In G. Gappert (Ed.), *The Future of Winter Cities* (pp. 233–250). Newbury Park, CA: Sage.

Tiebout, C. (1956). A pure theory of local public expenditure. *Journal of Political Economy, 64,* 416–424.

Tiebout, C. (1962). *The community economic base study.* New York: Committee for Economic Development. Tolchin, S., & Tolchin, M. (1987). *Buying into America.* New York: Time Books.

Tolchin, S., & Tolchin, M. (1987). *Buying into America.* New York: Time Books.

Turner, R., & Cole, H. S. D. (1980). An investigation into the estimation and reliability of urban shopping models. *Urban Studies, 17,* 139–147.

Up, L. (2004). Knowledge spillovers, agglomeration economics and the geography of innovation activity: A spatial econometric analysis. *Review of Region Studies, 34*(1), 11–36.

Valevanis, S. (1955). Losch on location. *American Economic Review, XLV,* 637–644.

Voith, R. P. (1992, September/October). City and suburban growth; substitutes or complements? *Business Review,* 21–33.

Warner, P. D. (1989). Alternative strategies for economic development: Evidence from southern metropolitan areas. *Urban Affairs Quarterly, 24*(3), 389–411.

Wasylenko, M. (1984). The effect of business climate on employment growth. In R. D. Ebel & T. McGuire (Eds.), *Final report for the Minnesota Tax Study Commission* (Vol. 2, pp. 51–73). Chicago: Butterworth Legal.

Weicher, J. L., & Thibodeau, T. G. (1988). Filtering and housing markets: An empirical analysis. *Journal of Urban Economics, 23,* 21–40.

Weiner, E., & Brown, A. (2005). The conscientious tourist. *The Futurist, 39*(5), 23.

Weiss, S. J., & Gooding, E. C. (1969). Estimation of differential employment multipliers in a small regional economy. In H. Richardson (Ed.), *Regional economics: A reader* (pp. 55–67). London: Macmillan.

Weiss, Y., & Willis, R. J. (1997). Match quality, new information, and marital dissolution. *Journal of Labor Economics, 15*(1), 293–329.

Wensley, M. R. D., & Stabler, J. C. (1998). Demand threshold estimation for business activities in rural Saskatchewan. *Journal of Regional Science, 38*(1), 155–177.

West, D., Von Hohenbalken, B., & Kroner, K. (1985). Tests of interurban central place theories. *Economic Journal, 95,* 101–117.

White, S. B. (1987). Reservation wages: Your community may be competitive. *Economic Development Quarterly, 1*(1), 18–29.

Wiese, A. (2004). *A place of their own: African American suburbanization in the twentieth century.* Chicago: University of Chicago Press.

Wiewel, W., Brown, B., & Morris, M. (1989). The linkage between regional and neighborhood development. *Economic Development Quarterly, 3*(2), 94–110.

Williamson, T., Imbroscio, D., & Alperovitz, G. (2002). *Making a place for community: Local democracy in a global era.* New York: Routledge.

Wilson, W. J. (1980). *The declining significance of race: Blacks and changing American institutions* (2nd ed.). Chicago: University of Chicago Press.

Wilson, W. J. (1985). The urban underclass in advanced industrial society. In P. Peterson (Ed.), *The new urban reality* (pp. 129–160). Washington DC: Brookings Institution.

Wilson, W. J. (1996). *When work disappears: The world of the new urban poor.* Princeton, NJ: Princeton University Press.

Wolaver, A., & White, W. (2006). Racial wage differences among young male job changers. *Growth and Change, 37*(1), 34–59.

Index

About the Authors

John P. Blair is a professor of economics at Wright State University, where he teaches courses in urban economics and local economic development. He has served as a consultant for a variety of state and local governments as well as private agencies. He has written numerous books and articles about urban issues and public policies. Blair's academic articles have appeared in journals such as *Land Economics, Growth and Change,* and *Economic Development Quarterly.* He received a Ph.D. from West Virginia University.

Michael C. Carroll is Director of the Center for Regional Development and an associate professor of economics at Bowling Green State University (BGSU). Before joining BGSU, he served on the faculty at Muskingum College and West Virginia State University. His business experience includes positions as corporate controller, operations manager, and president. His research interests focus on regional economic development and social economics. He is Editor-in-Chief of *Regional Science Policy and Practice* and Associate Editor of *Economic Development Quarterly.* His writings have appeared in a variety of academic journals, including *Journal of Economic Issues, Annals of Regional Science,* and *Industrial Geographer.* He also authored *A Future of Capitalism: The Economic Vision of Robert Heilbroner* in 1998. He earned his Ph.D. from Colorado State University.